ADVENTURES
OF A GARDENER

Adventures
of a Gardener

PETER SMITHERS

THE HARVILL PRESS
WITH
THE ROYAL HORTICULTURAL SOCIETY

First published in 1995
by The Harvill Press
84 Thornhill Road
London N1 1RD

135798642

© copyright Peter Smithers 1995

The author asserts the moral right to be identified
as the author of this work

A CIP record for this title is
available from the British Library

ISBN 1 86046 059 3

Printed and bound in Great Britain by
Butler & Tanner, Frome & London

TO

THE ROYAL HORTICULTURAL SOCIETY
MY MOTHER AND FATHER IN THE ART AND CRAFT
OF GARDENING

CONTENTS

PREFACE

It was shortly after my eightieth birthday that this book was conceived. The suggestion came from Susanne Mitchell at the Royal Horticultural Society. Without her help and that of Candida Hall at my publishers I could not have completed the work. In many respects this is their book.

Without her encouragement I would never have embarked upon the work. But was I not long past book-bearing age? I hoped not, for I have always revered and delighted in the English language, written or spoken: particularly spoken. Dean Selwyn reading the Collects in Winchester Cathedral in speech of faultless beauty: so perfectly controlled and yet moving was his rendering of the ancient English texts that tears sprang involuntarily to the eyes, the religious significance quite forgotten. Harold Macmillan in the House of Commons, directing the inflection of every syllable with faultless accuracy to bear its full weight with a critical audience. Winston Churchill at the microphone in wartime growling out the phrases which would echo around the world and still do so. These were the gods, masters of the spoken tongue, more direct and moving than the written word can ever be. Joseph Addison was the author of some of the most elegant English prose ever written. Like me he was a Member of Parliament and Undersecretary of State, and at the end of his life Principal Secretary of State. But he was too diffident to make a speech in public. Yet in his prose he did not write for his readers, he spoke to them. For two centuries he was a trusted friend and counsellor to English men and women, a living personality, a member of the family long after his death. In this book, attempting to follow my masters, I do not write for you: I speak to you.

CHAPTER 1

An Introduction to the Garden at Vico Morcote

IT SHALL BE A SOURCE OF PLEASURE
TO THE OWNER AND HIS FRIENDS,
NOT A BURDEN AND AN ANXIETY

"Think of yourself," said my doctor, "as a vintage motor-car: still serviceable, and in some ways perhaps more interesting than a new model. But it will not go as fast, it will need rather careful driving, and it will require more maintenance. It is certainly worth a little extra trouble." I had not previously seen myself in that light. On this occasion I had gone to visit Dr Schwarzenbach with a rather trivial complaint. A kindly and perceptive man, he had understood that although now an octogenarian I was indignant that I should have to complain of anything at all.

On reflection the remark struck home. There had always been two persons: there was my body and there was me. My body was not me. It was the faithful friend and companion which had served 'me' well through a long life. It had enabled 'me' to derive much pleasure from the physical world. True it had got me into a scrape now and then, but that had been 'my' fault not that of my body, and anyway the scrapes had sometimes been rather enjoyable. 'Me' and my body had gardened together, each doing our part for more than seventy years.

My parents employed two gardeners who possessed the strong bodies of Hampshire country folk. Those bodies and the whole of their working hours were available for maintaining the garden under the direction of my mother. She was a fine gardener and plantswoman. The world in which many such gardens existed throughout Britain dissolved rapidly after the Second World War. Sometimes it would be possible to afford and to obtain increasingly expensive help, but most people who wished to make a garden and to enjoy growing plants would have to do so in their own time and with their own bodies. With increasing age the time available might be greater but the ability

I

of the body to make use of it would diminish. Unless the entire operation was carefully planned what should have been a pleasure might easily become a burden.

Many books have been written about how to design and make a garden and about how to fill it with interesting plants. This book is about how gardening may relate to the rest of life in such a way that it is an acceptable and enjoyable part of the whole. This was the problem which confronted me when at the age of fifty-six I set about the task of making a garden at Vico Morcote, on an empty terraced hillside at the southern foot of the Alps.

If a garden is to take account of the wishes of the owner and to reconcile those wishes with the facts of life in the real world, then it must be governed by clearly defined principles. This is not the same thing as deciding the kind of garden which you wish to possess before you begin to make it. That is only the first step, though one of great importance. The second step is to decide how you are going to achieve that result. It is here that the principles are needed. This sounds complicated. In fact it is mostly common sense. The following twelve principles were established for the garden at Vico Morcote. They have justified themselves in practice during a period of twenty-four years.

Principles for my Garden

I   It shall be a source of pleasure to the owner and his friends, not a burden and an anxiety.

II   It must therefore be designed and planted so as to reduce labour to a minimum, and the work involved must diminish as the owner grows old.

III   All plants must therefore be of a permanent character: no annuals, biennials or plants requiring lifting in winter or attention of a special kind. They must be a self-sustaining plant community, an ecosystem of exotics, within which, as in nature, the plants support and maintain one another without the intervention of man.

IV   Fragrant and aromatic plants have preferential admission to add a fifth dimension to the garden; the fourth, of course, is time/motion.

V   Plants which flower early or late in the year, or in July the green month, also have preference, to extend the flowering season.

VI   The planting must be of a dense kind, so that the plants live intimately together with little space for weeds to grow or need for support. The plants themselves must do most of the garden work.

VII   'Difficult' plants, if not successful after a fair trial, are abandoned: there are plenty of easier subjects.

VIII   The design is that of a Japanese Stroll-garden. The owner and his friends are led by a winding path which, with short side-spurs, carries them through the entire garden and back to the starting point.

IX   The plantings, sixteen in number, are varying compositions of plants according to the lie of the ground. The visitor is surprised at every turn of the path, with a new plant community different from what he has seen so far.

X   No plant is added to the garden if there is in existence an obtainable superior form.

XI   Excluded from the main landscape of this garden are conifers and palms, which would divorce it from the deciduous forests of oak and sweet chestnut across the lake.

XII   No plant is ever sold or exchanged. All are available to serious gardeners, stock and labour permitting. The pleasure of owning a fine plant is not complete until it has been given to friends.

*   *   *

After giving some account of my earlier gardening life this book describes the application of these principles in designing and developing the garden at Vico Morcote and in its evolution from bare ground to a fully functioning ecosystem. It describes the extent to which the principles have proved workable and some of the mistakes which I made in their application. The principles were drafted to take account of my own preferences in the choice of plants, of the conditions existing on the Italian Lakes, of my age and of the resources of time and money which were available. They by no means prohibit me from pursuing my own gardening hobbies, special plants in pots and so forth, which have nothing to do with the ecosystem; on the contrary they are designed to relieve me of much of the otherwise inevitable work in the main garden so that there may be time for favourite specialities.

I believe that these principles can be adapted to suit any climate from the tropics to the desert to the sub-arctic and that their application can be varied to meet the tastes of different owners. There will be a different selection of plant material for a particular climate. The time necessary to arrive at maturity in the ecosystem will vary. On the Italian Lakes growth is rather fast. In the sub-tropics or tropics it would be even faster. In the desert or in the sub-arctic growth will be very slow indeed but the garden will reach the stability of an ecosystem in the end. Every stage of development from planning and planting until maturity will be exciting and delightful.

CHAPTER 2

Look Back to See Forward

THE LOVE OF GREEN AND GROWING
THINGS TOOK ROOT AT AN EARLY AGE
ALONGSIDE A FASCINATION WITH POLITICS

The great adventure which Nikita Khruschev called 'Life Itself' did not begin until I went to Magdalen College in Oxford, but the adventure of gardening began long before with Nanny. The 1914–1918 war broke out when I was nine months old. Both my parents were swept away in the war effort. I was left with Granny and Nanny in Yorkshire. I must have been three or perhaps four when I saw a German zeppelin, making an ugly buzzing noise, flying low over the garden at Donisthorpe House. At least, Nanny said that it was a zeppelin and she was generally right. She had grown up a country girl (see p. 6). In the England of those days this meant that she had lived in intimate contact with nature. She it was who made my first tiny garden, who taught me to nibble the young shoots on the hawthorn hedge, who taught me how to press and dry wild flowers, who – *pace* to the conservationists of today – served me a tiny poached blackbird's egg with breakfast. Throughout a life engaged in the political discords of an increasingly violent world there has always been a tranquil continuo: the love of green and growing things which Nanny implanted in her charge. It has never faltered to this day.

At the age of nine I was to go to boarding school, a year later than was usual in those days. My parents doubted I was tough enough, and at age eight they had replaced Nanny with a governess: 'Tom' she wished to be called. Tom was no naturalist but she would teach me some harder lessons than Nanny had done. The very first morning in the schoolroom when I contradicted Tom flatly to her face, she doubled up her fist and knocked me flat on the floor. I remember Tom with gratitude for that salutary lesson: it never needed repetition.

Peter and Nanny. She had grown up a country girl, in intimate
contact with nature. 1918.

Nevertheless Hawtrey's School in bleak Thanet by a cold chalky sea was
unfamiliar in almost every way. Even the clothes were unfamiliar. There was
a bowler hat, to be worn six times a year, on the train from Victoria to
Westgate-on-Sea at the beginning of term, and on the train back again at
the beginning of the holidays. There was a silk top hat for wear on Sundays
with an Eton jacket and striped trousers. Every day there was a starched Eton
collar and a tie, and a suit with matching trousers and waistcoat. This was all
new. But there was one continuity. I was permitted to share a garden plot
with another boy. Fortunately he was not interested in it: I had all twenty
square feet to myself. It was late April when I joined the school: just the
time to plant some bedding plants and to sow some annuals in the thin
chalky soil.

My father was a fine sportsman and amongst other things an excellent shot with gun and rifle. The school was told that I was to be taught to shoot. The rifle range, a small green lawn, was in a walled garden. A few vegetables and some roses grew there. But that summer a wondrous thing burst into bloom against the brick wall, though I must get there before mid-afternoon – escaping from cricket – if I was to see it. It was a shrub about five feet high, with large white blooms, each petal with a brown blotch at the base, and an entrancing aromatic scent to the sticky leaves. Amongst the lobelias, marigolds and petunias it was a being from another and a much better world. Its memory is a pleasure to this day. How *Cistus ladanifer* had penetrated the school precincts with their forbidding red brick and dark green paint I cannot imagine.

Apart from old Mrs Hawtrey who really liked and understood small boys, and the Reverend and genial Mr Hobbins, who taught classics and was known to his pupils as 'Hobbinos', I cannot remember any other attractive feature of my four years at Hawtrey's School – except for the superlative meringues at the local hotel. These were accessible twice a term when my parents were permitted a visiting weekend.

Now I was ten years old and home for the holidays. Nanny was still writing letters to me. Looking back I now know that I meant as much to her as she did to me. For three years immediately after the war my parents lived in a pleasant old house at Hartford Bridge in north Hampshire. It had the most delightful feature which a garden can possess: a stream running through it. It was only a little stream, perhaps three feet wide, a 'cut' from the River Hart. But in it was a small water wheel which pumped water up to a pond. There were also diminutive gudgeon swimming up and down. The splashing of the wooden paddles of the water wheel as it drove the little pump made a cheerful background noise. The water trickled back to the stream through a series of three small ponds in which I kept goldfish and golden orfe. There were frogs and all sorts of pond life besides. Somehow the whole thing seemed to be alive. By good fortune every garden in which I have lived has been endowed with the magic of running water.

By the upper pond was a rustic summer house thatched with heather. It was an attractive rather mysterious place over which towered an immense and ancient elm tree. I would rise at seven o'clock to enjoy the garden and its delights before breakfast. On such a morning, sunny and without even a breath of wind, I was standing by the pond watching my fish. Suddenly there was an immense shattering crack followed by sounds of smashing and splitting as a giant branch from the elm fell upon the summer house, destroying it completely and for ever. From that day I learned never to trust an elm. Now nature has had a terrible revenge on these magnificent but treacherous trees: almost all are dead from the Dutch elm disease.

In the garden at Hartford Bridge there were two small plots which were my own. In one of them, hanging over the edge of a dry wall, was a plant of the golden alyssum, *Aurinia saxatilis*. With its cheerful display of bloom and lovely fragrance it had delighted me every spring for three years. Three years is a long time at age ten and also in the life of an alyssum. Now my plant was growing old and one day my mother, with the best of intentions, had replaced it with a young plant of the same kind. It would be a surprise for me on getting home from school. It was just that and much more. I wept for a whole day. My parents were finally indignant: they thought it unmanly. Perhaps they were right, but I could not dismiss from my mind the memory of the much-loved beautiful plant, my friend, gone for ever beyond recall. It was a first brush with the finality of death. The early love of plants is evidently not just a romantic fabrication of my old age.

Plants and fishing for trout in the River Whitewater were a large part of home. Home was heaven itself. Why would I want to be in any other place on earth? When my father's brother officers would ask: "Well, little man" – they actually used those words sometimes – "I suppose you are looking forward to going back to school?" I would reply indignantly, "No!" This was quite the wrong answer and most definitely unmanly: no good would come of the 'little man'. But who would want to be at boarding school in bleak Thanet when he could be at my wonderful home? Absurd!

Today, after seeing eighty-four countries, home and the garden are still the best place to be and plants are my constant companions. They talk to me, and I begin to understand something of their language: "I would like more sun", "I am too dry", "I don't like that cold wind", "Your soil is too acid for me" or "I am perfectly happy, for goodness sake leave me alone". I sometimes read of romantics who talk to their plants. In what Nepalese dialect, I wonder, should I address my *Daphne bholua*? Would my lapagerias understand me better if I spoke to them in Spanish or in the Indian language of southern Chile? Or have they learned English from me or Italian from my part-time gardener? It will be more useful to the plants if I understand their language and respond with the appropriate action. People who do this are said to have 'a green thumb'. This is the dialogue of the garden. It does not have much to do with the thumb.

As a boy I had learned much in the potting shed from our head gardeners.

Peter with Lonsdale, head gardener at Donisthorpe House. 1918.

I use the plural because my Aunt Evelyn North had in succession two splendid men, masters of their craft. In our own garden where my mother was really head gardener, a lesser breed would do. Old Lonsdale, a very broad Yorkshireman in a peaked cap and green apron, was head gardener at Donisthorpe House, my grandfather's home in Yorkshire, then at Frimley Park, his post-war residence near Camberley, and finally at Star Hill, Aunt Evelyn's first house in Hampshire. If I transgressed by hammering crocks on the potting bench to provide drainage for a pot, I would be corrected with a gentle rap over the knuckles.

Lonsdale was a master grower of potted plants for the house: schizanthus, calceolarias, cinerarias, godetias, streptocarpus, cyclamen, and gloxinias. Each plant seemed to have the shining pristine perfection of a new motor car. He not only grew them: he arranged them in place in the house and did it very well. He had learned his craft as a garden boy under an earlier generation of head gardeners who had learned in the same way. No doubt all had been gently rapped over the knuckles if they were caught breaking crocks on the potting bench. There were no horticultural schools in those days that I know of. As I grew older I would sometimes entertain Lonsdale with an account of what I had read in a gardening book, if only to enjoy the inevitable response: "Ee, Master Peter, I doant maak nowt o' bewks". But he knew far more about how to grow plants than many a modern garden writer.

Payne was Aunt Evelyn's head gardener at her second house in Hampshire, Pelham Place, where I spent much of my time, bicycling over from Itchen Stoke House where my parents now lived. Payne had all of old Lonsdale's skills and was also perfect master of the art of growing fruit for the table: grapes, peaches and nectarines, under glass in the cool English climate. By now I was fourteen or so, and Payne and his smooth-haired fox terrier, Pat, were great friends. Payne and his wife, who was a superb maker of cakes, lived in the lodge at the park gate. Opposite was a public house, the Horse and Groom. It sometimes happened that a few of the patrons of the bar in need of fresh air would stray into the park and fill the place with inarticulate noises. I happened to be there on one such occasion. Payne suggested that they leave. One of the revellers was so unwise as to be impertinent to Payne, a big burly man. Payne put his hands on his hips, fixed the man with a glare and said in measured terms, "I've killed worms like you." The group of revellers melted away. For Payne, a soldier in the trenches in the 1914–1918 War, there had been other things in life besides gardening.

At home at Itchen Stoke House I was able to take some part in my mother's gardening activities and to pursue my own growing enthusiasm as a plantsman. In a long rectangular bed in the kitchen garden I planted bulbs which took my fancy, and my parents gave me a three-quarter span frame for special plants. Not all of them liked the chalk soil, but a number of unusual things established themselves. Some were more curious than beautiful but all were interesting. Few of our neighbours went in for such things, though there were some magnificent gardens in Hampshire at that time. My efforts were not really worthy the attention of their owners. The exception was Sir Hubert Miller. He was a Baronet of the first creation by King James I, a bachelor, and much sought after by the county ladies. He had a delightful house and garden at Froyle and a small palazzo in Venice. But he it was who never failed to ask to see what I had to show him in my trial bed. He would look at some entirely unfamiliar bloom of modest beauty, and through a very large white moustache would come the words, "Very intereshting, very intereshting - but not a real fflower". A 'fflower' had to be conspicuous and

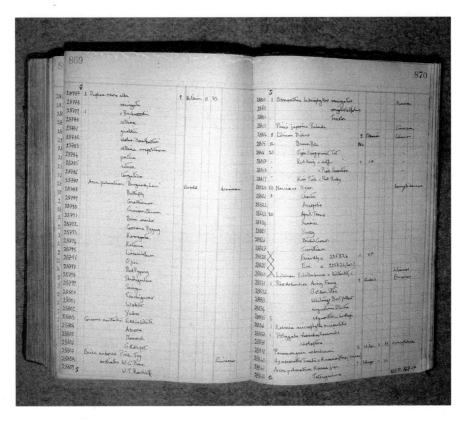

A last act at Harrow was to buy a very large index book at the school bookshop, to record my plants. It was filled in 1993 with entry No. 32,147. It is now supplemented by a computer.

brightly coloured. A man of marked character, when he was knocked down in the road outside his house by a motor-cycle, but fortunately not hurt, he lay still, pretending to be dead, "to teach the young man a lesson".

I loved Sir Hubert for his sympathetic interest in something which I now suspect really rather bored him: perhaps I loved him even more than General Herbert, a brother officer of my father and by no means a rich man, who never left Itchen Stoke without pressing five shillings into my hand when nobody was looking. In those days five shillings would buy several interesting plants.

I had grown up in the world of the English manor houses, a nice thing to do. Harrow School to which I went at age thirteen was another matter. Except for the Engineering Workshop, of which I was the Secretary, and for rifle shooting in which I shot for the school, Harrow was bleak and slightly unpleasant, relieved by a house master who gave me permission to go to the

Chelsea flower show and allowed me to keep a few pots of rarities in his garden frames.

It was at age fifteen that a new form master presented me with the hitherto stale facts of history as the thrilling story of mankind. I was electrified. This was the great game. I would be a player in it if I could. Until now gardening, dry-fly fishing and engineering had been all of life. They would remain with me in the years ahead but in the background. The real business of life had begun. I subscribed to *The Times*, read the parliamentary debates and had finished the books for the term at the end of the second week. I went to my house master, who, quite unwittingly, was about to do me another good turn. "Sir, I would like to go in for an open history Demyship at Magdalen College, Oxford."* He laughed in my face. "You, a scholar! I never heard such a thing." Furious, I persuaded my parents to let me leave Harrow and go to read history for a year with A. D. Innes, a distinguished Tudor historian. There were three open Demyships in history each year and a very large number of entrants in the examination. Just after my seventeenth birthday – to the astonishment of my former house master and somewhat to my own surprise – I got the second of them.

A great change came over my life and gardening as I left Harrow for Oxford. The University, or more specifically Magdalen, was a love affair, all absorbing (see p. 13). Life seemed to have begun, and it was exciting. Amongst other things I squeezed into a packed hall at All Souls College to listen to A. L. Rowse, then a left-winger, lecturing weekly on Marxist-Leninism. It was fascinating. At that time in intellectual circles in the University anybody who was not a Marxist-Leninist, or at least a socialist, was a fool. But the whole thing seemed to me unreal. This was an economic not a political theory, predicting the 'outpouring of socialist plenty'. Would it really pour out? In my political philosophy paper in final schools I said that I doubted it. And if it did not do so the whole system would fall to bits. I never changed this opinion. Thirty years later, in 1961 when I was a delegate to the United Nations General Assembly, I drove my own car, with my wife and daughter, through much of the USSR. The economics of Marxist-Leninism had failed and the Soviet economy was hopelessly overburdened with a vast military establishment and onerous obligations worldwide which it was too feeble to support. The Moscow Government was driven up against the frontiers of the economy. The whole edifice

---

* A Demyship – a 'half' Fellowship – is a scholarship on the fifteenth century Foundation of the College by William of Waynflete, Bishop of Winchester. It carries with it certain privileges beyond those of an undergraduate.

Magdalen was a love affair. The view from my bedroom. 1932.

must collapse one day though I could not say when that would happen. I expressed this view to the Foreign Office. Our ambassador in Moscow, a very clever man, disagreed, politely. I cannot to this day understand why what was perfectly obvious to me at that time was not obvious to those whose business it was to know.

But to return to the delights of Magdalen. By a happy chance the University Botanic Garden stood opposite the College lodge, just across the High. The venerable Institution still preserved its seventeenth-century specimen beds and it also had well stocked modern greenhouses. In no place that I know of, except perhaps Cambridge, does the damp chill of winter bite so savagely as it does in Oxford. Magdalen had no central-heating system in those days. The Tropical House, with a splendid plant of *Victoria amazonica*, had great allure. How delightful must life in the tropics be if it was always like that.

Down from Oxford with a 'First' I wrote to the Chairman of the Conservative Party to say that I would like to enter politics. He replied that I was much too young and should get some experience, then think about it again in ten years' time. He was right, of course, though foolish to turn away a rare Conservative intellectual in a generation in which socialism was fashionable. Nevertheless up to this point life had indeed spoiled me. My grandmother would say: "My dear boy, you have much to be thankful for."

Elizabeth, a great favourite of mine in those days, now herself a grandmother, put it somewhat differently. She looked up at me with kindly blue eyes and a sweet smile and said: "You know, Peter, the wonder is that the way your family spoil you, you are not worse than you are."

Then the war came, I assumed my Commission as a Lieutenant in the Royal Naval Volunteer Reserve and went off to service in HMS *Radiant*, Lord Iliffe's yacht, newly converted to an armed patrol vessel testing anti-aircraft devices in the English Channel. Young reserve officers, doing their best to become the professionals which they certainly were not, were generously treated by the Royal Navy, but certainly not spoiled. Winning the war came before every other consideration. Life was exciting and very interesting. I was fascinated by and loved the sea for its own sake. That was why I had joined the Royal Naval Volunteer Reserve, colloquially known as 'The Yachtsman's Navy'. My dream was to become a skilled navigator. The war at sea should afford plenty of opportunities. To this day the first sight of the sea after a long absence is deeply moving. I had been thrust into a new and fascinating world different from any that I had known before.

It did not last long. Convalescent after being dangerously ill for the first and last time in my life in the bitter winter of 1940, I was declared unfit for sea service. It looked like a boring administrative job in a bowler hat for the rest of the war. But, astonishingly, the Navy joined my family's club, and spoiled me. Kitty, a pretty and delightful blonde girl whom I knew, had several other admirers. One of these was a Commander in the Naval Intelligence Division of the Admiralty. He worked with Lieutenant Commander Ian Fleming, Personal Assistant to the Director of Naval Intelligence. Ian, in spite of his modest rank, was at the very centre of the British Intelligence machine. He spoke with the authority of Admiral Godfrey, the legendary Director, who was known in the Intelligence Services as 'Uncle John'. Ian telephoned Haslar Naval Hospital at Portsmouth. "Lieutenant Smithers is not to be discharged: he is to report to the Director of Naval Intelligence immediately." Such are the chances which alter the entire course of life, as this one did.

In London my orders were to report first to 'Uncle John' and then to 'Broadway', the headquarters of MI6, the Foreign Intelligence Service. There, after a brief indoctrination, I was instructed to report immediately to MI6 headquarters in Paris as Naval member of the staff. I jotted down my instructions in my diary. "Just give me that, will you," said Jimmy Blythe who had been giving me the details. He took the diary, tore out everything that I had written, threw it into a basket labelled 'Secret Waste' and handed back the remainder. I got the point. This was serious and dangerous business. I have never kept a diary since, preferring to rely upon what was once a prodigious memory.

The fall of France lay three months ahead. I witnessed the whole discreditable spectacle from within. The little Hôtel Vouillement was a quiet place in the Rue Boissy d'Anglas. It was frequented by elderly French couples up from the country. A Russian artist named Marc Chagall lived there. He seldom appeared, but when the air raid sirens would sound, the inhabitants of the Hotel, including Marc, would descend to the entrance Hall and sit comfortably in armchairs until it was all over. Marc would appear in pyjamas, dressing-gown, and a very large black hat with a tall crown. Once settled in his armchair he would pull the hat right down so that it covered both his ears and his eyes and would thus insulate him from the disagreeable world outside. When the 'alerte' was over one of us would nudge him gently and the hat would rise slowly as Marc rejoined the world around him. I was to know this delightful man later when he lived on Lake Waramaug in Connecticut. He never greeted me in any other way but with a military salute.

Paris was never more beautiful than in the wartime blackout. Unlike the London blackout, it was not particularly black: the lights were blue in colour, which added an air of mystery to the materialism of that city. But with the collapse of the French defences the staff of MI6 had to be put out of the reach of the Germans. One day 'Biffy' Dunderdale, head of MI6 Paris, entering the office, took the photograph of Generals Gort and Gamelin which adorned the entrance table, turned it with its face to the wall, and without a word walked into his office. Next day I was dispatched in advance in a French Army truck loaded with our files and accompanied by an armed guard, to make the necessary preparations. First base was to be at the Château le Chêne in Sologne, where for a couple of weeks I became Commandant de la Place. My 'staff' consisted of Germaine Duchesse de Gantot-Biron and her domestics and gardeners. A friend of Commander Dunderdale, she had volunteered her house as our first retreat in case of need. While making the physical arrangements to receive our people in due course I enjoyed the luxury of a French walled garden full of the disciplined culture of fruit trees, something in which the French excel.

After about ten days of unexpected bliss in that sunny summer, the MI6 staff arrived from Paris and moved in. They were rather more numerous than I had provided for. Of many nationalities, some of them had formed romantic attachments previously unknown to authority. Now the attachments came along too. They were right to do so. Before our staff left Paris the concierge at our office building and his wife had been given a wad of francs and were told to disappear into central France and never to appear in Paris again. A new couple was appointed in their place. They arrived after our departure and never saw any of us. The Germans went straight to the unobtrusive office in an apartment building in the Avenue Charles Flocquet. The new concierge and his wife could tell them nothing. We heard that they had been shot out of hand.

The German advance continued and again I was sent ahead to make the arrangements for a last base in France from which our people would be evacuated to England. The Dupuis and Rothschild villas at Le Pyla agreed to receive them. For Philippe de Rothschild this was an act of considerable courage. From there the party drove in convoy of their own cars to the dockside at Le Verdon where the cruiser HMS *Arethusa* was waiting for them. I slept in *Arethusa* that night expecting to sail with her next morning for England. The Germans bombed the anchorage, the bombs bursting in the water making a sharp metallic sound within the ship. The Captain sent for me at breakfast. "You speak French, I think? Commander Fleming is in Bordeaux. You are to go ashore to join him before reporting to the First Lord of the Admiralty as his temporary Flag Lieutenant."

When Winston Churchill became Prime Minister The Rt Hon A. V. Alexander, MP had replaced him as First Lord of the Admiralty. He had flown to Bordeaux to negotiate with Admiral Darlan for an agreement that the French Fleet would sail to Britain to continue the war. In the event, it was to slink off into ignominy for the rest of the hostilities.

Ian and I spent the day burning papers left in the deserted British Consulate. I found the seal used for sealing diplomatic bags and took charge of it. When I returned it to the Foreign Office in London they were rather indignant. I had no business to have it! No doubt the Germans would have made better use of it. Ian took the key of the British Consulate to the American Consul. Mr Waterman refused to receive it: he had no instructions. Over his protests Ian rammed it into his coat pocket and we walked away.

Dinner next night was with what remained of the French and British General Staffs at the magnificent Chapon Fin restaurant in Bordeaux. The Germans were advancing and the proprietor was determined that we should drink his very finest wines, the bottles of a century, before the enemy arrived. None of us had much heart for food or drink on that sad occasion. A group of broken men sat around the table. I was cheered to hear that at the Château le Chêne Germaine had opened the cellar doors and had invited the village to come to help themselves before the Germans got there. She had a fine cellar, which I had much enjoyed, and the village had responded with alacrity.

But to return to Bordeaux: I was now temporary Flag Lieutenant to the First Lord. After dinner we set off in the dark in a French Navy car with minimum lights and the full moon, to drive to the lake at Biscarosse. We twice narrowly missed disaster in the ditch. Finally the First Lord told me to order both drivers to get into the back seat. He and I would sit in front and I would drive, cautiously, English style, in the middle of the road, by the light of the moon. He had to get back to Cabinet at all costs. The drivers obeyed somewhat reluctantly. It was fortunate that the First Lord did not understand French and thus missed the substance of their observations.

At Biscarosse a heavily armed RAF Sunderland flying boat was waiting on the lake. The huge craft had but one pilot, which was not surprising at that moment. No doubt one of the officers in charge of the armament could have taken over at a pinch. So the co-pilot's seat was empty. The Wing Commander suggested I sit in it. I had never flown before. As we taxied across the lake in the moonlight the pine trees drew nearer and nearer. I could not believe that we would leave the water, or France – but of course we did. Approaching Plymouth in daylight we had a fighter escort and then a special train to London. In the train I took down Mr Alexander's notes for Cabinet. We were both exhausted and woke each other up by turns. From Paddington Station straight to Downing Street. I had been lucky to get out. It would not have been nice for a member of MI6 to fall into German hands. I had had a grandstand view of great events. I have had one ever since.

That was the splendid sunny summer of the Battle of Britain, but I spent much of it in the underground Operations Room of the Admiralty and with 'W' section of MI5 which was engaged in collecting German spies parachuted into England. We had broken their codes and had a reception committee waiting for them at the appointed places. There were occasional brief visits to Itchen Stoke to see my parents and the garden, but for the present plants had to give place to many other thoughts. Much of my time was spent in security operations devised by Ian who became a lifelong friend and partner in many adventures.

Naval Intelligence knew that the Germans had an interesting new air-sea rescue craft, now operating from Dutch harbours. Ian felt that we should try to secure one. We had a complete German light bomber, captured in working order, and plenty of Luftwaffe uniforms from airmen shot down over Britain. I was sent to collect a set of uniforms from Cardington where they were stored. These would be sufficient for the RAF men who would fly the aircraft and for Ian and myself. We would fly out to sea, come down off the Dutch coast, be rescued by the Germans, knock them on the head and drive the captured boat back to the Thames. A simple straightforward operation! But by extraordinary good fortune 'Uncle John' got wind of the plan and, to my considerable relief, instantly vetoed it. Ian knew far too much for there to be the slightest risk of his falling into enemy hands. Thus was 'James Bond' already waiting in the wings, to be an outlet years later for Ian's frustrated longing for adventure. It was not a longing shared by me.

In the autumn Ian discussed with higher authorities a very different kind of adventure. This was my appointment as ADC to the Duke of Windsor, now Governor of the Bahamas. No doubt in view of what were believed to be HRH's political opinions the idea was that I should keep a discreet eye on him and report if necessary. It would have been a delicate and rather unpleasant operation.

But then Admiral Godfrey decided that he needed an officer at the British Embassy in Washington whose sole task would be the exchange of intelligence with the US Navy Department. I would join the staff as Assistant Naval Attaché. I would fly to Lisbon with the head of the US Bureau of Ships, Captain, later Admiral, Earl Mills, who was already planning the great new US Battle Fleet which he subsequently built. He was carrying with him the plans of the latest battleship then building for the Royal Navy, HMS *Prince of Wales*. It struck me as an insecure way to transmit such a vital secret of the war. The Americans did not yet understand security, something about which I had been learning rather fast. My father came to see me off in the British Empire flying boat from Poole Harbour. I never saw him again.

In Lisbon we would join Lord Lothian on his way back as Ambassador in Washington, but things did not go smoothly on our arrival in the Tagus. For safety the unarmed flying boat had flown in darkness and it was late in the evening when we arrived. Every hotel was full of refugees from France. Finally a kindly concierge gave us an address saying that we would probably get lodging there. The door was opened by a charming lady and we explained our predicament. No problem: we were shown to a double room which we would share. It had no bath. Captain Mills returned from a trip to the bathroom. "Lootenant, I don't know what kind of an establishment this is, but there sure are some interesting ladies walking about with very few clothes on." He put the battleship plans under his pillow and we went to sleep. I doubt that their Lordships of the Admiralty would have slept well if they had known the location of the plans of their newest capital ship.

With Lord Lothian we flew to New York in the Pan American Clipper on the two hundred-and-thirty-seventh transatlantic air crossing, stopping at Horta and Bermuda to refuel the huge flying boat. A nervous Portuguese officer paced continually up and down the aisle all the way to Horta. "Lootenant, I guess that guy is walking to Horta for a bet," remarked my travelling companion. At 2,000 feet I watched the skyscrapers of New York arising out of the sea. In view of what I had left behind and of what lay ahead it was a moment of overpowering emotion never to be forgotten. Ahead lay hope. In Washington I heard that Mr Alexander had asked for me as Flag-Lieutenant to the Board of Admiralty. That, too, would have been fascinating.

Lord Lothian died almost at once and was succeeded by Lord Halifax. A former Viceroy of India and Foreign Secretary, and a very devoted churchman, Halifax was a truly great ambassador. In the critical months ahead he would capture the confidence not only of the government in Washington but of the American people as a man of total and unswerving honesty. His only relaxation from a crushing work schedule was tennis. I became one of his tennis four on the Embassy court. As the Ambassador had a defect of one arm, for service he was obliged to hold both the ball and the racquet in one hand, with which he would throw and then hit the ball: a difficult feat which resulted in quite frequent double faults. But being a man of deep religious conviction, instead of uttering a four-syllable word such as in other circumstances any of his three partners might have done, he would emit a long deep inarticulate groan. We had to remember to do the same when, with less excuse, we would serve a double.

The rest of the Embassy staff was a hand-picked galaxy of diplomatic stars, all to become ambassadors in due course. Washington was the key to the future of Britain. If at the end of a couple of weeks a new member of the Embassy team seemed not to 'get on' with the Americans, he would find himself unceremoniously bundled onto the next transport back to Britain. With such an assembly of talent, and with the Foreign Office telegrams on my desk, this was a grandstand view of a world in crisis. Such it remained for two fascinating years during which I saw and met almost 'everybody'. (PLATE I)

My tiny frame house on 28th Street in Georgetown had been newly renovated: rescued in fact from collapse. It had a strip of garden behind it as wide as the house, that is to say about twenty feet. It was newly laid out with rich-seeming bare earth, asking for plants. The fresh soil was loose and needed no digging so I set about planting such things as I could find and all went well until summer began. Then I discovered my mistake, one to be repeated, inexcusably, much later in my gardening life. The soil dried out with alarming rapidity, and on examination it appeared that beneath a top-dressing of less than a foot in depth there lay layer after layer of oyster shells. They were probably disposed of by a restaurant in a city which consumes great quantities of oysters from nearby Chesapeake Bay. My Georgetown garden never developed as it might have done: the Embassy workload in wartime was too heavy to permit of a major operation of garden construction.

These were times when every morning the Foreign Office telegrams would bring news of triumph or disaster or of both. Across the Atlantic Britain was fighting alone for survival, the Royal Navy battling tenaciously to prevent strangulation by the German submarine offensive. Looking back to those days I marvel at the daring and skill of the German U-boat commanders. In Washington I knew that few of my friends believed in their hearts that Britain could survive. Ian Fleming was a frequent visitor from the Admiralty and would stay with me. Relentless in his determination to win the war, he was a dynamo of creativity in intelligence operations. He it was who came to impart to 'Wild Bill' Donovan some of the specialist knowledge which went into the OSS, later to become the CIA, and which years later would go into the making of Ian's novels.

A manly, handsome and romantic figure, and very rich, Ian was much admired by several young ladies but too busy to offer them more than passing though certainly exciting attention. He was wholly absorbed by the conduct of intelligence operations worldwide but also fascinated by the minutiae of irregular fighting techniques. From Lord Suffolk, an expert in such matters, he had learned how in close combat one might kill one's opponent by biting him in the back of the neck should the opportunity to do this offer itself. For the duration of hostilities the ladies, though not forgotten, had to take second place.

One of my duties was to collect US intercepts of the Japanese diplomatic coded telegrams from the Navy Department. So secret was this, lest our knowledge of the codes be compromised, that the Director of Naval Intelligence forbade me to discuss the matter even with him. I was permitted to pass on their sense to the Ambassador in paraphrase but might not copy or touch the strips of paper put before me on a tray. I must bring my own typewriter and paper.

One day there lay before me the message from Ambassador Oshima in Berlin to the Foreign Ministry in Tokyo, informing the Japanese Government that Hitler was about to attack the USSR. The idiot! Had he not heard of Napoleon? On that day, for the first time, I was sure that Britain could not be beaten. Nobody but a fool could have been convinced of this hitherto.

Pearl Harbor day was a day like no other in life. My colleague in the Navy Department, Commander Al Kramer, had been on duty alone in the intercepts department all Saturday. Astonishing. We now know that both the Army and Navy Commanders in Hawaii had been warned of an imminent danger of war, that they failed to consult one another and failed to order a state of readiness. Hawaii was a long way from Japan. On Saturday in the intercepts department Al had received thirteen of fourteen parts of a long message from Tokyo to the Japanese Embassy in Washington. They were to await the fourteenth part which would give precise timing for delivery of the message to Secretary of State Hull. No car, astonishingly, was available, so Mrs Kramer had driven Al round Washington, delivering the thirteen parts to the White House, to the Secretary of the Navy and to various Admirals.

At one am on Sunday Al went home to bed ten minutes away. He instructed the watch officer to call him immediately if the fateful fourteenth part was intercepted. It came in at five minutes past three on Sunday morning. It said that the whole message was to be delivered to the Secretary of State at one pm precisely. Nobody called Al. No intelligence officer in his right mind could doubt that it meant an impending Japanese attack somewhere. Next morning Al said this to everybody he could get hold of. There were consultations amongst senior officers, but staff were not on duty on the weekend and nothing was done.

On that sunny Sunday morning I went to my office in the main Embassy building to see if there was anything from the Admiralty which needed attention. There was nothing. I collected a girl from her family in George-town and drove out in my open car to the Blue Ridge Mountains where so many wonderful plants grow wild, including species of *Lilium*. At that time of year there might be a few seeds. A Press car recognised me, drove alongside and told me to switch on my radio. A torrent of confused reporting and comment poured forth. Our outing ended abruptly. As I drove up

Massachusetts Avenue to the British Embassy we passed the elegant Japanese Embassy building. The smoke was curling from every chimney in the house as they burned their documents. I knew now that we would win the war.

My equivalent at the Japanese Embassy, the Assistant Naval Attaché, had also gone in to his office that morning, to see if there was anything from the Admiralty in Tokyo. He found nothing, took in the milk which was on the doorstep, and went off to play golf. Tokyo was not risking any leaks by informing anybody of what was about to happen, other than those obliged to know.*

It has never been stated but it was a fact that after the news broke panic reigned in parts of the United States. Glued to my communications radio I listened to a New York Station announcing that hostile planes were believed to be approaching the city. From whence they might be coming was unclear, but something of an exodus had begun. One's friends said, "We've lost the fleet, it's all over isn't it?" This kind of thing lasted for several days. Then it happened. The entire American nation seemed to arise, shake itself, and set out with grim determination to seek revenge. An amazing and unforgettable spectacle, and a beautiful illustration of the mercurial American temperament with its violent swings of mood. It is so unlike our own.

In one of the series of long personal letters which Ian would write to me from the Admiralty, he commented upon Pearl Harbor. "It must have been fascinating seeing America go to war and we were delighted with Mayor La Gardia's [*sic*] instructions to the American people not to scream. It has cheered everybody enormously over here. It was perhaps a good thing for the relationship between our two countries that *Prince of Wales* and *Repulse* were sunk because otherwise I don't believe the Americans would ever have recovered from the disgrace of Pearl Harbor. I hope they will have the guts to shoot Kimmel and the General. It might put good ideas into Winston's mind." His views on current events were never dull.

Now a British Joint Staff Mission under Field Marshal Sir John Dill was integrated into the American war effort. My one-horse show was taken over by a staff of five naval officers. What I had been doing for the past two years would have provided material for a book. I could not imagine any posting more fascinating for a junior officer. What would 'Uncle John' do with me now?

---

* I have checked and refreshed my memory of these events, not easily forgotten, by reference to: Clausen, H. C. and Lee, B. *Pearl Harbor: Final Judgment*, Crown Publishers, 1992. ISBN 0–517–58644–4.

CHAPTER 3

Adventures in
the American Tropics

THE SPLENDOURS OF THE TROPICAL
FLORA AND THE EXCITEMENT
OF NAVAL INTELLIGENCE

"Smithers," said the Naval Attaché, Admiral Pott, "I suppose you speak Spanish?" I knew that it was not a question but an order for my benefit. "Yes, Sir." (I went that afternoon to the Berlitz School.) "The DNI wants you to go to Mexico to look into the possibility of German submarines refuelling down there. There have been sinkings in the Yucatan Channel, you know." Mexico was full of oil. The Naval Attaché was a very severe, reserved and rather remote figure, as a serving Admiral should be with his staff. But with time I had come to realise that he was an extremely good friend in disguise. I became Acting Naval Attaché at the British Diplomatic Missions in Mexico, the five Central American Republics and Panama, and Honorary ADC to Sir John Hunter, the Governor of British Honduras. No other officer from the Volunteer Reserve had been or would be given a territory of his own in the course of the war. Though nominally under Washington two thousand miles away, it was up to me to carry out my mandate in this vast fascinating territory in whatever way I thought best. It would mean travel out from my seven capital cities to any point on the coast where information might be available. I would supervise a system for the collection and transmission of Naval Intelligence.

This would oblige me to pass through some of the world's richest flora. It ranged from the tropical jungles of sea level to the cloud forests and cactus deserts of the Cordillera. In between was a splendid orchid flora as well as an array of temperate flowering plants at the higher elevations which would have furnished a garden without any other additions: dahlias, lupins, penstemons, scarlet lobelias, many amaryllids and endless other delights. Ian Fleming, who had certainly engineered the appointment, said that 'Uncle

John', who knew his officers, was heard to murmur, "He must remember that he is a naval attaché and not a botanical attaché." I cannot express the excitement with which I set off in my car on the long drive to Mexico to assume my fascinating new kingdom. In Washington I had been a small but significant part of a great machine dealing with the world crisis. Now I was all on my own with a limited but fascinating responsibility in a vast area which approximated to my idea of Heaven.

My territory comprised some of the world's most interesting and dramatically beautiful countries which seemed overloaded not only with the excitement of my daily work but with attendant delights which were not strictly part of the Naval Intelligence routine. Around it swirled the Pacific Ocean, the Caribbean Sea and the Bay of Mexico. Above it towered the great snow-capped volcanoes of the Cordillera. Nature, though very beautiful, was cruel and violent: earthquakes, erupting volcanoes, violent storms, poisonous snakes and spiders, forbiddingly armed plants and deadly diseases. Mankind was welcoming and talented. The great Mexican painters and architects were working all around me and some became lifelong friends. The lilting Mexican music, so gay and yet so sad, was in the air everywhere. But mankind seemed to set little value upon human life which was readily expendable. The extraordinary contrasts of beauty and violence only served to enhance the value of the former. It was an experience never to be repeated or equalled and always to be treasured. It lasted for four years.

The British Ambassador in Mexico City was a notoriously difficult man. My colleague the Military Attaché, Colonel Wright, a stickler for doing things in the approved manner, would have an almost daily quarrel with His Excellency, insisting that the latter read and discuss his reports to the War Office. When I returned from my first journey to the Pacific Coast and drafted a short report for the Admiralty, as a matter of proper routine and courtesy I sent a copy to the Ambassador. "Why bother me with this bloody nonsense?" he minuted in red ink. Excellent, I was even more on my own than before. I never troubled him with a report again and we always got on well together: our contacts were purely social.

The Mexicans knew perfectly well why I was there and were helpful. Nevertheless faces had to be saved. My enthusiasm for tourism to study the Mexican flora and the great wealth of Spanish colonial architecture, both of which had the advantage of being perfectly genuine, suited both sides. As a result there are a few palm specimens in the British Museum Herbarium, and there are over a thousand photographic transparencies of Spanish colonial churches and monuments in the Victoria & Albert Museum archives. Some of the beautiful buildings in remote villages recorded in them no longer exist.

Most of my work lay down at the coast on the Gulf of Mexico and the Caribbean. This was quite another world from the uplands of Mexico or of Guatemala. My position as Honorary ADC to Sir John Hunter, the Governor of British Honduras, provided some variety and excitement. (PLATE I) The American Intelligence services had been caught unprepared by the war. They had plenty of money and enthusiastic but inexperienced staff. They now became convinced that a German submarine was being refuelled by an organisation operating out of the Colony. This was just what I had been sent to Mexico by 'Uncle John' to detect. I was able to provide the US Naval Attaché with conclusive evidence that the submarine which they cited had been sunk by us in quite other waters some time ago: we had clothing of survivors. I also knew that enough oil to refuel a long range submarine could not have been transported on the coast without the fact being reported to me. But it was all to no avail. The US General commanding the Sea Frontier from Panama became quite excited. If we did not arrest the fifty or so suspects he would come and do it himself. The British Intelligence authorities, reflecting that we were at war with Germany, not with the USA, decided to waste no more time in argument. Sir John ordered the arrests. About fifty of the suspects were sent to Jamaica for interrogation. They were subsequently returned to Belize to continue their accustomed trade of smuggling. In the Caribbean this is a well accepted occupation even today. It has nothing to do with submarines.

But British Honduras was not only a smugglers' paradise but also that of a botanist. The remains of the great mahogany forests still grew there. Cocoa was still growing wild in certain areas of the interior. There was a fine orchid flora including the famous *Brassavola digbyana*, since rechristened *Rhyncholaelia digbyana*, which has given wonderful fringed and bearded lips to many modern cattleya hybrids. In the far south of the Colony there was an almost incessant rainfall and wonderful wet tropical vegetation which merged as one moved further north into the drier vegetation of Yucatan.

Transport up and down the coast from Puerto Barrios in Guatemala to Belize was by a small motor vessel, the *Heron*. There was, as I recall, but one cabin on deck which I occupied. We sailed out of the bay at Barrios, surrounded by tropical forests, in the early evening. During the night I was awakened by a warm breeze in my face carrying an unwelcome smell with it. In the darkness I saw a very large head and horns. These belonged to a cow which had pushed open the cabin door. I managed to push her out again and went back to sleep. Next morning *Heron* stopped offshore the small port of Blair Atholl and the cow was hustled unceremoniously overboard. She swam happily off to the beach where a reception committee was evidently expecting her.

Back in Mexico the United States Naval Attaché, Captain Conover, had a staff of four Assistant Attachés. He was a delightful man and it was at his house, a former convent, that I met my wife. She was on holiday from St Louis, Missouri. We were married three weeks later. Our honeymoon in Missouri lasted but two days since there was nobody to 'hold the fort' for me. But in reality the honeymoon lasted for three years, the duration of our stay together in Mexico. Since then Dojean has been a diplomat's wife, a politician's wife and a gardener's wife. All three positions require exceptional qualities which she possesses. Much more difficult in these times, it appears, is to remain married at all. In a life of good fortune this has been my greatest blessing.

After very extensive travels in all seven of my Republics and many adventures, the information system which was required seemed to be running well and it was less often necessary to leave the Embassy in Mexico on long journeys to the coast or to travel to Central America. Weekends became a possibility. We rented a cottage in a compound in Cuernavaca. In those days it was indeed paradise. The Rancho Almanalco had originally been the property of the Conquistador Alvarado. It had been provided with a stream of pure water which flowed from the volcano high above and which could be used to irrigate the garden. The house was of the simplest: no more was needed in that perfect climate. The bath consisted of a machine of elegant simplicity called the 'Rapido', a vertical boiler fired by wood. If when in the bath one needed a little more hot water, one leaned over the side, picked up a piece of wood, and lobbed it into the 'Rapido'. I feel sure that Adam and Eve, before making that fatal if understandable mistake, had a 'Rapido' in the Garden of Eden.

Though Mexicans lived in a country in which almost anything could be grown somewhere or other, and though it was packed full with one of the world's richest flora, they were not connoisseurs of plants. The flower markets were filled to overflowing with tuberose, calla and gladioli. Most other plants, if one asked for a name, were 'tulipan'. There were some fine Mexican botanists: men of science. But when it came to horticulture the few masters were, inconveniently, Japanese or German. Interesting planting material was difficult to find except for two great families: the orchids and the palms.

The garden at the Rancho Almanalco soon began to fill up with orchids, mainly natives of Mexico and Central America. *Laelia, Stanhopea, Gongora, Lycaste, Masdevallia, Catasetum, Epidendrum, Cypripedium, Oncidium* and many minor genera. At an elevation of about five thousand feet a wide range of orchids could be grown. They filled the balcony of the house and then filled a slat-house contrived on the roof. They were attached to every likely tree. I had never lived with or grown orchids. Now was the chance to do so. There was much to learn.

An early lesson was about symbiosis. During the spectacularly beautiful drive down to Veracruz on a naval mission I had noticed an orchid in full flower growing on a silk cotton tree in an accessible position. Just the thing for the garden at Cuernavaca. On the return journey I detached the very large plant of *Schomburgkia tibicinis* from the tree and loaded it into the boot of my car. It seemed surprisingly light. I did not know that the pseudobulbs of this orchid are hollow. Neither did I know that it was symbiotic with a particularly large and aggressive ant which lived inside the pseudobulbs. To my extreme discomfort I discovered this on the long drive back to Cuernavaca.

Orchids come from so many different altitudes, climates and local environments that more than any other family, they oblige the gardener to study the conditions in which they live in nature. I soon learned that it was useless to bring an orchid back from the cloud forest in Costa Rica, cool and damp throughout the year, and to expect it to grow in Cuernavaca. There it rained every evening for half of the year and not at all for the other half, with swings in temperature from chilly in January to the nineties in May. Of course the same reasoning applies in some degree to all cultivated plants, but no family that I know of has such a wide range of requirements as the Orchidaceae. Almost all can be depended upon to grow well, provided that they are given exactly the conditions which they like. All can be depended upon to dwindle and die if they are displeased. I do not share the view of some modern photographers who find beauty in a dead or dying flower: it is always painful to see the process of death and never beautiful.

The stanhopeas could be relied upon to grow and flower on our balcony with little attention, for they were local inhabitants. The oddest of orchids, the large handsome leaves not unlike those of an aspidistra, would grow vertically from the wooden basket in which the plant hung. The flower spikes would make their way out of the bottom between the wooden slats, hanging downwards. One's first sight of a stanhopea in bloom gives the impression of a plant gone quite mad. The explanation of the phenomenon is that in nature a stanhopea will probably cling to the debris in the fork of a tree, a position which facilitates its particular style of acrobatics. Usually about breakfast-time the very large globular buds would suddenly explode, releasing the powerful fragrance of vanilla characteristic of the genus and perhaps not entirely compatible with the world's best breakfast: fried eggs, black beans and scorching hot chiles all covered with tomato sauce and displayed on a tortilla: 'huevos ranchero'.

Perversely, no doubt, I wanted to grow a group of orchids which were manifestly unsuited to the climate of Cuernavaca. I had much to learn about gardening. I would not attempt such a thing today. These were the dendrobiums, Indians and south-east Asiatics, which even strayed as far north as southern Japan and south into Australia. Certainly some of the species of that very large genus would have grown in my garden, but it was *Dendrobium nobile* which caught my fancy and still does so. Why I cannot tell. There are

A stanhopea gives the impression of a plant gone quite mad.

other orchids equally beautiful. The latest suggestion of the scientists is that individual men and women are mutually attracted by compatible DNA. Perhaps. Men, fortunately no doubt, do not inevitably fall in love with the most beautiful available woman. However that may be, this orchid has always looked at me with a beckoning expression not entirely unfamiliar amongst our own species. I did my best to respond, but Cuernavaca was much too warm in autumn when *D. nobile* would have welcomed a Himalayan chill. I gave up, but the spell remained upon me to revive in other circumstances far from Mexico.

More successful was my romance with the Lycastes, natives of Mexico and of much of Central America. Like other of my attachments to a genus of plants, it began with an entrancing fragrance. *Lycaste aromatica* was accurately named by the eminent botanists involved in its description: Lindley and Hooker. They might indeed have used the word 'fragrans' and have remained in order. The *New RHS Dictionary* says that this orchid is 'sweetly scented'. But the *Oxford Dictionary* adds to the meaning of the word 'aromatic' the epithet 'spicy'. This exactly describes the unique aroma of this pretty little orchid; Lindley and Hooker got it right. The scent seems to have all of the ingredients of a well spiced Rum Punch with cinnamon predominating. One sometimes sees this rather hardy orchid in displays at the RHS flower shows at Westminster. I always make straight for it. Nothing better recalls the past than a fragrance recaptured. For a brief moment I am aged thirty and back in my garden in Mexico.

My other adventure with plants in Mexico was with the palms. Few species were available for planting and there was not much room in the small irrigated garden. I planted several and collected herbarium specimens of *Brahea dulcis* in the wild. Hoping one day to expand my interest in these plants into a wider cultivation, though unclear for the time being how that might come about, I wrote to Liberty Hyde Bailey, the greatest living authority on the Palmae at that time. He responded kindly as all good plantsmen do, and sent me a collection of his publications, individual pamphlets in the series of *Gentes Herbarum*. Like the Orchidaceae, the Palmae is an immense family with hundreds of genera and thousands of species, many of which have not yet been identified or described, and some of which will probably be destroyed before this can happen. There is also a lively science in fossil palm species which are now long extinct.

Palms are fast growers. Some ten years after leaving the Rancho Almanalco we returned to look at it. On entering I was struck by the increase in shade since my time, but for the moment I could see no sign of my palms. Then I looked up, and there they were, far overhead. Once I had looked them in the eye: now I only saw the underpinnings. One day, somehow, I would grow palms in earnest.

It was at Cartago, in Costa Rica, that I saw a garden which was unique at that time and which was to have a lasting influence on my ideas of what my own garden should be. From this experience there grew the concept which was to take form many years later at Vico Morcote. Mr and Mrs Lankester, elderly English people long resident in that most delightful country, invited me to tea. It was an almost perfect replica of tea on the lawn at Elvetham Hall with old Lady Calthorpe, which I had sometimes enjoyed on my way back to Itchen Stoke from Oxford in June at the end of the Summer Term. The silver tea things, the light flickering under the silver kettle, the pretty china, the thin cut sandwiches and the little sugar-covered cakes. Delicious! In the near distance across the lawn was what appeared at first sight to be a neglected and broken down woodland.

Broken down it was, and was intended to be, but neglected it most certainly was not. It had been left in its natural state, with fallen and decaying trees amongst a younger generation. Ways had been cut through this natural cycle of life and death, and on every available branch and log an orchid had been planted. Almost all were species native to Costa Rica. There were even some from the cloud forest. The beauty and interest of the garden, for such it was, were unique in my then experience. It was not, of course, what I later attempted in Vico Morcote, the creation of an ecosystem of exotics where nothing existed before. A native ecosystem was already there and the Lankesters had used it to house the best collection of orchid species in Central America. I understand that by good fortune the 'garden' is preserved to this day though the Lankesters are dead these many years.

In Mexico the telegram arrived from Winchester inviting me to submit my name as Prospective Conservative Parliamentary Candidate for that constituency. It was a surprise. My wife and I knew that acceptance would mean the end of a fascinating and delightful period in our lives and the beginning of a new and more sombre chapter. Besides the politics of the post-war period it meant a return to Hampshire and to what might remain of the garden at Itchen Stoke after the war. My father had died and Itchen Stoke without him could never be the same again. But the painful decision to accept was made easier for us.

The Rt Hon Leslie Hore-Belisha was visiting Mexico. He had been defeated in the 1945 election after an illustrious career as a senior Cabinet Minister. He it had been who as Minister of Transport had introduced pedestrian crossings in England, 'Belisha Beacons', which gave the pedestrian an absolute priority of way. The handsome orange globes on black and white standards were collector's items for the young and tiresome until the novelty of stealing them wore off. At the critical time before the beginning of hostilities Hore-Belisha had been Secretary of State for War. Greatly daring, he had fired a number of well-connected and popular elderly generals, replacing them with younger men, greatly to the indignation of the establishment and to the benefit of the war effort. I showed him the Winchester telegram. His face became grave. He turned and looked me straight in the eye, and I remember his exact words: "Young man, I would go on my BENDED KNEES" – and he spat out the words – "for anything HALF as good." He never again secured a seat in the House of Commons or the Peerage which he richly deserved.

I telegraphed my acceptance to Winchester and a fascinating chapter in life closed therewith. I had been enthralled by Mexico in a dozen ways. The extraordinary combination of beauty of every kind with tragedy of every kind had sunk deep into my being. Having travelled more widely in Mexico than any other diplomat that I knew and for that matter more than any of my Mexican friends, I found the Mexicans more difficult to comprehend at the end of my four years in that country than at their beginning, but I felt an affection for the extraordinary land which nothing could extinguish to this day. It was in bitter sorrow that we drove up the mountain-side leaving Cuernavaca. We knew that nothing in life would ever be the same again. It never was.

But Hampshire was home and I knew my ground. Fifteen years as Member for the Winchester constituency were nothing but a pleasure. A Saturday afternoon round of village fêtes in the Test or Itchen Valleys was as enjoyable a way as could be imagined of passing the time and doing business all at once. I never had the slightest controversy with my electors and supporters, and very little with the local socialist opposition. In fact it sometimes happened that at a public meeting the principal socialist heckler, having had a good time, would get up to propose the vote of thanks, to the consternation of the loyal lady supporter who was waiting prepared to do just that. There is a great difference between finding a constituency because one needs it in order to sit in Parliament, and sitting in Parliament because that is what one's friends wanted one to do.

The garden at Itchen Stoke House had survived the war so far as its main features were concerned, but almost all my rarities were dead. A new beginning was needed. Our old gardener, Bull, had been in charge through the war but without the accustomed assistant. My father's collection of apples and pears was in reasonable shape. Two seasons of planting put the whole garden well on the way to recovery. Then my Aunt Evelyn North gave us her house, 30 Wilton Crescent, in London, and herself moved to a smaller house nearby. There were altogether too many houses in the family. Lord Ashburton had always wanted to buy Itchen Stoke House, which lay surrounded by his properties and which had been built by a member of his family. When my mother moved to Colebrook House in Winchester it seemed sensible to use that as our political base in the constituency. I sold Itchen Stoke to a delighted new owner, who flew the flag of Lord Lieutenant of the County of Hampshire from what had once been my garden. Well – not really my garden, for it was my mother who had made it and I had only inherited and restored her work.

CHAPTER 4

Adventures in a Cathedral City

CREATING A WATER GARDEN
IN THE SHADOW OF
WINCHESTER CATHEDRAL

My mother died in the cruel month of January, 1950. I buried her beside my father in the churchyard at Itchen Stoke, fifty yards from the garden which she had made and loved. I had thought my parents faultless. I still do so. Now both were gone. It had never occurred to me to blame them for my own mistakes.

Before the war my mother had purchased a small plant of *Mahonia bealei*, then a novelty from the Himalaya, for the price of a guinea – that is to say, one pound and five pence in modern currency. It was thought by her and by my father to have been a great extravagance: the highest price they had ever paid for a plant. But the pleasure which they derived from the lovely fragrant yellow sprays produced unfailingly every midwinter, followed by blue berries with a 'bloom' like that of grapes, made it a good investment. Now Lord Ashburton kindly provided me with a flowering branch from my parent's plant. I cast it upon my mother's coffin as it lay in the open grave while the sexton stood ready with his spade.

Colebrook House in Winchester was now mine. In the immediate post-war years work upon it had been almost impossible. Now we set about its restoration in earnest. In much earlier times it had been two houses. Later it had been the Cathedral Choir School for which purpose the two houses had been put together to make one larger house. Recently it had been put to wartime uses. Its location was interesting. Winchester – Venta Belgarum in the Roman Empire – had been one of the earliest and most important centres of the greco-roman culture in Britain. It had been so nearly extinguished in the Dark Ages after the Romans left and was revived, notably from Winchester, both before and after the Norman conquest. In the course of various

33

city building operations many traces of the ancient Roman buildings had been uncovered. I had a trial hole dug in the garden at Colebrook. The remains of a collapsed Roman house were found, with pieces of pottery and other relics. Colebrook Street had been a Roman street. Mediaeval remains also abounded. More than once, elderly former choirboys returning in sentimental mood to the site of their old school told me that there was an underground passage which led from beneath the ancient staircase to what had formerly been the Benedictine Monastery attached to the Cathedral. Diligent search never discovered it. It must have been a very wet affair if it ever existed. The water table was only about five feet below the surface of the ground.

The house of 1950 faced west. (PLATE 2) It had been heightened at some point by the addition of a third floor. The windows looked directly into the east end of the most venerable of all the English cathedrals: the retro-choir, then the choir and finally the Norman tower which overlooked everything. I discovered to my astonishment that the centre of the front door at Colebrook House lay precisely upon the central axis of the choir. Surely this could be no accident. As in some other cruciform mediaeval cathedrals, the choir was upon a slightly different axis from that of the nave, symbolising the drooping head of Christ upon the cross. Research now showed that in the early mediaeval period the building which then stood on the site of Colebrook House had belonged to Augustinian canons. I often thought of them as I crossed the threshold.

But how much of the mediaeval building remained? The façade was William and Mary or perhaps early Queen Anne. But if one looked at the house from the east side it was a different building. (PLATE 4) Tudor chimneys, heightened when the extra storey had been added to the house, dominated the scene. They were topped by nineteenth-century chimney pots. To the back of the house two towers had been attached. One contained the staircase (PLATE 3) and the other 'closets'. Both had been additions to a mediaeval house. Inside the house the rooms were wallpapered and were furnished with coal-burning fireplaces from the nineteenth century. The past was concealed. With Wilfred Carpenter-Turner, the Cathedral Architect, and his scholarly wife Barbara, the City Archivist, we set about the stripping down and restoration of the whole building.

When Henry VIII dissolved the English monastic orders and confiscated their property, the house of the Augustinian canons had passed to the crown. So we had been a royal property, no everyday fact of life. More was to follow.

Over the garden wall to the south lay the grounds of Wolvesey palace, the magnificent residence of the bishop, and the ruins of the mediaeval palace which had preceded it. (PLATE 2) An improbable couple, King Philip II of Spain and Queen Mary Tudor of England had 'celebrated', if that is the proper word, their unhappy marriage in Winchester cathedral and had 'honeymooned', certainly an improper word, in what were now the ruins of the old Wolvesey palace. The City of Winchester had been put to some inconvenience and expense by these events, and Philip and Mary then and there gave the former Augustinian building to the city fathers as part of the recompense for their out-of-pocket situation. The document which they signed, preserved in the city archives, constituted one of our title deeds. So we had passed under hand of a King of Spain and of his wife a Queen of England! There may be another house in England of which this could be said, but if there is it has not come to my attention. It remained to discover how much of the mediaeval house had survived behind the modern, that is to say late seventeenth- or early eighteenth-century façade.

In the records the two principal downstairs rooms, either side of the doorway, were named *aula magna* and *aula coquina*. We started work on the 'great hall' which was in fact a modest nineteen feet square with three windows. The 'kitchen hall', now to be my library and study, with two windows, was left for a later stage of the work. *Aula magna* had a small metal coal-burning fireplace on a wallpapered chimney-breast. I gave instructions for it to be stripped and the work began early.

Coming down to breakfast I looked into *aula magna* to see what was going on. Through the dust there appeared a broad chimney-breast of eighteenth century brick. Nice, I thought, and the search for an elegant mantelpiece of the period passed through my mind. Then some angel spoke to me. Vandalism or no, I heard myself saying to the bricklayer, "Knock me out four bricks just there," and I pointed to the centre of the chimney-breast. Peering into the hole I saw a V-shaped stone structure. It was unmistakable. It was the apex of the arch of an early Tudor stone fireplace. Within an hour the whole of the brickwork was gone and there stood revealed a real beauty – something beyond my wildest dreams – a Tudor fireplace, clearly of the earliest period when chimneys had just been invented and were tacked on to the back of existing buildings. (PLATE 3)

But what was the situation on the same chimney-stack on the floor above where, in the principal bedroom, there was another small coal grate? This was quickly removed and there stood revealed a second elegant Tudor fireplace. (PLATE 3) It was of smaller dimensions and fewer pretensions than the one in *aula magna* but beautiful and in perfect condition. In the back of the fireplace was a miniature stone arch just over a foot wide. Behind it was a small chamber two and a half feet deep. Wilfred, an expert in old buildings, had never seen anything like it and had no suggestion to make as to its purpose. Barbara consulted the City records. In Queen Elizabeth I's reign it appeared that the house had been occupied by the apothecary to the Dean and Chapter of the Cathedral. We had before us an apothecary's still of the Tudor period. If another existed we had not heard of it.

But where had the elixirs from the still gone to? The little arch had been closed against the fire, probably by a metal plate. Behind the bedroom was a closet now converted into a tiny bathroom, just large enough to contain the modern machines of hygiene. It occupied a tower, probably attached to the back of the house at the same time as the chimney. From the chamber in the fireplace we found a channel leading into what was now the bathroom. Clearly the elixirs from the still had landed up there to be dealt with by the apothecary.

It remained to test the fireplace in *aula magna* which we intended to use to burn wood logs. These included plentiful ancient oak beams, no longer serviceable, which were available from repairs to the Cathedral roof. The Dean and Chapter were glad to sell them. So for the first time for a couple of centuries a fire was lit on the hearth. The chimney absolutely refused to receive the smoke which soon filled the room. A specialist architect was consulted who installed baffles and other devices but without the smallest success. "Beg pardon, mister," said the old bricklayer who had been putting in these gadgets, "Beg pardon o' that ther harchitec, but ee be throttled." I was not quite sure whether he meant to throttle the architect and asked for clarification. He explained that the Tudor chimney was meant to burn wood but that the chimney pot on top of it had been put in along with the much smaller coal-burning fireplace which we had removed. The chimney was throttled. "Say nothing to the architect," I said, "but just go up there and take off the pot." It was no sooner said than done. The fire drew away splendidly.

In the old dining-room, now disused, there was another small coal-burning fireplace but older chimneys stood above. Our appetite for Tudor fireplaces was now insatiable. The coal grate was removed only to reveal a gaping hole. The ancient fireplace which had certainly stood there had been destroyed. It must have been quite a small one.

William Symonds, a Winchester Mayor and patriarch of the Tudor period, had built a fine half-timbered and jettied house on Winchester High Street. It was one of the most attractive features of the city. Now it had been purchased by a shoe shop. They asked for permission to demolish it and to build a nice new building for their business. This was too much for the city fathers, but to my distress they finally agreed that the interior of the house might be destroyed and rebuilt provided that the new façade would look just like the old one. The shoe shop closed the deal with alacrity.

One day I walked up there to look at the demolition which was far advanced. Amongst the debris stood a small stone Tudor fireplace probably of the reign of Henry VIII. "What are you going to do with that?" I asked the contractor. "I thought of putting it into my bungalow in Fair Oak," he replied. Remaining as calm and unmoved as I could manage I said, "I shall be glad to buy it from you: then you could get a nice new one for your bungalow." The fireplace now stands in the small former dining-room at Colebrook House.

Not everybody shared our admiration for our discoveries. Henry McIlhenny, collector of modern art and benefactor of the Philadelphia Museum, when told that we had found Tudor fireplaces, advised, "Cover them up as quickly as possible." It did not seem proper to advise him what to do with some of his modern pictures.

While sitting in the House of Commons during the week, I seemed to be spending the weekends in a house filled with the spirits of an earlier day. It even passed through my mind that there might be a ghost: perhaps that of the apothecary? As a county, Hampshire was rather rich in ghosts. While I was a small boy I remember the word passing from mouth to mouth in the village of Itchen Stoke that 'the thing', sometimes also called 'the worm', had appeared in the nearby village of Tichborne. 'The thing', which nobody could describe but which was not pleasant, appeared only when the reigning Tichborne was about to die. Tichbornes had lived there from time immemorial and had acquired quite a family of ghosts. On this occasion Sir Joseph Tichborne was away in East Africa hunting big game. In those days before portable radio penetrated the jungle and the bush it was assumed that the lion had got him. No doubt 'the thing' had its own superior communications. However, to the confusion of 'the thing' Sir Joseph returned home shortly afterwards and everybody agreed that he had never looked better. He died 'unexpectedly' some weeks later.

It must have been in 1952 at an early session of the Council of Europe in Strasbourg that I sat next to Cosmo Russell at lunch. He was a member of the newly constituted Secretariat, one day to be my own though I did not then dream of such a thing. What do you say to a Member of Parliament meeting him casually for the first time? Surely, "Where do you sit for?" I replied "Winchester." "Ah," said Cosmo, "that is where I saw my only ghost." Another boring ghost story, I thought, but I listened politely. "In the war," Cosmo continued, "I was billeted in the Abbey Mill House." I now listened intently, hanging on every word, and said nothing. The Abbey Mill House, inhabited by my friend Robin McCall, the Town Clerk, faced Colebrook House across the narrow street. "It was at dusk one evening," Cosmo continued, "that as I returned to my billet I noticed a woman standing in the doorway of the house opposite." The house opposite was Colebrook House. I still said nothing and Cosmo continued: "There was something very odd about her and I looked again. She was wearing old-fashioned rough clothes, as though they were hand-sewn; and she seemed somehow out of proportion, too short, as though her lower part was missing. Then I realised that I was looking at something extraordinary. I rushed into the Abbey Mill House, called my hosts, 'Quick, quick, to the window,' and I rushed to the window overlooking the street. But the old woman had gone, and so had the doorway. Just the plain brick wall of the house opposite remained."

At this point Cosmo's story ended. That was all he knew. What he did not know was that early nineteenth-century illustrations show a doorway just in the place which he had described (see p. 39) that the present Colebrook House had then been two houses, the entrance to the smaller one being through this doorway which had been bricked up leaving no trace of its former presence when the two houses were united: and that when my mother had put in an extra bathroom and the street had been excavated to receive the necessary downpipe, the old level of the street had been discovered slightly more than a foot below the existing street level. The floor in what was now the pantry in Colebrook, formerly the entrance to the smaller house, was still at that level. So the old woman 'seen' by Cosmo had been standing in a doorway which had once existed but no longer did so, at a street level which had once existed but was now much higher. Obviously the old woman also no longer existed.

So we owned a ghost! Or did we? My own belief is that even after Einstein and quantum theory we have but a poor understanding of the nature

PLATE 1 The British Embassy, Washington DC in wartime, 1941. A grandstand view of a world in crisis.

Government House, Belize, British Honduras, 1943. My work as Honorary ADC to the Governor provided some excitement.

PLATE 2 Over the garden wall of Colebrook House lay the ruins of the mediaeval Wolvesey Palace. King Philip of Spain and Queen Mary Tudor lodged here at the time of their wedding in Winchester Cathedral.

Colebrook House: the west front. The centre of the entrance door lay precisely on the axis of the Choir of Winchester Cathedral

PLATE 3 The early Tudor fireplace of *aula magna*, discovered behind the existing chimney breast and dating from the time when chimneys had just been invented and were tacked onto the back of existing buildings.

The staircase, constructed in a tower attached to the east side of the house.

On the floor above *aula magna* was another Tudor fireplace into the back of which had been built an apothecary's still. The elixirs were led out by way of a channel at the back of the still.

PLATE 4 Seen from the east the earlier origins of Colebrook House were apparent.
The staircase tower stands next to Tudor chimneys.

The entrance to Colebrook House. On the right of the doorway is an American tree peony 'High Noon'.

PLATE 5 St Ethelwold's Stream, created by a Saxon Bishop of Winchester to drive the Abbey Mill. The dining-room balcony overlooks the stream with the knapped flint wall beyond the garden bridge.

The Colebrook cascades into St Ethelwold's Stream.

PLATE 6 From the open kitchen window we would catch eels.

The water garden in which the image of the Cathedral is reflected.

Dwarf rhododendrons and other ericaceous plants defy their alkaline surroundings. They are growing in a bank of peat bricks supported by masonry discarded from the Cathedral.

PLATES 7 The water staircase with four shallow steps, each broader than the preceding one. This 'forced perspective' gives an illusion of greater distance.

In the water eye the water wells up gently as though from a spring, before flowing down the water staircase.

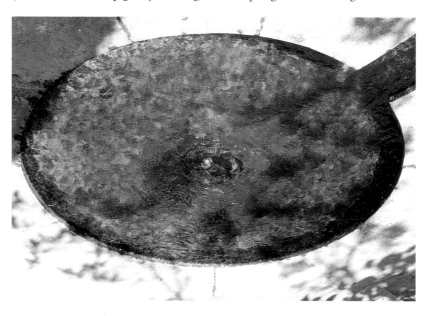

PLATE 8 *Dendrobium superbum* (*left*) and *Dendrobium thyrsiflorum* (*right*) at Colebrook House. Orchids could so easily take over the whole of my gardening life.

Colebrook House, Winchester, early 19th century. At that time there were two houses, later combined into a single Colebrook House which served as the Cathedral Choir School. The doorway of the smaller house, shown here, was bricked up and no hint of its existence remained. Cosmo Russell saw his ghost standing in this doorway which no longer existed.

of time. We cannot understand it because we live within and not outside the system of which it is a part. Sometimes by accident a person will stumble upon a 'bug' in the system, which like a 'bug' in my computer will suddenly reveal something from another programme, something in the past or perhaps in the future. If this were so, then the old woman's ghost belonged to Cosmo, not to me. At any rate, none of us ever saw her.

The garden at Colebrook was about half an acre in extent. It was entered by an elegant doorway from the street. (PLATE 4) It was separated from the garden of Wolvesey Palace by a wall of knapped flints. This, and the puddled chalk wall, were the walling techniques of the chalk country. The flints had to be removed from the farmland where they damaged the plough. They were then split by the ancient technique of 'knapping'. The exposed black surfaces embedded in puddled chalk made an attractive wall. But the feature of the garden was water.

St Ethelwold's Stream, named for the Saxon Bishop of Winchester who excavated it as a branch from the River Itchen to drive the Abbey Mill, passed under Colebrook House and through the garden. (PLATE 5) Except occasionally in a winter storm it was a limpid chalk stream. It was full of trout, crayfish and eels with an occasional marauding pike. In some years a kingfisher would honour us with his presence, flashing through the garden and away down the valley. From the west St Ethelwold was joined by a small stream which had presumably sewered the Benedictine Monastery formerly attached to the Cathedral. From the east it was joined by the Colebrook, from which the street and the house took their names. (PLATE 5) None of the streams had been integrated into the planning of the garden: they were there, partly subterraneous, and both flowed surreptitiously into St Ethelwold. This must be changed!

We constructed a balcony to the dining-room, which overlooked St Ethelwold, and then a space at water level where one might sit to watch the busy life of the stream. The steep opposite bank we faced with a wall of peat bricks such as are used for burning, into which dwarf Rhododendrons and other ericaceous plants could be inserted, defying the alkaline surroundings of the garden. At that time part of the mediaeval balustrade of the cathedral was being replaced. We bought it from the Dean and Chapter and incor-porated it in the stream bank. The chalk-haters throve exceedingly in the peat. (PLATE 6)

Both the smaller streams were made to cascade into St Ethelwold with a splash instead of trickling in unobtrusively. But it was the stream from the

Cathedral precincts which offered the greatest possibilities. It flowed mainly underground, invisible. No longer!

Across the Abbey Passage, between Colebrook House and the Cathedral and on the course of the stream, there stood four small houses. These had been condemned by the City Council for demolition. We purchased the site, demolished the houses, and replaced them with the water garden which now occupies the area. So far from being invisible, the stream now flows through a rectangular pool in which the image of the Cathedral is reflected. (PLATE 6) Plants of *Calla aethiopica* 'Crowborough' which likes to grow in water, were planted in the pool and flowered with regularity. A pair of brick pillars designed by Wilfred and capped with stone obelisks would frame the view, thus opened to the public. Our reward came not from the City Council, which appeared not to have noticed a major improvement to the amenities of the area, but from the general public in the years ahead. Hardly ever would a visiting tourist en route to or from the Cathedral by way of the Watergate fail to pause to admire the perspective of the tower viewed across the pool. But this was only a first step in the exploitation of the stream.

The mystery of a spring had fascinated me since I was a small boy. Flowing water was exciting, but a spring, bubbling up gently from the earth, was a living being: something extraordinary and mysterious: important in every primitive religion: the abode of spirits. If I could not have a spring I would produce a passable imitation of one. It would be a water-eye.

After it flowed through the rectangular reflecting pool the little stream was tapped by a pipe which led underground beneath the Abbey Passage and into the Colebrook House garden. There the tube would enter the bottom of a circular basin five and a half feet wide and would end vertically about two inches below the water level. The water would well up as though from a spring, gently breaking the surface. (PLATE 7) The uninitiated would never guess the deceit, for there were indeed springs in this valley bottom, where the chalk downs drain into the gravel. The stream would then flow out of the basin and away down four shallow steps of a water staircase, with lawn either side. From a narrow exit from the water eye it would broaden out until it disappeared under the house. Viewed from the house this was a forced perspective giving an impression of much greater distance than was in fact the case. (PLATE 7) Finally the water would splash out into St Ethelwold.

It was a highly successful scheme and it provided shallow slow-flowing water-beds in which I could have grown watercress. But there was plenty of that in the local market: the Itchen is the greatest of watercress rivers as well as the most challenging to the skill of the dry-fly fisherman. So instead there thrived the beautiful varieties of the water Iris, *Iris laevigata*, a true aquatic: the pale blue, the dark blue, the pink and the white varieties and that with white-striped leaves.

All of this was planned, but there was an entirely unforeseen bonus. In a water-staircase it is essential that the water fall from level to level in a clean unbroken ribbon or curtain. The aesthetics demand this. The water-staircase was edged and stepped with elm boards, used for centuries in the Itchen water-meadows to construct hatches, and lasting the lifetime of most people. But the exit from the water eye had to be over smooth paving stones, and over the last of these the water ran shallow and broad before falling in the prescribed ribbon. It soon became apparent that we had inadvertently invented a luxury birds' bathing place. They must have come from far and wide and the fast-running shallow water would be full of them. Some even waited on the grass by the side until there would be room in the bath. Water from flapping wings flew in all directions. I took no credit from this achievement, only great pleasure.

Planting the garden was no problem. Its deep alluvial soil, so different from the thin chalk soil of Itchen Stoke, lent itself to such things as standard roses, at nose level, and many rarities which needed daily inspection. This could be given in such a small space. I also built a small greenhouse leading off the dining-room, for the specific purpose of growing dendrobiums. England of all countries demands a greenhouse attached to the house which can be entered on a bitter midwinter's day without going out of doors.

I have heard it said that every woman should have an Italian lover, but also, unkindly, that if she is an Anglo-Saxon she had better leave it at that. Somehow I felt this about my orchids. They were fascinating – utterly fascinating – and they could so easily take over the whole of my gardening life. In fact they very nearly did this. (PLATE 8) It was not so much their blooming, splendid though this might be, but their whole behaviour: the open visible daily development of the beautiful roots, the young growths, the ripening of the growths for flowering and then the appearance of the flower buds, the flowering and in a little sunshine the perfume. There was something new and exciting for every day leading up to the climax of blooming. There was a great variety of delicious fragrances. All seemed to run in rhythm like some elegant dance. Amongst the latest plants to evolve in nature and the most complex, there is something disconcertingly human about their behaviour. As long as they are given precisely what they require, they are the easiest of plants to grow. But make a mistake and then – they will not tell you: they will leave you to find out. Six months later when you do so – it will be too late. This makes success all the more satisfying. One of the happiest of my memories in gardening is of my great plant of *Dendrobium pierardii* var. *lantinifolium* in full bloom, the four-foot-long growths hanging down vertically and clothed throughout their length with the beautiful pale lilac and cream flowers. If my memory is right my plant received a Cultural Commendation from the Royal Horticultural Society. But the orchids were to be an episode, a fascinating one, and I would leave it at that.

So now was the time to realise my Cuernavaca dream of growing the hybrids of *Dendrobium nobile*. They were out of fashion. Their one great breeder had been Sir Jeremiah Colman, he of the mustard, who boasted that he made his fortune, and presumably financed his dendrobium breeding, from the mustard that people left on their plates. Some of the finest hybrids were called for his garden at Gatton Park. I began to assemble what remained of them, and then found a source in Germany, Herr Wichmann at Celle near Hanover. He had been breeding these plants with some success. As the greenhouse was regulated to give the nobile dendrobiums and a few compatible species of the same genus exactly what they wanted, there was no trouble with growing them. They gave us great pleasure with their masses of fragrant bloom in late January, February and March, just at the time when the winter has begun to seem eternal.

Then the breeding of *Dendrobium nobile* was taken up in Okayama in Japan by Jiro Yamamoto. He produced some magnificent yellows, far surpassing anything raised before, as well as some notable whites. I set off for Okayama with my wife. We talked dendrobium talk throughout the morning, through the lunch which was kindly offered to us and through most of the afternoon. It was a highly successful visit. But to somebody not familiar with the mores of gardeners, perhaps the most remarkable thing about it would have been that Jiro Yamamoto spoke no word of English and we spoke no word of Japanese. But both of us spoke dendrobium.

Colebrook House was really an integral part of the Winchester Cathedral complex. Though formally outside the Cathedral Close, the wall of the Close was one of my garden walls, and there was a doorway giving direct access, perhaps dating from the time of the choir school. The Watergate entrance to the close was adjacent to the private entrance to my garden. The condition of the trees in the Close distressed me. It must have been two centuries since any trees had been planted·in the extensive area. Soon those which remained, decrepit limes for the most part which had been ignorantly topped by some tree butcher looking for a job, would have to be felled as unsafe. I said this to the Dean. He heartily agreed and, good churchman that he was, added, "Why don't you undertake to replant the area for us? The chapter will be delighted and will give you a free hand." So that was that.

For several Sunday afternoons I walked about the Close and the Church-yard with a bundle of bamboos, sticking them into the rich black soil. I tried to see full grown trees standing there a hundred years later. It was an extraordinarily difficult operation. A mediaeval building, unlike a classical one, does not dictate the formal lines of planting with which it should be surrounded. So I began with a simple decision of principle. Around the great Norman Cathedral I would plant the large trees of the forest, natives, which would have been familiar to the men who from the eleventh to the fifteenth centuries had worked to build the structure. Only at the door of the monachorum would there be an Italian cypress, to remind the ghosts of the Benedictine fathers of their Italian origins. There would be a Glastonbury Thorn in homage to the legend of St. Joseph of Arimathaea from whose staff the Glastonbury tree, flowering at Christmas, is alleged to have sprung. But the placing of the trees was a matter of agonising difficulty and only succeeding generations will be able to decide whether I judged rightly.

The beautiful residential houses of the canons and others within the Close are mainly from the seventeenth century with a few later additions as well as much earlier interiors. It so happened that the Bishop of London, Henry Compton, had planted the garden at Fulham Palace in the last decade of the seventeenth century. At that time many new ornamentals were being imported from the Americas. The list of the Bishop's trees still existed. So this would be used as a guide to the selection of trees for planting in the residential areas.

When the sites had all been chosen, the holes had been dug and the trees to be planted had arrived from Hilliers nearby nursery, a day was assigned for the ceremony. Each tree would be blessed at planting: one by the bishop, one by the dean, one by each of the canons, one by each of the cathedral vergers and one by the head choirboy. Of course, an indispensable tree in such circumstances was the Judas tree, *Cercis siliquastrum*, so magnificent when its purple flowers spring from the naked bark in memory of Judas Iscariot's grisly and presumably well-merited end. I really did not like to ask

44

Amelia, Dojean, Peter and Sarah in Winchester, 1964.
The brooding presence of Winchester Cathedral set life
in a long perspective of centuries.

any of the religious dignitaries to bless the Judas tree, and so I just had it planted without a blessing. Of twenty-seven trees planted that day, it was the only one which, in spite of my intensive care, finally died. I believe that it was subsequently replaced and that the replacement survived.

In Winchester Cathedral, where our earliest kings are buried, there are commemorated many men and women who served their country in India, in the Far East, in Africa and in the Americas. Many died and were buried where they had served, supported by the beautiful liturgy of the Church of England which has now been virtually destroyed. I have no desire to be personally remembered, as they are, after my death, and there is scant reason why I should be. Nevertheless the trees in Winchester Cathedral churchyard will probably linger for a couple of centuries, and some a little more, before they too die. If nobody remembers who placed and planted them that will not matter at all.

The end came at Colebrook House in 1964 when, after a brisk campaign across Europe directed by Ted Heath, I was elected Secretary-General of the Council of Europe in Strasbourg. I resigned from the Government in which I had been the Parliamentary Undersecretary of State at the Foreign Office, and from Parliament, to assume my new post. The mandate was for five years. I did not even consider the possibility that I might not return to Colebrook House at the end of it. This, together with the excitement and importance of the work awaiting me in Europe, made the parting more tolerable.

I loved Colebrook, and the great Cathedral, very much. Both were a distillation of England, of her history, of all for which she had once stood and of the benefits which the men who built her empire, like the Romans before them, had brought to mankind in many far-off lands.

CHAPTER 5

Tree Peonies under Imperial Protection

BUILDING UPON
TWO THOUSAND YEARS
OF PLANT BREEDING

Tree peonies had been cultivated and selected in China for at least two thousand years before my mother planted some of them on the north side of the house at Itchen Stoke, just by the front door. They grew splendidly there. The idea that Chinese or Japanese tree peonies – 'Moutan' to the Chinese and 'Botan' to the Japanese – must have full blazing sun is mistaken, though they will be perfectly happy in it. In fact in a treacherous climate of late frosts a north or west wall is a good place for them, provided that they can see the open sky above. The latter point is essential. In England there so often is an 'unexpected' late frost. At the foot of such a wall the sun will not strike the new growths before they are thawed out.

I started to grow a few botan in my garden in Winchester. (PLATE 9) Their ancestors had come to Japan with travelling Buddhist monks from China in about the eighth century AD. In China the roots of the moutan were a valued medical material as they still are today. This has led to the collection and extermination of the wild plants in many areas. It is a classic example of ignorant destructiveness. By collecting the wild plants and selling the roots, the peasants destroy the source of their income. These are plants which are easily cultivated in areas where they grow wild and which could be used to provide a permanent source of income and employment. An appeal is now being launched under the auspices of Professor Hong Tao of the Institute of Forestry in Beijing, Dr Lupo Osti, the distinguished Italian specialist in tree peonies, and others including myself. This is addressed to the Chinese Government suggesting the establishment of a scheme to encourage the commercial cultivation of moutan for the pharmaceutical trade and the prohibition of the collecting of wild plants. It was probably for medicinal rather than for decorative purposes that the moutan were brought to Japan and became the botan.

In China at that early date the moutan already had an illustrious history as privileged garden plants for the rich and powerful. They were placed under Imperial 'protection' by the Sui Emperor Yang-ti some time between the years 589 and 618 AD. Many Chinese families had bred them and choice hybrids were sources of pride and were of great value. By the time of the Ming there was an extensive literature about moutan. Some of the names of these varieties survive. Top Candidate Red was a reference to the Chinese system of examination, central to the imperial administration. A top candidate was a man already marked for a distinguished career. Perhaps Dancing Green Lion, Seven Treasure Crown, Emerald Butterfly and Heaven's Fragrance are more evocative of the flower. Tipsy Immortal Peach is a reference to the imaginary sacred fruit illustrated in much of Chinese painting, perhaps suggesting that this particular 'peach' was suffused with more red than usual. Wang Family Greater Red reveals the pride and wonder with which the breeders of these plants regarded their product.

The Chinese bred for immense double blooms as they still do today. They breed so-called green flowers, white with green markings, though I doubt that a Dancing Green Lion is still to be found in the market. Loyang, an early imperial capital city, was and still is the centre of breeding. The Japanese had a different aesthetic. They bred for single flowers of great elegance. There is also a difference in the method of propagation between Chinese and Japanese tree peonies. It is important to the gardener. The Chinese grow their moutan into immense plants with multiple stems, and then divide them up for distribution. The Japanese graft their botan on to a wild understock as a means of multiplying them. Such were the plants received by me at Colebrook House. It did not occur to me to try to improve plants with such a lengthy, documented and illustrious ancestry, far exceeding that of any other cultivated ornamental that I can think of. It would be enough if a few of these aristocrats would agree to grow and flower for me.

Though I did not know it at the time, the truth is that tree peonies do not really like the English climate, a view shared apparently by some other misguided foreigners. That of the Eastern United States or of Continental Europe is much nearer to the conditions from which they originate: a sharp relatively dry winter and a hot summer. It is not surprising that, outside of Japan, the principal breeding programmes have been conducted in northern France in the last century and in Pennsylvania in the present one. Of course some notable plants have been grown in England since their introduction from China in the early nineteenth century and from Japan at its end. In most cases they have been in full sun and on alkaline soil. Lewis Palmer, then Treasurer of the Royal Horticultural Society, grew a fine plant of a supposedly wild tree peony, *P. rockii*. It was in his hillside chalk garden at Headbourne Worthy, a couple of miles away from Colebrook House. There was a famous plant of the same species in Sir Frederick Stern's garden at Highdown growing in a chalk pit. Sir Frederick, most generous of gardeners, did not like to see any enthusiast leave Highdown with empty hands. I came away with a seedling from his Rock's peony, as did many other people.

My Winchester garden was shaded part of the day by the giant plane trees of Wolvesey Palace which stood to the south. The winter of the Southampton basin is damp and mild and Colebrook House was down at the level of the water meadows. The three streams which flowed through the garden assured a high humidity. Water was everywhere. One morning I awoke to discern through the mist a giant figure sitting on my garden wall: a heron looking pensively at St Ethelwold's stream which held a good many trout. He was not the only poacher. One day Annie, our cook, looking from the kitchen window saw a young Wykehamist* there in the garden in the act of landing a trout. Before she could get out of the house he was away down Colebrook Street with rod, line and fish. Good luck to him! Like so many from Wykeham's foundation he is probably an ambassador by now. We would catch eels from that same kitchen window. This was a watery world quite unlike Highdown, Headbourne or, for the matter of that, Loyang. Not surprisingly botrytis was a problem with the peonies. So was nutrition. Lewis Palmer remarked that he had never seen a tree peony suffering from chlorosis until he saw one of mine. It was not exactly a compliment. The deep silt in the Itchen Valley bottom was altogether too damp and my garden too sheltered for these very hardy plants. Ah, well! I had a few nice blooms but the plants let me know that life was difficult for them: they were not happy, and neither was I.

When we went to Strasbourg in 1964 after my election as Secretary-General of the Council of Europe, that city kindly provided us with a large and stately official residence. It was in the centre of the former German area of the city, constructed in the interval between the Franco-Prussian War and the Great War of 1914, when Alsace was a part of Germany. Around it was

---

* 'Wykehamist': a pupil at Winchester College, founded in 1382 by Bishop William of Wykeham.

a small garden which contained nothing except for a large beech tree. This was the first time that I had gardened in a continental climate. The long grey cold winter seemed never-ending and I longed to see a green leaf. Ready to provide just that was the beech tree. I dreamed of the wonderful fresh green of the beeches in Selborne Hanger.* After the long wait the buds opened on my Strasbourg beech. The leaves were brown: it was a copper beech.

With the spring I set about planting everything which might add pleasure and interest to a dull if prominent place: lilies, clematis, and tree peonies amongst other things. I even managed to defeat part of the grey winter. Some of the new German hybrid rhododendrons are bred for very cold climates and flower in midwinter. I planted them along the railings which gave on to the great central square, the Place de la République. They flowered quite well, but my reward came from the populace. Two aged Alsatians, possibly peasant farmers, were gazing through the railings at the extraordinary phenomenon of bright red blooms in February. *"Non, non, mon vieux, ils sont en plastique."* Well, perhaps the beautiful blood-red bells did have a plastic look about them.

The tree peonies grew without the slightest problem. No sign of botrytis. No chlorosis. Plenty of flowers. Good growth. I was impressed with the wisdom of growing plants which like one's garden conditions, and forgetting about the rest however desirable. The clematis, too, did excellently and flowered profusely. I had planted them on the north side of a low stone wall which carried formal wrought-iron railings. The roots would be in shade and the heads in the sun clambering over the railings: an ideal arrangement. To the south, across the Fossé du Faux Rempart, the moat which was part of the ancient defences of the city, was the Prefecture. The clematis grew splendidly and clambered all over the railings. I never saw the flowers. They were all on the south side of the railings. The Prefect told me that he enjoyed them every morning as he shaved. Now I plant clematis so that I can look at them with my back to the sun.

At the end of my mandate as Secretary-General, five years from planting, the tree peonies were fine large plants. Now we were to move to Vico Morcote on the Lago di Lugano in Switzerland. The mayor, former prime minister Pierre Pflimlin, kindly agreed to let me take the tree peonies with me. The clematis and many other ornamentals would remain behind for my successors – and the Prefect. So we hired a truck and set off in convoy with

---

* A famous stand of beech on the slopes of a chalk down near the residence of the naturalist Gilbert White, in Hampshire.

The Residence of the Secretary-General of the Council of Europe in Strasbourg faced the Prefecture to the south across the canal. The Prefect enjoyed the flowers of my clematis as he shaved. I never saw them. They looked the other way.

the tree peonies in large plastic pots, perhaps thirty plants. It was early autumn, just the time to move them.

Unlike herbaceous peonies which hate transplantation and sulk for a couple of years thereafter, tree peonies do not mind it at all, provided that the rules are strictly obeyed. If not grown in containers, they can only be transplanted with the certainty of success in September or October. This is the brief period of the year when they are nearly dormant. At that time they can if necessary be sent by air parcel on bare root with the leaves cut off. Provided that they are properly planted on arrival they will produce an acceptable flower five months later without any detriment to the plant itself.

Unlike herbaceous peonies, tree peonies must be planted deep. Almost all the plants on the market today are grafted. If the junction of the root stock with the graft is at or near the surface, the root stock will grow, the graft will die out, and you will end up with a plant of *Paeonia lactiflora*, a worthy species but not what you intended. If the junction is buried about four inches below the surface of the soil, then over the years the peony scion will establish its own roots and new growths will spring from the base and will appear through the soil. The root stock will gradually die away. That is all there is to planting tree peonies in a climate and soil which they like. Any good garden soil will do, provided that it is not excessively acid. An annual feed with a general fertiliser in autumn when rooting begins, or in early spring when top growth begins, will be appreciated. If botrytis is a problem, the time to spray with fungicide is in early spring as soon as growth buds begin to move. However, these plants are hybrids of *P. suffruticosa* which, as its name suggests, is sub-shrubby: in spite of its name as a tree it is a semi-woody plant.

In such a plant a certain amount of die-back is natural. The last nine inches or so of soft growth beneath the flower will invariably die back at the end of the season, leaving a new growth bud at the top of what remains, or on a strong plant two or three such. These are the flowers for next season. It follows from this growth habit that shaping of these plants, if desired, is a complex business. At Vico Morcote they grew rapidly to six feet or more, altogether too high for comfort. If I cut back the long growths, I cut off next year's flowers: not a desirable outcome, though new growths will spring freely from below which will flower two years later. The Japanese, the master growers of these plants, have a solution – and apparently the labour to carry it out. After flowering, as soon as the new buds are formed in the leaf axils which will probably be in June, take a sharp knife and excise those buds in the upper leaf axils. Fat new buds will then develop in the lower leaf axils to provide next year's flowers. At the end of the season just before leaf-fall, cut back the upper part of the growths to the highest of the new buds which you have encouraged to grow lower down. Hey, presto! You have shortened your plant and you will also have flowers next spring. But if you have a lot of plants it is a lot of work and I do not myself do this.

English gardeners have had a long romance with the 'wild' Chinese tree peony, which has been grown under the name of *P. suffruticosa* 'Rock's Variety' or variants on that theme. Its own romantic story has been often told but briefly it is as follows. What was almost certainly a wild plant was sighted by Reginald Farrer in southern Kansu in 1913, but not introduced to cultivation. In the 'twenties of this century the American plant collector J. F. Rock sent back seeds from a plant growing in the Lamasery at Choni in south western Kansu where he lived. These seeds went to the United States, Britain, Sweden and Canada and their progeny became known as Rock's peony. The beauty of the large white flowers with conspicuous chocolate blotches at the base of the petals and a white seed capsule at the centre of the golden stamens, carried on a vigorous and floriferous plant, attracted much attention.

Seed from these plants was freely distributed as *P. suffruticosa* 'J. F. Rock's Variety'. Unfortunately, however, bees collect pollen from tree peony flowers to convert into the wax in which they will store their honey. Many of the 'Rocks' raised from seed and found growing in England today are certainly bee hybrids, often beautiful but bearing only some resemblance to the original plant. But it is possible that Chinese as well as English bees have been at work. In response to Sir Frederick Stern's inquiries of Dr Rock, it was confirmed that his seed had not been collected in the wild but from plants growing in the garden of the Lamasery where he lived. It is likely that other tree peonies were growing there. Meanwhile in 1928 the Lamasery had been burned to the ground and all the Lamas had been killed by Muslims. The original plants almost certainly perished in the confusion and destruction. Though J. F. Rock thought that the Lamasery plants 'looked like' a wild plant there was apparently no way of knowing whether this was so or not. Even if they were wild the seed which they produced might be the result of pollination by an ordinary cultivated moutan.

For the garden at Vico Morcote I received a plant of the form of Rock's peony most commonly grown in England, and apparently identical with the one in Lewis Palmer's garden at Headbourne Worthy. I also received from the USA a plant with Arnold Arboretum parentage quite different from the English plant. Of these two the former 'looked' to me like a hybrid and the latter 'looked' like a species. This diagnosis was at first confirmed when Professor Hong Tao of the Chinese Academy of Forestry, the leading authority today on Chinese wild peonies, visited my garden in 1992 and saw both plants in flower. The English plant he pronounced as undoubtedly a hybrid. The Arnold Arboretum plant he thought to be very close to the wild plant, perhaps the real thing. However, on taking a magnifying glass to the flower parts and the foliage, he decided that even that plant showed signs of hybridity. As Rock's parent was a garden plant and anyway is dead it is prudent to assume that all plants of *P. suffruticosa* 'Rock's Variety' in cultivation today are hybrids. Meanwhile Professor Hong Tao and Dr Lupo Osti are hoping to introduce to cultivation wild plants of the peony sighted by Farrer in Kansu. This has been described by Professor Hong Tao as *Paeonia rockii*. If his diagnosis is supported this will greatly simplify the writing of garden labels.*

---

* For the latest summary of the position of Rock's Peony and other Chinese species of Tree Peony, see: *The New Plantsman*: Vol. I, Part 4, 1994. Gian Lupo Osti: 'Tree Peonies Revisited'.

In any branch of life the accepted wisdom is by definition out of date. By the time it is accepted, the world has moved on. This proved to be true of the breeding of tree peonies. I was told by several 'authorities' that it was a waste of time growing tree peonies from seed: the Japanese plants were already so sophisticated. (PLATE 12) Nothing much was to be expected other than more of the same and it would take five to seven years to see a disappointing flower. Two things happened to disprove this.

With a couple of hundred different Japanese and American hybrids in the garden, I did not attempt to cut off all of the seed pods after blooming. A certain quantity of seeds fell to the ground and germinated successfully where they lay. Two of these plants were overlooked until, on discovery, they were near to flowering size. When they finally flowered both were outstanding doubles, with very strong stems holding the massive flowers in an upright posture. One, palest pink, was very beautiful and floriferous. The other was pure white, also beautiful and floriferous. I cannot even begin to guess which of my named plants the bees selected for breeding. Both these seedlings have been registered with the Registrar of Peonies at the American Peony Society and are being propagated by the Rivière nursery in France for distribution in due course.

A more important development was from the English plant which has passed under the name of *P. suffruticosa* 'Rock's Variety'. As this peony was much in demand amongst my friends and as my plant had grown to a considerable size carrying fifty or more flowers, I sowed some of the seed to raise plants to give away to visitors. One could not tell what the progeny might be, for many Japanese tree peonies were growing nearby. I kept a few seedlings and grew them on myself but, accepting the accepted wisdom, I did not expect much from them. After the years of waiting they began to bloom. I shall not describe them since the plates give some idea of what they were like. In summary, out of eighteen seedlings the following has been the result:

3   discarded as not worth growing

3   acceptable garden plants, given away to friends

1   retained with my rating xxxx

5   retained with my rating xxxxx

6   retained, named and registered with the registrar of peonies and in process of propagation and distribution in due course by Rivière. (PLATES 10, 11 AND 12)

PLATE 9 Botan – Japanese tree peonies.

Botan 'Renkaku' with azaleas. The tree peonies are part of the vegetation of the garden, not isolated specimens.

PLATES 10 & 11 Vico hybrid tree peonies from *P. rockii* 'Dojean'.

'Brigadier Lane'.

'Luella'.

'Ice Storm'.

PLATE 12 Vico hybrid tree peony from *P. rockii* 'Baron Thyssen-Bornemisza'. One of the largest tree peony flowers in the garden.

Japanese tree peony 'Shima nishiki'.

Amongst other people I had sent some of this seed to Ryoji Hashida, president of the Japan Botan Society. At the annual show of the Society in 1994 a seedling from this consignment gained the prize for best new seedling of the year. It was somewhat similar to 'Luella': notably redder in colour, but retaining the white capsule and dark flares typical of Rock's plants. If I had some doubts as to the ability of my bees as plant breeders, and if I feared that perhaps my selected seedlings might be geese rather than swans, these misgivings were instantly removed by this accolade from the home of the Botan.

The record thus shows that Japanese hybrid tree peonies with centuries of breeding behind them when crossed on to what is either a species, *P. rockii*, or a first generation hybrid from it, give most promising results, well worth the long wait. For anybody inclined to repeat the experiment, it is important to sow the seed immediately it is ripe while still covered with natural oils. The pots must be exposed to frost or at least to severe cold the following winter. Even with this treatment the seed may not germinate next spring so the pots should be retained for a second season. This is no doubt a mechanism for preservation of the species in the wild. If the first year's germination is destroyed a second may follow.

The naming of Japanese tree peony cultivars has been the source of much aggravation. The problem is partly due to the structure of the nursery trade in Japan. Botan plants are propagated by farmers and sold by them to nurseries. The propagators are not always as meticulous with their stocks as might be wished and the distributing nurseries do not keep all their plants to check them in flower. By the time they reach Europe the plants may be anything at all unless they have come from one of the few specialist suppliers who know their plants and take infinite pains with them. Now, however, we have an incontrovertible authority for the correct attribution of names, in the illustrated book published by the Japan Botan Society and largely the work of Ryoji Hashida.* With this book in hand I have made the circuit of my plants and have rewritten a good many labels. So far as I am concerned it is a final authority. If anybody says that I have a plant under the wrong name they may go to Japan and argue their point if they please. If I cannot find the exact image of my peony in the book, it is probably a seedling, and it will be labelled as such, citing the nearest matching image. When the plant is out of flower this will give some idea of what it is like.

* *A Photographic Book of Tree and Herbaceous Peonies in Modern Japan*: The Japan Botan Society, 1990, obtainable from the Society.

However, there are a few but good sources of supply for tree peonies outside of Japan. In France the Rivière nursery near Lyon is now in the fifth generation of tree peony growers with Michel. A sixth generation is about to take over. In consequence this nursery has an unrivalled collection of the early European hybrids raised mainly in France. If now and then in France one comes upon an immense old tree peony carrying fifty or sixty blooms, it will be one of these. They are doubles, the result of breeding from the original Chinese imports early in the nineteenth century, which preceded the arrival of the Japanese singles several decades later. The Rivière nursery also has a number of Japanese hybrids and will distribute all of my named hybrids from *P. rockii*. In addition Michel Rivière has written the best modern book on tree peonies.★ In these days when the conservation of good plants is much on people's minds it seems to me that the existence of a reliable source of supply and of a good textbook secures more than half the battle.

From the Japanese imports distinguished French breeders such as Lemoine gave us some nice yellow and bronze hybrids in the early years of this century, using *P. lutea* or *P. delavayi* as one of the parents. But the former is a poor head-hanging creature, though vigorous and easy and of a pretty colour. Unfortunately the head-hanging characteristic was transmitted to many hybrids which carried large flowers from the Japanese or Chinese side of the cross. Professor Saunders set about correcting this in his breeding work at Hamilton College in Pennsylvania. He also made extensive use of *P. delavayi* to introduce a number of dark mahogany-coloured flowers. He has been followed by Daphnis and Reath and now by a number of other breeders working within the orbit of the American Peony Society. Their products are more sun-loving than the Japanese parents: wonderful garden plants with new exciting colours and sometimes with gigantic flowers. They are expensive but worth their price if you have the money. They will probably acquire the elegance and sophistication of the Japanese plants after a century or two of further breeding. For these magnificent American tree peonies there is also a good source of supply: the Klehm Nursery in North Barrington, Illinois. Through the American Peony Society the breeders now working in this field can be contacted and their plants can sometimes be purchased direct. There is no book dealing comprehensively with American tree peonies.

Though tree peonies have made a large contribution to my garden, and

★ *Le Monde Fabuleux des Pivoines*, Floraprint France, 1992, ISBN 2 90069–35–1.

have given me great pleasure and some excitement, this is in no sense a 'Peony Garden'. It is a community of plants in which the law of nature prevails with only minor interventions by me. The tree peonies must find their place along with the rest of the vegetation. (PLATE 20) In the early years of the garden, when the entire area was a sun-blasted southern slope, large numbers of tree peonies flourished exceedingly. As the system has gradually transformed itself, according to plan, into a woodland of magnolias and other trees and shrubs, the available sunny locations have decreased dramatically. This inevitably has meant the decline and loss of many tree peonies. This is part of the price to be paid in establishing an ecosystem of exotic plants. In its evolution many genera have had their day of triumph before assuming a relatively smaller part in the mature system. It is not everybody who will accept the inevitable transience of the early stages of such a garden. In that case they will have to work hard or employ a garden staff to maintain their plants and the garden will have a different meaning and significance.

CHAPTER 6

In which the Plants Do Most of the Work

THE GARDEN WORK MUST DIMINISH AS THE OWNER GROWS OLD

Five and a half years as Secretary-General of the Council of Europe in Strasbourg had been a fascinating episode in life. I had found the Organisation of eighteen governments, a Parliamentary Assembly and what was probably the best international court in existence then or since, the European Court of Human Rights, in a state of mild confusion. The restructuring of the intergovernmental work had been an immense labour, but had been successful. I felt that my task had been completed. It would be better to have a fresh mind to take over for another five years. Though urged to stand candidate for another term, I declined to do so.

The leader of the British Delegation to the Parliamentary Assembly, Sam Silkin, suggested to me that it would be useful, in the light of a unique experience, if I were now to go to the House of Lords. This would mean return to England, to Colebrook House and to work in Parliament. It seemed to me the proper course. Harold Wilson, then Prime Minister, was consulted and readily agreed. He had been helpful to me during my time in Strasbourg. But he added that in accordance with British practice the Conservative Party leadership must be consulted: I had been a Conservative Member of Parliament. Nothing further was heard of the idea, so evidently it was not acceptable to the Conservative leadership. So instead the Socialist government put my name forward for a Knighthood in the Foreign Office list, which is not subject to party scrutiny. Knights have nothing to do, as such, except to enjoy their titles.

This was the moment for an important decision. I had never wished to spend my life entirely in one occupation: not for me a steady job with a pension at the end of it. The world was infinitely diverse and infinitely fascinating. Life should touch it at many points and should consist of different successive chapters. But now there seemed to be no choice but to open a new chapter. My former constituency at Winchester was represented by the delightful Member who had succeeded me on my departure for Strasbourg, Admiral Morgan-Giles. He should go down to history for his blunt sailor's advice in the counsels of the Conservative Party at a moment of crisis when holders of marginal constituencies seemed to be losing their nerve. Thus spoke the bluff British sailor turned politician:

> Pro bono Publico
> No bloody panico

The Winchester seat was well filled by the Admiral and the House of Lords was not available. To return to England to watch the world go by did not seem the right course. We would strike out afresh into a new life. Colebrook House would be sold – a heart-wrenching affair – and we would take advantage of an intimation from Switzerland. The Swiss had been constructive members of the Council of Europe and the President of the Confederation, Willi Spühler, with whom I had had many dealings when he occupied the post of Foreign Minister, intimated that we would be welcome in his country if we should decide to settle there. The world seemed to be full of people wishing in vain for permission to live in Switzerland: for us the door stood open. It would be a good base from which to use the Senior Research Fellowship which the United Nations had provided for me.

Now we had moved from the stately official residence of the Secretary-General in Strasbourg to a little hotel in Morcote on the Lago di Lugano. Our bedroom windows looked across the water to the mountain the other side, which was Italy. What at first sight looked like a tourist boat plied across the lake from the Swiss frontier post of Morcote to the Italian port of Porto Ceresio, a water-bus with a customs officer on board. It was the lovely month of September, when innumerable kinds of mushroom, many edible, flourish in the woods around the lake, when the grapes are ripening on the vines, when figs abound everywhere and the nuts are ripening on the trees. One glimpsed the Lombard plain in the far distance, a garden of every kind of delicious fruit and vegetable and stocked full with splendid cheeses.

I once heard a story told about the Italian Lakes. It was of an Englishman who settled there early in this century. After fifteen years he abandoned his residence and returned to England. He lunched at the club. "I say, old boy, we thought you loved it so living on the Lakes. What went wrong?" "Well, it was too much. Too much good food, too much fine wine, too much magnificent architecture, too much fine art, too much splendid music, too much lovely scenery, too much sunshine, too many beautiful women, too bloody much of everything, so I have come home to grey England." Perhaps unjust but with an element of truth. There was indeed a great deal all around us, and on the hillside above was an area of steeply sloping disused vineyard (PLATE 13) which we had purchased and on which we would build a house and make a garden.

It is twenty-five years since I sat here on the hillside contemplating our purchase. It marked a turning-point in life, the end of whole-time involvement in national and international politics. Now the tranquil continuo of gardening would move from the background to the foreground as we set about the design and construction of the house and the design and creation of a garden. With any luck it would be our last house and our last garden. How would the house relate to the garden and how would the garden relate to the surrounding scenery of mountains and forests? If harmony and unity between all three were to be achieved a great and sustained effort of imagination and creativity would be required.

The local architects, in the tradition of the chalet, liked to divide their houses into numerous small compartments, each sealed with a door. This would not do at all. We specified that the house should have an open plan with the minimum of internal partitions and with doors only where they were absolutely necessary. Accustomed to building on mountain sides, Swiss architects filled their houses with steps: three up here, five down there and then another four up somewhere else. All these different levels, often in the same room, were more than tradition and a response to steeply sloping sites: they were thought to add interest to the living space and to emphasise the function of different parts of it. Perhaps they did so. For a house which we hoped would one day be occupied by old people this would be absurd. We specified to the architect that there should be no steps within the house, and no steps entering or leaving it, not even one. There should be glass-to-ground across the entire front of the building. Most of the windows should slide open if desired. The house must sit upon a plinth, with the same paving material within as without. Not only must we be able to walk out of the house and into the garden without the intervention of steps – perhaps one day a wheel chair might need to travel easily from one to the other – but also the eye must travel without interruption from within the house out through the garden and beyond to the forests on the mountains across the lake. We would, as the Japanese say, 'borrow the scenery'.

The house would consist of a group of four separate pavilions, each performing a particular function. All would be grouped around a central patio and they would be interconnected with one another. The patio would be partly roofed and partly open to the sky so that there would be dry access and living space but also sufficient light and rain for plants to grow both in the earth and in pots. The stream would flow through the patio. In winter, spring and autumn the house would look outward across the lake. In the heat of summer, reaching 90 degrees by day, the outside of the house would be shuttered by its white roller blinds. Now it would look inwards to the shade of the patio, a living space easily accessible from the kitchen. A through current of air would pass up or down the course of the stream. The sound of water tumbling down the rock would be pleasantly suggestive.

We were attracted by two originals. One was the primitive architecture of the Caribbean Islands before the interior decorators got there. The Rice House on Mustique was a fine example: the beauty of wood and natural materials and of space and openness. The other was the elegant simplicity of modern Japanese house architecture. We spoke about this with the architect, and I added that I would like the house to look as though it would blow away in a storm, though I hoped it would not do so.

Bruno Bossi, a very experienced and distinguished Swiss architect, took all of this in good part and in fact relished the challenge of building something quite different from anything he had attempted before. But he was startled to find that the first structure to be erected would be the three-quarter span greenhouse. This must lead directly off our bedroom/study, so that I could enter it in winter without going into the open air, and could do so in pyjamas if so inclined. The greenhouse, designed for the site and prefabricated in England from western red cedar, would be the family on-site headquarters during the two years which would be required to complete the house. It was there that we received friends long before there was a house in which to welcome them. It would be my responsibility to design the garden, to relate it to the house and to the deciduous forests on the mountain skyline.

At the time of the Renaissance the Italians completed the conquest of nature and thoroughly subdued it, imposing order upon inhabited areas within the surrounding wilderness. The garden became a logical deduction from the geometry of the villa. Nature would not be permitted to escape

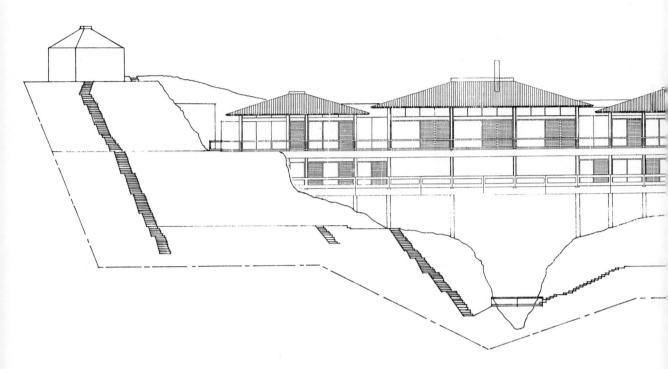

Architect's elevation of the house at Vico Morcote.

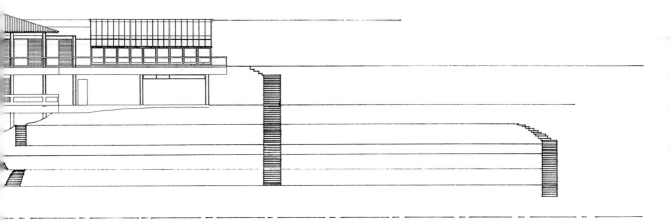

Early stages of building and garden construction. 1970.

again now that it had been brought under control. The boundary of the Italian garden was a clearly marked frontier within which all was ordered for the pleasure and convenience of man. Its design was permanent and its aspect need never change. Beyond the garden was savage nature.

In this Italian-speaking Canton of Switzerland the situation was somewhat different from that in Italy. There were few stately villas. Gardens were divorced from their surroundings less by the formality of their design than by the nature of the planting within them. A palm from China, *Trachycarpus fortunei*, or several of them, was an obligatory element in almost every garden, along with one or more Italian cypresses. Here and there a monkey-puzzle, *Araucaria araucana* from southern Chile, might be thrown in to make the divorce from surrounding nature absolute. These plants alone indicate to all beholders that the garden had nothing to do with the nearby deciduous forests of oak and sweet chestnut. So much was this the rule that the palm had become a troublesome weed, self-sowing with great freedom. Clearly if we were to 'borrow the scenery' no such incongruities must be permitted to meet the eye as we looked out from the house across the garden towards the mountains. The exotics which would make up our ecosystem would need to be carefully chosen so that although they were foreigners in a strange land, they would appear to be a part of the landscape.

So in this empty space Bruno Bossi would create our house and in it I would design my fifth and last garden. There were no constraints upon me for there was virtually no vegetation worth preserving. There were three decrepit walnut trees, two of which died while the third has entered upon a new lease of life while hosting a splendid *Vitis coignetiae* which has scrambled to its upper branches. With such freedom to design I already understood that it would be impossible to create or to maintain a successful garden unless it were based on certain principles. These would govern not only its design but also its subsequent development. This can be achieved easily in the Italian formal garden, the outlines of which need never change. But my garden would be an exercise in time/motion, continually changing and developing until it reached the stability of an ecosystem in the years ahead. In a surprisingly short period, a matter of weeks, its principles resolved themselves into the document which is printed in Chapter 1 of this book.

There is, however, a problem in the application of such principles. Whatever I may decide should happen, the plants may not have studied my principles with sufficient care; worse still, they sometimes fight against them. Principle IX, that there should be no repetition of planting material in different parts of the garden, has been difficult to maintain. Where a particular plant has indicated its dissatisfaction with its chosen location the temptation to try it somewhere else has proved overwhelming. The error of judgment was mine in the first place. It was not the principle which was at fault.

One plant in particular has positively trampled upon Principle IX. *Daphne bholua*, brought back by me from the Nepal Himalaya and described in another part of this book, is a treasured plant desired by gardeners throughout the temperate world. It is scarce and when found it is expensive. But in my garden, apparently imagining that it is still growing on the Daman Ridge, it has played the part of the invading exotic without enemies to control it. It has seeded itself everywhere and in clear defiance of Principle IX is to be found in fragrant bloom throughout the months of January, February and early March at every turn of the path. A weed is defined as a plant out of place. Perish the thought, but that is what this wonderful daphne might become.

The house would be built at the top of the steeply sloping site on a terrace created by much bulldozing. Earth and rock thrown out by the excavation would create enough flat space for three 'open air rooms' adjacent to the house and on exactly the same level (PLATE 14). The house itself would span the narrow ravine down which flowed the stream fed by a perpetual spring above the nearby village. The main pavilion would form a bridge connecting one side of the ravine with the other. The stream would flow through the central patio of the house and then cascade down the rock face to which the house is attached. The cascade would be visible from the back of the living space. The pleasant sound of falling water, rising to a torrent in heavy rain, would fill the room.

The south front of the house would look down upon the greater part of the garden far below and sloping steeply towards the distant lake. The plantings would therefore be seen from above as well as from the winding path passing through them. This was of great significance for the design. With the passage of time the exotics would grow up until they reached or surpassed the level of the main terrace. At that point the house would seem to float amongst the tree-tops, a spectacular situation at all seasons and particularly at the spring blooming.

The forest across the lake had a high canopy of oaks and sweet chestnuts beneath which was an under-storey of various shrubby plants, and on the forest floor a splendid array of native terrestrials: several orchids, hepaticas, anemones, *Helleborus niger, Muscari comosum*, primroses, cyclamen, some species of gentian and many other delights. The whole, a natural ecosystem, would have served for a garden. But nobody went in to spray, to prune, to weed or to sweep up the leaves. It was interesting and beautiful, but there was no gardener. The plants themselves and the insect and animal inhabitants of the forest did all the work. My purpose would be to create a similar ecosystem but using exotic plants suited to the climate and soil. As I also wished to inhabit the garden with my friends, I could not expect the plants to do the whole of the work. But except in the open-air rooms, where for the comfort and convenience of man strict order must be maintained, they should be able to do most of it.

An obvious choice for the high canopy was deciduous magnolias. In the climate of the Lakes these grow into trees with surprising speed, and because of the lie of the land they could be viewed from above. There would be an under-storey of camellias, rhododendrons and other shrubs. On the forest floor would be interesting terrestrials. Such a system would take time to grow, but growth in the climate of the Italian lakes is about twice that of England or of the Eastern Seaboard of the USA. This was 'old man's gardening country'. Nevertheless there would be a period of several years during which the garden would be passing from a sun-baked southern slope to its final destiny as a woodland. Extensive plantings of sun-lovers would be made to fill the empty spaces in the knowledge that they would eventually be crowded and shaded out of existence.

This was to be the main ecosystem covering about half of the garden. But there were to be others of quite different composition. Small shrubs such as Japanese azaleas filled certain spaces, deciduous azaleas others, deciduous flowering shrubs covered the east face of the valley, and in the outdoor rooms there was dense but careful planting of many treasures around the small lawns which formed the centre of each. There was a hot dry slope with little soil over the rock, which would be for Mediterranean and similar plants: labiates, cistus, tree heaths, yuccas and dwarf pines. There were several beautiful native plants which were already present and which would become per-manent features of the garden: primroses, the orchid *Cephalanthera latifolia* and wild strawberries, the latter in great profusion. All survive to this day, particularly the strawberries which have become a ground cover wherever they get a chance. Before Vico Morcote became a dormitory for Lugano, the inhabitants made a modest living from strawberry growing.

One ecosystem was a conspicuous failure. I have a gluttonous love of fresh figs, so on a steep slope there would be a planting of a collection of eight varieties. These would provide summer shade for various plants including many bulbs. The figs were obtained, planted, and grew prodigiously. Far too prodigiously. I should have reflected upon a visit which I once made to a fig plantation near Izmir in Turkey. The trees thrived in rocky soil with little earth, there was hardly any rain and there was great heat. They were never watered or fertilised. In consequence growth was slow, short and very hard. Each year would add a few inches. But those few inches would bear four figs. In the comparatively rainy climate of my garden and in the deep soil of a slope made up from excavations, the figs did indeed bear four fruits on each growth, but the growth would be two feet long. Soon the figs were out of sight up in the sky, greatly to the satisfaction of the blackbirds. They were removed and replaced with the same number of plants of *Magnolia macrophylla* which I had raised from seed from different clones selected in the USA.

The macrophyllas have been a great success, growing rapidly into trees with huge leaves and enormous white flowers, freely borne in June. Only hail is sometimes a problem for leaves which are thin and fragile. But the resulting mass of very large foliage is impressive and beautiful. An admittedly short-sighted lady visitor congratulated me on my splendid banana plants. As for figs, we buy them in the market.

Everything in a garden can be purchased except for time. We decided to make a great effort of planting in the earliest years, knowing that this would inevitably involve some mistakes. But it would bring the garden to maturity more quickly. After the preparation of the site a garden contractor was employed for three planting seasons. Under my direction he would set out the several thousand species and varieties of plant which were arriving from England, Japan and the United States. I had a full-time gardener to help me to maintain the garden. After three years the pace slowed somewhat and the contractor was no longer needed. After seven years the garden had begun to fill out and my gardener, Hansjürg Albrecht, accepted a post as head gardener at the Botanic Garden on the Isole de Brissago on Lago Maggiore. It was sad to see him go. We had been through exciting times together, but the plants were now beginning to take over and to do the garden work themselves. A half-time man, half in house and half in garden, would be sufficient. He would not need to be skilled so long as he could be controlled. This was important, for the most destructive animal in the garden is often the gardener. I would still direct everything that happened.

The system arrived at a functioning maturity after about twelve years, though continuing to develop. The plants had settled down and taken control. Where once there was a waste of weeds and emptiness now I looked out upon luxuriant tiers of foliage over which the forests across the lake could be seen. Twenty years from planting, nothing incongruous comes between us inside the house and the continuous vegetation ending at the skyline. No palm, conifer or monkey puzzle is in sight. The diverse parts in the scene are united.

Here I must explain that I have nothing against palms, conifers or monkey puzzles. The point is that they must be used in appropriate circumstances. One monkey puzzle in the average garden is an absurdity like an ostrich on a grouse moor. But in the splendid garden at Kerdalo Braz in Brittany, Prince Wolkonsky has planted a whole grove of monkey puzzles. You come upon them suddenly. The effect is dramatic and magnificent. Surely a dinosaur will stalk out from them at any moment, putting us to precipitate flight. An Italian cypress is a beautiful feature of any village in Tuscany. And who wants a tropical beach without a fringe of palms? There are indeed palms in the garden at Vico Morcote, but they are a group standing together in the depth of the ravine where they do not conflict with the surrounding scenery and look like a natural stand in their native China. The few conifers which are planted here, mostly dwarves, have been kept well out of the line of sight from the house. But there is no monkey-puzzle: I have no space for a Wolkonskian grove.

Twenty years from planting the garden embraces the house (PLATE 14) and the magnolias have grown up until the house floats amongst their upper branches. The dense array of bloom in the tops looks in at us as we lie in bed. The lake and the mountains are visible only through planned openings in the foliage. A panoramic view was never desired, indeed it was to be avoided. Instead the house and its inhabitants are part of the foliage, one with the mountain forests in the distance. On a warm summer's night with the windows wide open I lie in bed listening to the roar set up by a shower falling upon the big leaves of the magnolias, and I relish the scent of rain after a hot day. It is part of the stately procession of the seasons. I am back in the timeless forests of past millennia, but very comfortable.

I grew up in a country village in southern England and lived my youth in step with the cycle of the year. This has been a thing of beauty wherever I lived and most particularly in the garden. In Hampshire it was an almost imperceptible process, with occasional conspicuous markers along the way. The first aconite to flower, the wild snowdrops by the Itchen at Ovington, watercress in the gravel of the cold chalk spring by the river, the first daffodil, and then the cascade of spring began in chill beauty, passing into the heavy fragrance of the summer borders. The first new potatoes, the first asparagus, the first peas from the garden, the great excitement of the first strawberry, the soft 'May Duke' cherries followed by the solid 'Napoleon Bigarreau' and ending with the bitter but delicious 'Morello' hanging on the wall until it was almost black and at its best, the gooseberries ripening on the bushes, the August apple 'Beauty of Bath', and the little summer pear, 'Doyenne d'Eté' which must be picked and eaten straight off the tree, the first raspberries, the figs on the garden wall, reluctant ripeners in that northern climate and the more relished for that. Mushrooms popped up overnight in the park, the only species of that huge family which the English dare to eat though their country is stocked with plenty of other delicious ones. Then began the long procession of autumn apples and pears taking us up to and beyond the next year's aconites. All these things and many others came and then disappeared until next season. They were not yet devalued by the year-round availability of deep-frozen produce or of imports from the southern hemisphere or from California. Of course, much has been gained by the change, but something beautiful and exciting has been lost.

I was twenty-six when, invalided from active service in the Royal Navy, I arrived at the British Embassy in Washington as Assistant Naval Attaché. The Potomac river was frozen solid from bank to bank. This was indeed a new world. On the eastern seaboard the procession of the seasons had come to an abrupt halt with the onset of winter. The woods in Rock Creek Park through which I walked to the Embassy every day were lifeless as though there had never been a leaf on the trees. The ground seemed to be just minerals and dead leaves: so different from the winter in a Hampshire copse where life and motion continued at a barely perceptible pace until the spring.

One morning I went to my office in the Embassy in a fur-lined overcoat; when I came out at lunch-time the wind had changed and with it spring had arrived. There followed an impetuous onrush of foliage and flowers. Soon the splendid flora of the Blue Ridge Mountains set off upon its annual display culminating in the lilies and innumerable other delights. As I walked to the Embassy each morning through the dense foliage of Rock Creek Park I would pick and eat the wild mulberries from the bushes. A glorious golden autumn and then everything came to a dead halt again with winter.

On the Mexican plateau seven thousand feet above the sea the procession

PLATE 13 The site for the house and garden above the Lago di Lugano, 1970.

A few cold nights are followed by a rapid rise in temperature the next day. Conditions like this are found in the lower ranges of the Himalaya, and Himalayan plants grow well at Vico Morcote. Sometimes it snows heavily – wet, destructive snow which breaks the branches of evergreens.

PLATE 14 The dining-room terrace.

One of the three 'open-air rooms' adjacent to the house and on the same level. There is dense
but careful planting around the small lawns which form the centre of each.

PLATE 15 Spring blossom, with *Rhododendron yakushimanum* in the foreground.

PLATE 16 The big leaves of magnolias soon formed a rich humus layer,
but they smothered many beautiful small plants including *Calanthe striata*.

of the seasons had not been regulated by temperature but by the rains. From the end of October until the middle of May not a drop would fall. In my garden in Cuernavaca, where streams irrigated the whole area, it was perpetually green and full of flowers and luxuriant foliage. But on the mountains the xerophytes lost their few leaves and the innumerable species of cacti would become dormant. By April there would be dust everywhere. By early May the oppressive heat and the longing for the rains to begin would become almost intolerable. And then, one day, the rains would break at last and the air would be filled with the delicious scent of the first drops upon the parched earth. Temperatures would fall dramatically and would remain pleasant throughout the summer. From the bare ground there sprang up the scarlet flowers of *Sprekelia*, the cactus desert burst into bloom, and there followed a procession of splendid flora of many genera until the rains ceased again in autumn.

In the wet tropics of Central America, though growth was very rapid, the procession of the seasons slowed to a crawl. The nearer I drew to the equator the less was the difference between midsummer and midwinter until in southern Belize or Panama it was hardly perceptible. But who could complain of this, given the marvellous wealth of the wet tropical flora and silva?

The procession of the seasons, the return every year of old friends at their appointed time and the appearance of new ones, is one of the principal delights of a garden. The art of garden design consists in part in assuring that in so far as the climate permits there will always be something of interest going on. In Vico Morcote the procession of the seasons seemed to be ideal for growing a wide range of plants to flower throughout the year, even in midwinter. The guide to the Swiss climates called it a 'low stress area' where human longevity was the rule. The sun was king. On our mountain side facing south-east, sunrise would be followed by a gentle flow of warmer air up from the lake below, bringing a rapid rise in temperature. Sunset would be followed by a barely perceptible movement of cooler air down from the mountain above. There would be plenty of very hot days in summer, in the upper eighties or low nineties, but always followed by a cooler night. In winter there would be some very cold nights but few very cold days. Even in January or February when the sun chose to shine, lunch in the open air would be enjoyable. In a word, there was a wide temperature differential. It was not unlike the montane climate of the lower ranges of the Himalaya. Himalayan plants should be at home in the ecosystem. This proved to be the case.

Sometimes it would snow, heavily: wet destructive snow which would break the branches of ornamental shrubs. (PLATE 13) In a region where summer thunderstorms would echo magnificently from the mountain sides, thus greatly increasing their power to impress, in winter there would sometimes be a snow thunderstorm in which the flakes would fall in great cascades, for it was a heavy rainfall area. But it was not gentle English rain. With Swiss thoroughness, when it rained it was a serious matter, sometimes too serious. In one August storm we were to have more than twenty people drowned in a torrent, including a man and his dog. In spite of warnings he went back to the house to save the dog and both perished.

If rain is sometimes of subtropical intensity, fog is unknown, but clouds drift up and down the mountainsides. The weather and the procession of the seasons are nothing if not dramatic. At the southern foot of the Alps there is thus a mild winter and a sub-tropical summer. There could be flowers in the garden in every month of the year and plenty of them, provided that the right plants were selected. The garden could be a different garden every two weeks. But the enigma of 'hardiness' was particularly baffling.

Attempts have been made in the United States to classify plants according to the regions in which they are thought to be 'hardy'. Perhaps this is a rough guide to planters, but it can never be more than that. Hardiness is not a matter of absolute temperature. The hardiness of a plant depends more than anything else upon its native climate to which its growth is attuned. In the case of a hybrid this may, of course, be variable with the mixture of genes. Some plants which will pass through a night of thirty degrees below freezing Fahrenheit without harm would succumb to a frost of five degrees below which lasted for a week and penetrated deep into the soil, freezing the roots. Hardiness also depends upon the degree of ripening which the plants have had in the garden in late summer and autumn and upon whether the frost occurs in damp or dry conditions. There are too many variables for hardiness to be predictable with any accuracy.

Perplexed by this problem, I wrote to a well-known authority on Maddenii series rhododendrons for advice as to the hardiness of various species. I received the scathing but perfectly correct reply: "Every plant is hardy until I have killed it myself." I quote these wise words to everybody who consults me about the hardiness of plants. Lionel de Rothschild used to put it in another way when asked for advice. That great and generous gardener would reply that he never gave advice. He could only say what he knew to be true for the garden at Exbury. This might not be true in some other garden with different conditions. Within the bounds of reason there is always a good chance that the surprise following an experimental planting will be a pleasant one. I never dreamed that gardenias would grow here in the open where temperatures often go down to 20 degrees Fahrenheit at night, and sometimes lower. But one has flourished for seventeen years on a north-west wall and has flowered freely every season. In the sun fifteen yards away a sister plant dwindled to ultimate death.

In this garden the procession of the seasons provides for a very long growing period and hence for rapid growth year to year. It also provides an extremely thorough ripening of the wood in late summer and autumn. This increases hardiness and assures a profusion of bloom on flowering trees and shrubs such as cannot be approached in less sunny climates (PLATE 18). A garden which would take twenty years to develop in southern England will produce the same result in half that time on the Italian Lakes, it will produce twice the display of bloom, and it will grow a wider range of relatively tender plants. Also it will only rarely experience the bitter disappointment of a late frost.

After the evolution which I have described, and except for the open-air rooms adjacent to the house, you might think that the ecosystem, my garden if you would allow it to be that, looks neglected. You would be right. It is indeed neglected. That is what it is intended to be now that I have arrived at old age. It no longer needs my daily care. It can safely be left to itself with only a small adjustment here and there from time to time to facilitate passage through the dense growth. I am free to pursue undemanding hobbies suitable to an 'old gent' whom London cabbies sometimes address respectfully as 'Guv'. Breeding hybrid nerines is the chief of these hobbies.

Although this 'neglect' was planned and foreseen, after a lifelong association with carefully manicured gardens I found it at first difficult to accept. Then I reflected that in the beauty of a natural woodland, whether it be the rain forest in Dominica or a bluebell wood in England or the redwoods of the Pacific coast, I would not criticise it because it was 'neglected'. So much in our perception of the world around us depends upon our own assumptions and prejudices. If we are to play the great game of creation we must be prepared to discard some of the mental luggage of the past in order to live in a new present. A dandelion is a beautiful flower. Why should I be offended by it so long as it is controlled by the ecosystem? But there are one or two dangerous exotics which must be watched: the palm seedlings, *Robinia* and one or two others which if permitted would get out of control. And certainly none must be introduced. Mercifully there is no ground elder, *Aegopodium*, that I know of this side of the Alps. A friend who brought me a small pot with a plant which turned out to be a rare variegated leaf form of that vegetable plague was startled to be told to burn it at once. These minor worries apart, in old age I am free to contemplate the beauty of my mature plantings and to relish a sense of unity with them and with the system of nature of which they are now a part.

But my wife and I and our friends are not the only beneficiaries of the ecosystem. The dense foliage of deciduous trees and shrubs which covers the entire area of the hillside below the house has become impenetrable to man except for the narrow circular path with many side spurs which leads through it. It is now a refuge for many humble creatures driven from their natural habitat elsewhere. Birds, of course: tiny birds seldom glimpsed amongst the foliage: a splendid chorus of blackbirds. The beautiful black and orange salamander, only to be seen in a rainstorm, proceeding with the slow deliberate steps which are safe for a poisonous animal. Several species of lizard including a large green one with a blue head which freezes in his tracks to stare at me and then disappears in a flash. Three species of snake, one of which, *Viperus aspis*, is very poisonous. But all three are gardeners: great consumers of slugs. I seldom see them: only an unexplained movement of the foliage suggests their presence. A nameless large nocturnal animal hunts grubs in the lawn and is hardly ever glimpsed though often heard at night. Fireflies dance on a warm summer evening. A shy black squirrel leaps from one magnolia to the next. This year a fox has become a frequent visitor. Nothing menaces these creatures – except for cats. These have sometimes been a serious threat to our birds and hence to the ecosystem; but it has been much reduced. In this part of Europe and in certain villages of which this is one, when there is an 'r' in the month cat is welcome on the dinner table, though not on mine.

Interestingly there seems to have been a successful control by the ecosystem of some common pests. For example, there used to be a very serious nuisance, the rhododendron beetle, which disfigured the leaves of a majority of the rhododendrons. It has gradually diminished with the growth of the ecosystem. It is still there but not significant. Possibly this has something to do with the growth of a deep humus layer from the heavy leaf fall, in which we are now host to one of its enemies. Slugs, once a very serious plague, seem to be less numerous. As pointed out in the chapter on lilies, the lily beetle, an exotic, has arrived here and is the only insect outside the greenhouse against which I am obliged to use chemicals. In its original environment no doubt it had enemies to keep it in check. Here it seems to have none, except for me.

It is easy to describe but difficult to estimate something which is of one's own creation. The problem is one of philosophy. The garden has given me great pleasure at every stage of its development and I see it not as a snapshot taken today but in the perspective of the years past. The only reality for me is what I myself perceive. When I die the universe dies with me. It was hard to guess what the perception of others might be if my project came to fruition. The view of a visitor in the garden for the first time would be a snapshot of that moment. An early visitor, an Italian lady who grew up in a stately villa, lunched with us in the green month of July. On the terrace after lunch, coffee cup in hand, she said, "I hear you have an interesting garden. May I see it?" I motioned to the dense foliage below the terrace. She followed my gesture but was puzzled and then embarrassed. No vistas, no statues, no fountains: just plants. Not many flowers, either. Not much of a garden. Then she looked at me and saw that I was delighted with her reaction, and she was alarmed. The English were known to produce great eccentrics: doubtless her host was one of them. Perhaps she was right? Who knows? Or cares?

Many visitors come to the garden, from many countries near and far. All are interested in the plants, and many are interested in the ecosystem and in the concept that the plants must do the garden work. All are lovers of gardens or of nature, otherwise they would not seek out this mountain side. They are welcome. From many of them there is something to learn. Nigel Nicolson recently wrote that the visitors to the garden at Sissinghurst were as welcome there as the birds and the bees. It was well put and it is the case here. But although there is a spectacular indeed perhaps an excessive display of blossom at certain seasons, at others I fear that visitors may be as disappointed as the Italian lady was. Interestingly this has never again been the case, so far as I know, not even once. It is not the individual plants which draw the comment, though plantsmen have plenty to say about them. What seems to impress visitors is the spirit of the garden, the overall effect, the sense of unity without formality, the sense of unity in diversity, something which they never experienced before in a garden.

This is pleasing but for me not important. The art of gardening is a complex and difficult one in many dimensions. It cannot be collected or sold at Sotheby's, but it is art none the less. For a garden is a personal thing, a part of its creator. Like any true work of art it is his own expression of the meaning of existence, but unlike the plastic arts it is ephemeral: with him it will die.

CHAPTER 7

A High Canopy of Magnolias

THEY REPLACE NATIVE FOREST TREES AS THE MAIN STRUCTURE OF THE ECOSYSTEM

It certainly did not begin as that! It was apparent that in our climate growth would be so fast that it would be better to plant small and to plant well rather than to transport larger specimens. Besides, it would be much less expensive and in any case the new hybrids would not be available as big plants. On the bare terraces as the building of the house proceeded the little magnolias were hardly visible.

In 1970 most nurseries were selling the old soulangeana magnolia hybrids. Let me make it clear lest I needlessly hurt the feelings of their owners, that a fine tree of any of these old friends is a treasure to possess and a magnificent sight in full bloom. Moreover it has the value of the years grown into it, something which the newly planted modern hybrid, however splendid, cannot aspire to. The Chevalier Soulange was one of the greatest benefactors of the garden. But even a superficial examination of the market, such as it was, convinced me that newer and superior hybrids were now to be found, though not easily. It was these that I would plant. It would be in the nature of a 'trial' of magnolias.

Only one true soulangeana now remains in the garden: 'Brozzonii', now a large tree. It is still the latest in bloom of the spring flowering group and valuable only for that reason. There is one other so-called soulangeana which remains: 'Burgundy'. (PLATE 18) Its magnificent colour differs from all other magnolias that I know of, and it is extremely weather-proof. In this garden its blooms easily survived a late snowstorm. It clearly has much liliiflora blood but its origin is shrouded in mystery.

Hillier's catalogue listed a good many magnolias, including numerous species. Treseder's nursery in Cornwall listed far more of the campbellii and sargentiana families. These and their hybrids were what really interested me. The preface to the Treseder catalogue said, very sensibly: "If you wanted to plant a Cox's Orange Apple you would not dream of buying a tree raised from a pip. You would buy a budded or grafted tree of the named clone or cultivar which would eventually produce true Cox's Orange Apples identical to those of the original plant." This was exactly my opinion. Numerous plants were ordered from Treseder and planted. On average they must have been about three feet tall, if that is the proper word.

It is not my purpose to write a treatise on magnolias, but only to note one or two points which may be of interest. The first is that magnolias which are not planted from containers sometimes have a tiresome habit of sulking for a year or two. I suspect that the tops are waiting for the roots to get going and the roots are waiting for the tops to do so: stalemate. I procured a very fine foliar feed made in those days by the Murphy Chemical Co. of St Albans. It contained numerous trace elements. As soon as a few leaves unfolded they would be sprayed above and below with this feed with the addition of a 'spreader' to ensure good coverage of the leaf surface. The results seem to have broken the stalemate in almost every case, and vigorous growth began.

Of course the young plants, mostly a single cane, were carefully tied to bamboos to assure their safety and to keep the roots still in the early years. About the third season, a mysterious agent appeared to be eating the young leaves. Not slugs, not the rhododendron beetle, not caterpillars, nothing in fact that was visible by day. A lady visiting the garden discussed the situation with me. 'Have you thought of earwigs?' But where would they be? Bamboo canes are hollow. I fetched insecticide and poured a little into the tops of the bamboos. Out swarmed the earwigs. I had created a luxury housing estate for these unattractive insects. The remedy was simple. The tops of the canes were plugged with wax, and my future forest trees were no longer in danger of destruction by earwigs.

Another lesson was learned at an early stage. I received a young plant of the truly splendid *M. campbellii* 'Werrington', one of the very best clones. For some reason, perhaps because the terminal bud of the single cane had been injured, in early April I cut off a couple of inches at the top of the single growth, leaving a lateral bud to grow as leader. Bleeding began at once. I tried everything I could think of to stanch the flow of sap. Everything failed. The plant bled to death under my eyes. Now I never prune a magnolia in spring until it is carrying a substantial amount of flower or leaf. Why not prune in autumn anyway? Because cutting off all those flower buds goes against the grain. Magnolias do not normally require any pruning, only shaping sometimes to make an elegant specimen.

The magnolia year begins with the flowering of *M. stellata* in its many variants. Thinking in terms of the small specimens usually seen in gardens I ordered them all for planting. It soon became apparent that in this climate they would grow into miniature trees. As the trial proceeded the outstanding plants identified themselves. Amongst the whites 'Harvard Centennial' seemed to me to be superior. Amongst the pinks two from Japan were far better than any others. The first to arrive came with the name of 'Chrysanthemumiflora'. It has thirty or so petals and their outer surface is a good dark pink, not the washy colour of so many others. But what a name, even if it is truly descriptive! Propagating material was sent to Ken Durio, then president of the Magnolia Society, who grows a fine collection of magnolias at his nursery at Opelousas, Louisiana. He also thought the name preposterous and suggested renaming the plant 'Red Mum'. To me the most heinous offence in gardening is to create confusion by renaming plants just because one finds an existing name troublesome. Besides, 'Red Mum' was even worse! It suggested a character from the barricades of the Bolshevik revolution. I explained to Ken that if he committed this terrible offence he would sizzle for ever in the plantsman's hell; and so 'Chrysanthemumiflora' the plant remained.

Then there arrived from Japan a plant so similar to 'Chrysanthemumiflora' that I am hard put to it to know whether it is distinct or not. In my garden it appears to be superior. It came under the name *M. stellata* 'Rosea 32 petals' and as such it has grown into the best pink stellata that I ever saw, a dense columnar miniature tree clothed to the ground and about sixteen feet high. (PLATE 20) This and 'Chrysanthemumiflora' are the only two pinks retained.

There is a third stellata which is a remarkable and favourite plant. It is *M. stellata* 'Norman Gould' FCC. This is a colchicine polyploid raised by Janaki Amal at the Royal Horticultural Society's garden at Wisley. Its white flowers resemble those of *M. kobus*, but with broad petals. Unlike typical *M. stellata* they are extremely weather-proof. Its growth is strong and rigid, different from that of any other magnolia that I know. It puts on a fine display of bloom. In this climate, which favours growth, in twenty-four years it has attained a height of about eighteen feet with a stout trunk. This slow growth probably accounts for its rigidity. It must be structurally very strong and is probably very hardy. To anybody despairing at the frequent destruction of the flowers of typical *M. stellata* by bad weather, this offers a good though very different alternative.

Some of the new American and a few English hybrid magnolias were planted in the early years of the garden. I had become highly dissatisfied with *M. × soulangeana* 'Lennei'. A very fine colour and flower but a floppy growth. Pickard's 'Ruby' did not have the same voluptuous flowers, but they were very fine indeed and the growth was rigid and unexceptionable. In the same colour range Gresham's 'Royal Crown' promised to grow into a fine tree on a strong trunk, and this it has done. From the name you will guess its American origin. Denied the entertainment of royalty in Washington those great republicans have filled the garden with a crowd of kings, queens, princes and princesses – but very few presidents.

Amongst the new American arrivals was a mere commoner, 'Grace McDade'. Grace carried one of the most beautiful flowers that I have ever seen on a magnolia: luscious pink and cream bowls, elegantly borne on the horizontal branches. But after several years it was all too plain that the growth of the plant was impossible: twiggy and weak. Oh, dear! In a small garden there is no room for failures. Then I remembered my Aunt Evelyn's house in her later years, Pelham Place. There had been a magnificent Lebanon cedar, one of the largest I ever saw, in perfect health. But it stood on the south side of the house, completely shading the main rooms. A terrible error of planting a century and a half before. After much discussion and dissension in the family, Aunt Evelyn decided to fell the cedar. She went away while the operation took place. Neither she, nor I, ever missed that noble tree after it was gone. I have retained this bitter lesson throughout my gardening life. I gave instructions for 'Grace McDade' to be cut down and dug out and avoided that part of the garden until the work was completed and a substitute planted. Well, I do not 'miss' but I do regret those marvellous cream and pink bowls.

The magnolias grew rapidly in our favourable climate, aided by foliar feed. The first of the Treseder plants to flower was *M. sprengeri* 'Claret Cup', a splendid deep purple seedling from *M. sprengeri* 'Diva' raised at Bodnant. The buds on my tree were suspiciously large for *M. sprengeri*. When the first one opened it was an uncertain blush colour: nothing like the colour of claret cup in my Oxford days or like that of the Bodnant plant. The large buds and floppy flowers suggested sargentiana parentage. This was disconcerting. Then the campbelliis began to bloom eight years from planting. This was a welcome change from the twenty years which they sometimes require in England. The first to flower was 'Ethel Hillier'. This is a most elegant white cup-and-saucer flower, the 'cup' being almost imperceptibly flushed with pink. A delightful effect. The others followed during the next four years. An exciting day was to be the flowering of *M. campbellii alba* 'Caerhays' received from Treseders; surely one of the finest white magnolias in existence. I watched the shedding of the outer casings of the fat buds, and then one day, the remaining ones split, revealing the petals: they were pink. My only consolation was that I had not had to wait twenty years to be disappointed and very angry. The same story was repeated with a number of other magnolias from the same source. The nursery had sent out seedlings when, on the strength of the preface to the catalogue, I thought I had paid for grafts. It had not occurred to me to examine the plants when I received them to make sure that they were in fact grafted.

This was a major disaster. My most important garden project, a plan to flower and evaluate the best of the campbellii-sargentiana-sprengeri clones and hybrids, could never now be realised. It was too late. I suggest that an examination should be standard practice whenever a hybrid magnolia or a named clone is purchased to determine that it is in fact a graft and not a seedling.

Incomparably the best source of information on magnolias, particularly on new hybrids and selections, was the American Magnolia Society, now simply 'The Magnolia Society', a world-wide organisation. I read its bulletins with fascination and procured some of the new plants described in them. I began to write about my own experimental planting. Then one day Otto Eisenhut, a nearby nurseryman selling the ordinary run of mass-produced plants, came to the garden at magnolia time. He was astonished. He had no idea that such plants existed. He asked me if he might propagate from my collection, and I at once agreed. As a propagator he is a genius. Today as a result of advertisements in the Magnolia Society's publications, he has a worldwide business in propagations from my magnolias and from others which he has added to them from many sources. This is a development which gives me great satisfaction. It has secured the distribution of many of the finest magnolias which would never have made it to the garden centres. Now they will probably do so. I applaud the current effort to preserve first-class plants by means of National Collections under the auspices of the National Council for the Conservation of Plants and Gardens (NCCPG). But by far the best means of preservation is to get good plants widely distributed in cultivation. Many plants from my garden have now gone around the world in this way.

In 1970 there were very few hybrid magnolias which were the result of careful breeding. Most were selected seedlings from open pollinated flowers. The reason for this is simple. To evaluate a cross one should raise at least twenty plants and preferably many more. Even one cross would occupy a fair sized garden. It will be ten years or so before one can know anything about the results, and twenty in many cases. So the deliberate breeding of magnolias is for those who are patient, rich and young. However, some institutions are patient and rich and they do not age. At Kew the late Charles Raffill raised and selected a number of very fine plants from carefully calculated crosses several of which are available today. Brooklyn Botanical Garden did the same. In the United States a private individual, Todd Gresham, in California, embarked upon an ambitious programme of crossing *M. campbellii* with old commercial hybrids. He aimed to combine the beautiful clear pinks, true whites and large elegant flowers of the former with the hardiness of the latter. This evoked no interest in the United States, but it caught the eye of Harold Hillier,* who marketed half a dozen or so of the resulting plants, all of which were installed here. They had been the earliest to be selected by Gresham so probably they had fewer campbellii genes than some others which took more time to reach the flowering stage. All were a great improvement on comparable soulangeanas.

I wondered where the rest of Gresham's magnolias were to be found if indeed they still existed. In the search for them a curious drama unfolded. Todd Gresham had died and nobody cared about his young magnolias. Nobody, that is, except for Mr and Mrs Frank Gladney who owned a piece of woodland not far from Baton Rouge in Louisiana. They hired a truck, drove to California, and loaded into it all the Gresham seedlings that they could carry. I went to their arboretum, and there were the trees, now about seven or eight feet tall, growing under Gresham's seedling numbers and in poor condition: the Gladneys were neither young nor rich and looked after the arboretum themselves as best they could. This was a heroic exploit still inadequately acknowledged by the gardening world.

I exploded in a letter to The Magnolia Society; here was a priceless heritage about to be lost for ever. They overlooked my indignation and rose nobly to the task of salvation. Now, thanks to the work of Tom Dodd, a

---

* The late Sir Harold Hillier, the most distinguished English nurseryman of his time, with five nurseries in South Hampshire.

nearby nurseryman, who planted out several rows of Gresham's hybrids, and of Ken Durio at his nursery in Opelousas, a series of truly magnificent new magnolias has been distributed. Most of them received a trial in my garden and were then propagated and distributed by Otto Eisenhut and of course by Ken Durio and Tom Dodd.

On the east coast, American breeding at Brooklyn Botanical Garden specialised in the very hardy summer-flowering deciduous magnolias, mainly based upon *M. acuminata*. Some fine yellows, creams and oranges have resulted. Shortly before their arrival on the scene I received from friends in Japan three plants which had resulted from similar breeding lines in that country. One of these, a bright yellow named 'Koban-dori', which the Japanese translate as 'Yellow Plate Bird', proved exceptionally attractive, was distributed by Otto Eisenhut from my plant and recently received an Award of Merit from the Royal Horticultural Society. However, I think that the Brooklyn plant named 'Yellow Bird' is even better. The two birds can easily be distinguished if seen side by side.

Also from Brooklyn a plant which has given great satisfaction in this garden is 'Elizabeth'. The flowering comes just after the spring-flowering magnolias and just before the summer ones. This is a useful characteristic. Unlike all the latter, 'Elizabeth' flowers without leaves. The colour of the flowers is cream, just short of being yellow. The plant is a vigorous grower and free bloomer, probably destined to become a large tree.

In the mild climate of New Zealand there has been important work with *M. campbellii* by the Jury family, well known for their camellias, and by Os Blumhardt. The latter raised what I consider to be the best magnolia to plant in a garden today, particularly for those which the Book of Common Prayer tactfully refers to as 'of riper years'. It is called 'Star Wars', for a long forgotten movie, not for President Reagan's anti-missile system.

A plant of this magnolia about two feet high arrived from New Zealand in an air-mail parcel. It grew two feet and next year it carried two very large flowers and grew nearly three feet. The flowers were of a good bright-reddish pink with none of the purple shades which are to be found, and in my opinion regretted, in all soulangeanas and most Greshams. The flowering season extends over an unprecedented five weeks, and there is a very acceptable second flowering in July. Like its liliiflora parent, it propagates easily from cuttings. But a warning! This plant was propagated from here and distributed by Otto Eisenhut. It obtained an Award of Merit from the Royal Horticultural Society as a large shrub. In my garden it is already a forest tree! It is not for the small garden. Has it inherited all the hardiness of *M. liliiflora*? So far no frosts have touched it here when they have damaged *M. campbellii*, its other parent. Sadly, this almost perfect and most obliging magnolia has one defect: no fragrance.

To me fragrance in a plant is of the greatest importance. Many years ago at Itchen Stoke House I had read about the wonderful fragrance of *Magnolia × watsonii*. I tried to grow it there, but the strongly alkaline soil over the chalk displeased it. Since then it had fallen into the hands of the taxonomists. Kew had acquired the first English plant of this magnolia from the Paris Exhibition of 1889. The Curator, Sir Joseph Hooker, described it with his accustomed precision and named it for the Assistant Curator W. Watson, with a fine citation of his work in the field of botany. But eighty-seven years later it was pointed out that the plant had been described one year earlier by the French botanist Carrière, though with a discrepancy in the description which in my opinion ought to have invalidated it. But the International Rules are interpreted with absurd rigidity, so now this magnolia has been conquered by the French. It is *M. × wieseneri*, the name used by Carrière. Ah, well! I cannot help noticing that the new railway under the Channel ends at Waterloo Station.

M. × wieseneri was planted at Vico Morcote and grew well into a straggling plant twenty feet high and wide. The famous fragrance, carried upwards by the morning current of rising air, was noticeable on the terrace above as soon as a single bloom opened. But the plant was of mysterious origin. Introduced from Japan, it has never been found in the wild. It was only recorded as having seeded once, and then no seedlings seem to have been raised. Authorities have speculated that it is a hybrid but this remains only speculation and does not warrant a conclusion that this is so.

In this garden the Magnolias seed with great freedom, the branches sometimes weighed down by the heavy pink seed pods. But *M. × wieseneri* was not expected by me to seed, and it had never done so. Then, one day, I noticed a small pink seed pod: certainly it would be on the neighbouring plant of Magnolia × *loebneri* 'Merrill'. Binoculars were fetched. The pod was on *M. × wieseneri*. Astonishing! And most exciting! I watched its development day by day. Ambrose Congreve, creator of the magnificent garden and magnolia plantings at Mount Congreve near Waterford in Ireland, was visiting just then. There had been a big hailstorm. When we went to look at the pod on *M. × wieseneri* it was not to be seen. It was found, lying on the ground, still not quite mature. Ambrose suggested putting it in a shallow dish of water, and this was done. Presently dehiscence began and good bright orange seeds were revealed. These were divided with Otto Eisenhut for greater safety and a number of seedlings resulted. What would they be?

Most of them were of extremely vigorous growth, with leaves much larger than those of the straggly seed parent. Was this a throwback to a parent in a hybrid past, or, more likely, pollination from a nearby tree of *M. hypoleuca*? The most vigorous of my plants rushed up into the size of a small tree and showed flower buds. When they opened, far above the ground, they were reminiscent of the parent plant but larger and different in shape (PLATE 19). The important point to establish was whether the famous scent had been transmitted. A ladder was fetched and teetering on top of it I nosed the bloom. It had indeed received the famous fragrance.

Here then was what promised to be a large tree in the style of *M. hypoleuca* but with a more interesting flower which wore the wieseneri perfume. In my small garden now full of plants I had no room for it. The tree was cut down to a stool to be used for propagation and perpetuation by Otto Eisenhut. Perhaps one day some learned cytologist looking for a subject will unravel the mysterious origin of *M. × wieseneri* and of its progeny in my garden. My bet is that my plants are *M. hypoleuca* pollinating *M. × wieseneri*. The hybrid origin of *M. × wieseneri* remains unproven.

And now an injustice, as I see it, shall be righted and the shades of the great Hooker and of the Assistant Curator whose fine work at Kew he sought to commemorate shall be appeased. This very desirable new magnolia is published and illustrated here with the clonal name of 'William Watson', and is being registered with the Registrar of Magnolias.

Prominent as a feature of gardens and public places on the Italian Lakes are very numerous trees of *Magnolia grandiflora*. It seems to luxuriate in the climate and soil and grows rapidly to the size of a large and very tall forest tree. Such specimens abound and have become typical of the region along with the palms and the Italian cypresses, though more magnificent than either. In or out of flower they are monumental in the landscape. Almost all of them are seedlings, and the fine selections which have been made in the United States, over two hundred in number, are unknown. I was determined to try some of the best of them. However, so prominent an evergreen could not be given a place in the scheme of planting between the house and the skyline: like a palm or a cypress, it would be a notice of divorce. So selected forms of *M. grandiflora* were given places at the back of the garden where they would be seen against the silhouette of the old village high above.

The numerous recorded variants of this magnolia differ in size of flower, shape of leaf, colour of the underside of the leaf and growth habit. The delicious fragrance also varies. For such a large fast-growing tree it is worth taking the trouble to plant the best form available. I selected over a dozen for trial. Surprisingly for a plant which is none too happy in the English climate, easily the best clone turned out to be the English selection 'Goliath'. It well deserves its awards of Award of Merit, First Class Certificate and Award of Garden Merit from the Royal Horticultural Society. It flowers young, it is floriferous, the flowers are very large and very beautiful, its foliage is unmistakable: comparatively rounded and slightly waved. I see that a recent publication on magnolias* describes this plant as having a compact growth habit. In this garden two trees of it have proved as fast in growth as any of the other large clones. The height is already thirty-five feet and going up fast.

Easily the most disappointing was the 'Exmouth Variety', also widely planted in England. It is a good grower, but compared with other clones a shy bloomer. 'Ferruginea' and 'Russet' have a magnificent rufous under-surface to the leaf which gives them a special attraction. 'Angustifolia' has small flowers of poor shape though distinctive narrow foliage. 'Little Gem' is a pretty miniature for a garden which cannot accommodate a large tree. 'Nanatensis flore pleno' is not after all double, though it occasionally produces a pretty ring of petaloids in the centre of the flower. 'Millais Form' has a good large flower and grows well. A variegated leaf form from Mr Pickard was pretty as a foliage plant, but after twice reverting to plain green it was abandoned. 'St George', an English selection (PLATE 19) and 'Samuel Sommer', an American selection chosen for hardiness, run 'Goliath' close for first place but do not overtake it. In the light of experience I would plant 'Goliath', 'Samuel Sommer', 'Russet' and 'Little Gem' and leave it at that.

As these magnolias are very floriferous in this climate and bloom from the end of May until the frosts come in late autumn, they are a useful source of cut flowers for the house. Their delicious rather sharp fragrance makes them admirable table centre pieces, bearing in mind that the flowers of 'Goliath' open to a size well over a foot in diameter. At the other end of the scale, a gigantic tree of this species with its spectacular flowers and beautiful foliage is one of the most magnificent spectacles in nature.

For a mild climate the magnolia cousins, the michelias, are an elegant

---

* *Magnolias*: D. J. Callaway, 1994, ISBN 0 7134 7569 2.

PLATE 17 Magnolias seen from the terrace.

PLATE 18 *Magnolia* × *loebneri* 'Merrill'. With plenty of sun a profuse flowering of the magnolias is assured.

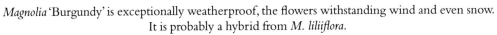
Magnolia 'Burgundy' is exceptionally weatherproof, the flowers withstanding wind and even snow.
It is probably a hybrid from *M. liliiflora*.

PLATE 19 *Magnolia* × 'William Watson', a seedling from *M.* × *wieseneri* raised at Vico Morcote. It wears the superb wieseneri perfume.

Magnolia grandiflora 'St George'. One of the best selections from this species.

PLATE 21 In this century breeding has transformed the camellias: Margaret Davis.

Camellia granthamiana grows wild only in Hong Kong. It flowers at Christmas at Vico Morcote if the weather permits.

PLATE 20 *opposite*
Magnolia stellata 'Rosea
32-petals'. It arrived from
Japan and is the best pink
stellata that I know of.
A small columnar tree
sixteen feet high and
covered with flowers.

PLATE 22 The giant bamboo *Phyllostachys pubescens*, *Embothrium coccineum* 'Norquinco Valley' and Exbury azaleas.

Rhododendron linearifolium, a beautiful eccentric in the rhododendron family with strangely distracted pink flowers.

PLATE 23 *Pawlonia fargesii.* A grave error in planting. Blue flowers should be seen against a green background, not against a blue sky.

Several terrestial orchids were established including *Cypripedium calceolus*.

PLATE 24 Many of Miss Ballard's *Helleborus orientalis* have settled down and multiplied.

Scilla natalensis from South Africa, a stately sculptural beauty, the exact opposite to what most gardeners think of as a scilla.

option where evergreen trees are desired. In the Orient they have a special significance. The deliciously fragrant flowers of several of the species are offered in temples and incorporated in garlands. My introduction to this genus of relatively little-known plants was thanks to Harold Hillier. He sent me *M. doltsopa* which grew quickly into a tree twenty feet high and produced its fragrant white flowers in abundance. They are preceded by the most beautiful unopened flower buds on any plant that I know of. They are covered with a shining silky ginger-coloured indumentum. But the great frost came in 1985, killing all the eucalyptus. The michelia was lifeless, or so it appeared. The wood showed no green cambium layer: it was brown and dead. But a plant must never be sent to the cemetery without a proper certificate, and patience is indispensable in such cases.

Michelia doltsopa had been planted at the foot of a wall. One day I chanced to look at the trunk at the back of the tree, only a foot away from the wall. About five feet from the ground there were two tiny green points no larger than the head of a pin. Not since my mother threw away my treasured plant of the golden alyssum when I was a schoolboy had I shed a tear in the garden. Then it had been a tear of sorrow for the death of a friend. Now they were tears of joy that a friend, contrary to all expectation, lived after all. But it was only just alive. Only a strip of cambium next to the wall was still green.

Now I made a grave mistake. I cut the tree trunk through just above the green pin points. They are now twin trunks, and measured as I write these words each has a circumference of twenty-five inches and the tree stands at thirty-five feet. The root system was undamaged and an immense surge of growth propelled the two pinheads to these proportions in ten years. But the trunk which bears them is only half sound: the outer half never recovered, and the tree remains structurally weak. When the pin heads appeared I should have taken my courage and a saw in both hands and cut the tree to ground level, growing a single new trunk.

Michelia doltsopa grows on the Tibet–Burma border and is one of the species of that genus used for temple offerings. The Dalai Lama, visiting the Thyssen Villa recently, planted a propagation of my tree outside the Thyssen Museum. We had cleaned off my stainless-steel spade for him but the head gardener stood ready to do the work after the benediction. But no! His Holiness tucked up his robes, went down on his knees and planted the plant with his bare hands. I doubt if any Michelia ever had such an auspicious start. It is growing splendidly.

Michelia figo is a large bush with inconspicuous small flowers: inconspicuous, that is, to the eye. But to the nose they are startling. Their fragrance is that of acetone or, if you please, ladies nail varnish. This is a hardier species than *M. doltsopa*, and Mr Jack Fogg in the USA has produced a series of hybrids between the two. These are *M.* × 'Foggii' and in this garden we grow his selections from that cross, 'Jack Fogg' and 'Allspice'. They are free growers and bloom profusely, but the beauty of the flowers does not rival that of *M. doltsopa* and their fragrance is neither startling nor particularly attractive. Of the two, 'Allspice' is the better.

Some years ago I received a plant of *M. maudiae*. It was said to have come from Shanghai Botanic Garden, where it certainly grew under glass. It had large broad leaves, and looked as though it would be tender. I could find no reference to it in any of my books. It was planted between the giant bamboo *Phyllostachys pubescens* and my tall plant of *Embothrium coccineum* 'Norquinco Valley', both of which back onto the house. It was thus in a very sheltered position. The michelia grew long and spindly as might be expected in such circumstances, and I had no serious expectation of seeing flowers. It was in fact forgotten entirely, almost invisible amongst its lush neighbours.

One day in March 1995 standing on the terrace I was surprised to see great trusses of white flowers which in the distance seemed to be those of a white rhododendron. But no rhododendron had been planted there, neither could it have attained such a height. Then the truth dawned. It was *M. maudiae*. The flowers were about five inches in diameter, fully twice the size of those of *M. doltsopa* and borne in clusters. Furthermore, unlike the latter plant, the petals were beautifully rounded, like the petals of a small *Magnolia campbellii*. Indeed they had something of the cup-and-saucer form which distinguishes the flowers of that elegant magnolia.

My plant had come originally from Otto Eisenhut. He was telephoned at once. His plants had not flowered: all had died. This very beautiful michelia, far surpassing any of the four species and hybrids growing here, will be propagated by him next autumn.

On the whole the magnolias and michelias have been a great success and a source of much pleasure at every stage of their growth. (PLATE 17) Now at twenty-five years or so from planting, some of them are forest trees forty feet high and I have a woodland of exotics. But there was one disastrous error which, had I thought of it, could have been avoided. All my gardening life I had worked in valley bottoms: the Itchen valley in Winchester; the Rhine valley at Strasbourg. The question of the depth of soil never arose: so far as I was concerned it went on down to Australia. I did not sufficiently explore the site at Vico Morcote to determine whether there was sufficient soil over the rock to carry large trees. I should have noticed that in the surrounding forests there were relatively few large specimen trees, whereas on the nearby Lombard plain were some of the largest temperate deciduous trees that I have ever seen. The warning was there but I did not see it.

In the event, at the top of my garden where great quantities of earth had been deposited from excavations made to accommodate the house, the Magnolias have grown faultlessly down to the present day. But at the bottom of the garden they grew well enough for fifteen years, and then began to find that there was not enough depth of soil to sustain them in dry weather. Watering in such circumstances in this climate is dangerous. I have a few dead trees on my hands and the area will have to be replanted with plants which rest content with eighteen inches of soil and sometimes less, over the rock. This is the only major failure in the development of the garden, but a very serious one. The fault is mine, not that of the principles on which the garden is based. The most important part of the gardener's body is not the muscles or even the brain, though he needs both in reasonable working order. It is the eyes which make or break a gardener.

Since planting in my garden began, much important work has been done with magnolias. It is slow to reach the gardening public, but one day it will do so. Extensive breeding programmes by August Kehr and Phil Savage in the United States are producing many exciting new plants using a wide range of species. The astonishing growth of interest in gardening in the United States and elsewhere, and the enthusiastic support received by the Magnolia Society, make it clear that these new hybrids will do not risk being lost to cultivation as did Gresham's plants. Indeed they will be eagerly snapped up by propagators and the public. One of my few regrets about gardening is that I will not live long enough to enjoy growing the results of such work. But that applies to other things in life as well as to plants, and, after all, of magnolias I have had more than my fair share.

CHAPTER 8

Fragments from the Gardener's Palette

A MASTERY OF THE PLANT
MATERIALS IS NECESSARY IN THE
ART OF GARDENING

It is impossible to practise the art of gardening successfully without an adequate mastery of the materials. This is true of all the arts. A lifelong reading of nurserymen's catalogues and the planting of four previous gardens gave me a good idea of what I needed and where to find it. Records, also, were a help. In 1930 I had purchased a very large leather-backed index book (see p. 11) such as might be used for the inventory of a small business. This would serve as my Garden Register. As it has 970 pages and each page contains 33 lines, it seems that at that time I had no doubt that I would garden for many years. From what was then a prodigious memory – would that I had it now but my computer serves instead – I was able to backdate it to 1928. Just before my eightieth birthday I filled the last line in the book, with item 32,147, seed of *Leucojum autumnale*, a garden gem, from Wisley. But long before that the computer had taken over and had assisted in the sorting of information. A garden without records – and there are some large and famous ones which have none – loses a whole dimension. A large collection of plants cannot be surveyed simply from memory however good that may be. Also there is much to learn from the intelligent use of garden history.

Some of the main elements in the garden at Vico Morcote and their acquisition are described in other chapters of this book. In the garden register everything was included: every plant or bulb, every packet of seed, every propagation, along with the date, source of supply and a reference number which would appear upon a label. As an exercise in education I also placed against each entry the natural order to which the plant belonged. This was a great help in understanding the relationship between different groups in the garden.

About 15,000 entries went into the index for the garden at Vico Morcote. But for the broad range of plants the process of acquisition has changed greatly since 1970 when the assembly of materials began. In those days some of the old specialist nurseries were still in existence in Britain. Many of them are now only memories. Others exist with the same name but, like Bottome the Weaver, they are 'translated' into something quite different. The growth of popular interest in gardening has produced the garden centres, most though not all of which stock a limited range of plants mass-produced by mass-producers. The system has no interest in rare or special plants to be sold to a small market of dedicated gardeners. Today I would find it difficult to assemble some of the plants which went into the making of my garden in the early 'seventies.

But there has been a compensating development. Numerous very small specialist nurseries have come into existence, sometimes just a man and his wife. Within their limited scope they are experts. Finding one's way to what one is looking for in Britain has been simplified out of all recognition by the annual publication of *The RHS Plant Finder* under the auspices of the Royal Horticultural Society. I suppose that one day soon this invaluable work will be on a compact disc, which will make its information even more easily accessible.

Another important change is the growth of specialist groups and societies: the Magnolia Society, the Iris Societies in Britain and the USA, the Aril Society, the Clivia Club in South Africa, the American Hibiscus Society, several Cactus Societies, numerous Orchid Societies worldwide, the Palm Society, the American Peony Society, the Cyclamen Society, the Hardy Plant Society, the International Bulb Society and many others. The specialist groups established under the umbrella of the Royal Horticultural Society are also valuable sources of information about plants which are not obtainable in the garden centres and about current developments amongst specialists. Membership of any of these bodies is indispensable and most helpful to a gardener seriously interested in their particular subject matter. In fact serious gardening in any part of the world without membership of the Royal Horticultural Society is, in my opinion, to subject oneself to an unnecessary handicap. It offers a range and quality of services not approached by any other organisation. The establishment of its successful branch in Japan is an important step into a new age of international gardening.

The wild and cultivated materials of the gardener's palette are distributed throughout the world. With improved means of communication and transport the market for plants is becoming a global system. I await with excitement the further development of international contacts in gardening on the Internet. Already I am able to join a Gardening Forum on Compuserve, a network of two million computer owners, some of whom are gardeners and nurserymen. Though at present most members of the Forum are in the United States this will change quickly as the miracle of such communication becomes more widely used in other gardening countries such as Japan, Australia and New Zealand.

When this garden was planted no such thing existed or was even in sight, but by careful inquiry and research I managed to assemble important plants from many parts of the world. These would not have been available in any one country. It would be both more difficult and yet easier today. Many plants formerly available and which figure in my garden records are now impossible to find. But in so many genera splendid new species have been introduced and new hybrids have been raised. The gardeners palette has been changing constantly ever since the early botanists defined it in the sixteenth and seventeenth centuries. On balance it is richer now than ever before and the process continues. This is the supply side of gardening. On the demand side it is notable that public interest in gardening has increased rapidly in recent years, particularly in the United States. When I first went to that country in 1940, if I said that my main interest outside of daily life and work was gardening, I would get a sidelong look. It is not so today. In Italy gardening is no longer only an adjunct of architecture but is becoming a plantsman's domain as well. In France after the great achievements of the nineteenth century, progress slowed between the two world wars. Now there is a very substantial revival.

This means good business for the nursery trade worldwide and the planting of a garden such as mine is certainly just that. But labour, not plants, is the expensive item nowadays. A magnolia will go on working for its owners and their successors for a century or two without anything except one down payment of the purchase price. A gardener has to be paid every week. Money spent on plants in my garden has proved a good investment over a period of years as the plants have assumed the greater part of the garden work.

The labelling of plants in the garden has been a matter of difficulty. What is the good of meticulous records if the plants cannot be identified? I must admit that this problem has never been solved to my satisfaction. When at school at Harrow I had bought a labelling machine which handled 'Serpent' labels. For permanence and ultimate legibility these were the finest labels ever devised for flowering shrubs. They were narrow strips of lead on which the machine would impress names by means of an engraved wheel carrying the alphabet. The long soft lead strip could then be twisted round a branch of the shrub. As the shrub grew and the branch thickened the lead would gradually give way to the pressure within but would never fall. The trouble was that by the time I arrived in Vico Morcote the label blanks were no longer available: the firm had gone out of business. Labels made with this machine fifty years ago are as easily legible today as they were on the day that they were made and they will remain so indefinitely. With the wisdom of hindsight I should have arranged for blanks to be manufactured from sheet lead. This would have been expensive but it would have solved the problem so far as trees and shrubs were concerned.

Instead I tried purpose-made labels, but they were expensive and never available when I wanted them. Besides, they got lost if stuck in the ground and if attached to the shrub by a wire they would damage the bark one day. Then I tried aluminium labels. These were excellent for shrubs but got lost on the ground in the heavy leaf fall. It took me a year or two of experimenting to discover that out of some twenty different label-writers, only one had any permanence: I now know that its writing lasts at least six or seven years or perhaps more. Its name is 'Edding 780 extra fine' and I use it for writing all my labels to this day. But, unlike the 'Serpents', the labels would have to be re-written in due course. A burdensome undertaking. Various embossing techniques have appeared but they all have the disadvantage of wire attachment. The aluminium labels can be twisted around a limb as with the original 'Serpents', but I doubt their permanence in the long term. The truth is that over the years the problem out in the garden has slipped from my control. In the greenhouse the nerines, in which I am intensely interested, are all labelled with meticulous care, the colour of the plastic label indicating the year in which the particular cross was made. But they are in pots and are no problem. The magnolias only need labels for visitors: I can remember their names. But the large numbers of rhododendrons, azaleas and miscellaneous shrubs which are left to themselves in the ecosystem have a distressing tendency to anonymity though with some research I can identify most of them if necessary. On the ground, many terrestrials, buried under the heavy leaf fall, are nameless. I do not shed too many tears over this, but it is a failure, to be regretted.

The new plants had to begin work right away. Wherever there is bare soil a weed will find it. I must get there first with my chosen plant to forestall the choice of nature. Elsewhere the native vegetation of grass with some native sun-loving flowers would be left in place as long as possible and the magnolias would be planted in it. But on the new terraces of bare earth with no existing cover, and new slopes vulnerable to weeds and to heavy rains, the plants must be got into place as quickly as possible. These early plantings were sun-lovers, set out in the knowledge that except in certain areas they had at most ten years of life ahead of them before the shade began to close in.

The printed materials at the disposal of the gardener today are of vast extent. The Royal Horticultural Society's bookshop list is a revelation to most people who have not previously seen it. The Society's *New Dictionary of Gardening* and the five volumes of Bean's *Trees and Shrubs Hardy in the British Isles* are the foundation of my gardening library. It is kept as small and selective as possible. After the two encyclopaedic works come the monographs on particular genera or particular gardening techniques. The literature left by those collectors who were articulate, such as Kingdon-Ward, is also valuable in so far as it gives the gardener an idea of the conditions in which particular plants grow in their natural habitat. To these must be added the catalogues of the specialist nurseries around the world. Most important of all were the publications of the specialist societies. From their members plants which have just been bred and will not be in commerce for some years are often obtainable direct from the breeders. A new hybrid iris, for example, may be obtained in this way perhaps ten years before it will arrive on the market in Europe, if indeed it ever does so. Then there are the gems of gardening which are in the hands of a few dedicated specialists, handed from one to another, material which will never appeal to the mass market or which cannot be propagated for it. Japan is full of such things, and this garden is enriched by innumerable plants from generous Japanese friends. In fact there exists a kind of benevolent plant mafia with members around the world known to one another at least by name if not in person. Japan and England abound in such mafiosi and I like to think that I am a member of the net. Few of us exchange or sell a plant, or expect anything in return for what goes out from our gardens, other than the satisfaction of distributing a fine plant to somebody who will appreciate it.

It is the shortcoming of garden architects and designers that extremely few of them are masters of this vast palette of materials. An excuse is that, designing for others, they are constrained by what is locally available where the garden is to be made. This is nonsense! Today the transport of plants around the world is not a problem. Even the barriers erected by governments against the import of plants, sometimes with justification, can be overcome with a little careful study of the rules. All but a handful of the plants in this garden have been brought into Switzerland, a country into which it is absolutely forbidden to import a fruit tree or a cow, and for entry to which plants coming from all but a limited area must have the roots washed bare of earth. If plants have been lost in the process of importation, and not many have, it has almost always been because of incompetent packing. No, the vast worldwide palette of plants is open to any gardener or garden architect who knows what he wants and is prepared to take the trouble to get it.

More convincing is the plea that so many clients will not know the difference between a superlative plant and a good one. To obtain the superlative will occupy time and cost money. Why encounter this when the result will not be appreciated? All that the client wants is 'a nice garden'. There is substance in this argument. It also explains why some gardens designed by famous garden architects are visually satisfying as landscape and pleasant as living space but boring to the dedicated gardener. Alas, there are no short cuts here. If a garden is to be of superlative quality it has to be the work of the owner, who has lain awake at night for many years, pondering the next move and accepting no compromises.

Aside from the question of quality, the art of gardening depends in the first place on the selection of those plants which will grow in the location for which they are chosen and which will achieve the purpose for which they are intended. This is not at all easy. From the Principles of my garden which were stated in Chapter 1 of this book it will be seen that at the outset, in my own selection of plants, whole categories, such as annuals, were excluded. There are many superb annuals but they require much attention to grow to perfection, and they require it annually. With the onset of winter one's labour is lost for ever. Then there were personal prejudices, plants heartily disliked such as berberis. And then there were the love affairs. I have conducted these for many years with four great families of plants: the Magnoliaceae, the Liliaceae, the Amaryllidaceae and the Iridaceae. There have been flirtations with particular genera along the way: *Wistaria, Viburnum, Ceanothus, Hibiscus, Camellia, Rhododendron* and many others. Between love and hate lay a grey area inadequately explored. In this many gems have been discovered in the course of planting the garden.

The planting of under-storey shrubs proceeded at the same time as the planting of the magnolias. Slower growing, they would be left behind as the magnolias overtook them until they would be growing in half or in full shade. A surprising success for this purpose was with American high bush blueberries. Ten commercial kinds have grown without the slightest trouble and survive and fruit even now that they get less than full sun. They attain about eight feet in height and after an elegant if unspectacular display of bloom they give a succession of fruit for my breakfast – and for that of the blackbirds – lasting for a couple of months. I do not grudge breakfast to the best musicians in the bird chorus.

Camellias would obviously be a major element in any garden in an area where they thrive in full sun and require no attention. They would also survive into the shade but perhaps would not flower quite so freely. However, I counted without the enthusiasm with which they would grow. After fifteen years they were competing with the magnolias. *Pace* to camellia lovers – I cut a number out. One or two were a problem. I had planted 'Dream Girl', a bright pink Californian hybrid between *C. sasanqua* and *C. reticulata*. Dream Girl indeed! I dreamed about that girl for ten years and never a flower. Finally I did what my mother used to do. I walked up and down before her with a saw. She burst into magnificent bloom next season. The explanation for this phenomenon is that the point at which the gardener has become truly exasperated with a plant probably corresponds with the time when the plant was due to perform anyway. Now she stands thirty foot tall and is smothered in flowers from mid-January to early March. Some girl! Worth the wait? Her sister hybrid, 'Show Girl', at twenty-five feet high, with flowers in a slightly paler pink from mid-December to early March, bloomed right out of the pot. But 'Dream Girl' is better today.

In Japanese taste the Higo Camellias exceed all others: single flowers with flat smooth petals and a very large boss of golden stamens. Sometimes a white flower will be striped or margined with red. Tsuneshigo Rokujo sent me a fine collection of tiny propagations, packed with expertise, every one of which survived and grew into a healthy plant. They seem to me the most elegant of a family which is sometimes a trifle crass.

If crass it must be, then let it be very crass indeed. The Kunming reticulatas with their colossal double or semi-double blooms could never be described as elegant, but magnificent they certainly are and they flourish exceedingly in this climate, growing into small trees. Some Californian hybrids from them even exceed their parents in size of flower. 'Mandalay Queen' never ceased to astonish me with its enormous double pink blooms –

until one winter it collapsed under the weight of wet snow, snapping at the root. I doubt it snows much in Kunming – or in Mandalay.

We have succeeded with *C. granthamiana* from Hong Kong which opens its magnificent single white flowers with a splendid golden boss of stamens in early December and flowers through Christmas if the weather is at all favourable. (PLATE 21) At that time I remember the Secretary of State's room in the Colonial Office. On the table lay a very thick volume between plastic covers. It was the petition signed by thousands of inhabitants of the Colony of Hong Kong asking that the great Governor, for whose wife this camellia was named, be given a third term in office. The book was sometimes shown to other visiting Colonial Governors to encourage them. When last in Hong Kong I looked on the Peak to see if I could find a plant of *C. granthamiana* in the wild, but was unsuccessful, though I saw one in a garden. As it grows in no other locality it is probably now extinct in the wild though widely distributed in cultivation.

Surprisingly, the small-flowered sasanqua camellias have been disappointing. Beginning to flower in October they carry the blooming season through Christmas and are available in many variants and quite a range of colours. But they are snow-tender. My favourite amongst them is 'Narumigata', white with quite a large bowl-shaped flower edged here and there with pink, and carrying a very good though not first class fragrance. It is also one of the earliest to bloom, sometimes opening a flower in the first week of October.

Visitors who are not camellia specialists are always interested when I pause to show them an evergreen shrub carrying small fragrant white flowers. It is China tea: *Camellia sinensis*. Tea is often thought of as a tropical crop, but in the tropics it grows at higher altitudes. In the Italian Lakes it would be perfectly possible to cultivate tea gardens – if plentiful cheap labour were available to tend the plants and to harvest and cure the crop.

The camellias in this garden have been trouble free and entirely rewarding. They look and are perfectly happy, untouched by any maladies. They seed freely beneath the trees and neighbours like to take away the seedlings, in spite of my warning that in doing so they are taking a ticket in a lottery: a long wait may end in delight, disappointment or worse still, indifference. They are, however, doing me a valuable service. If left to themselves, the camellia seedlings would take over the ecosystem.

Rhododendrons have been less successful than camellias. Several hundred kinds were planted at the outset, but where the soil is shallow these shallow rooting plants would not tolerate watering in hot weather, and they were decimated by Honey Fungus, *Armillaria mellea*. Swiss law has created a paradise for this terrible enemy. When a tree is felled in a natural woodland on a mountain side it is forbidden to remove the stump. The idea is to prevent soil erosion. The result is to promote the spread of *Armillaria mellea* which is now invading the Swiss vineyards. This has not been a triumph of environmental protection.

Unfortunately I made matters worse. To provide shelter for the young ecosystem in the early years of the garden I planted a dozen species of eucalyptus. They served their purpose, growing with great speed, providing ornamental foliage and flowers for my bees in a very barren garden, and breaking the north wind coming over the alpine snow. Some were very beautiful, particularly the fine-leaved *E. nicholii*. Some were already large trees – *E. viminalis* and *E. nitens*, both with a trunk two feet in diameter – when in 1985 the great frost struck. It killed olive trees of immemorial age in nearby Italy. All the eucalyptus were killed stone dead.

This was sad but timely. They had served their purpose and were no longer needed to furnish and protect. I would probably never have had the courage to fell them all. In a way the frost seemed to have carried out a necessary garden operation. But now the poor trees had a terrible revenge. Removal of so many large stumps would totally disrupt the garden. I funked the issue, telling myself that the stump of an exotic and highly aromatic tree would be unlikely to serve as an *Armillaria* host. I was wrong. Honey fungus moved in. Somehow, when, trowel in hand, one plants a seedling from a three inch pot, it is difficult to persuade oneself that in fifteen years it will have a bole two feet in diameter and will be a large forest tree. I would never plant a eucalyptus, beautiful as they are, in this climate. However, honey fungus is quite welcome in the kitchen, where it is grilled with herbs and served on toast, or incorporated in a pasta. As I munch it for breakfast I savour the flavour of my revenge.

In spite of honey fungus and problems created by a climate which has become much drier and hotter during recent years, the rhododendrons have given much pleasure. If there is a good spring rain they look extremely healthy in the early part of the year. Some of the dwarf species and dwarf hybrids have combined to form a dense ecosystem of their own which would do honour to a Himalayan mountain side. One or two of the eccentrics have been a great success: *R. linearifolium* (PLATE 22) which never ceases to astonish me with its narrow leaves and strangely distracted pink flowers, and

R. serpyllifolium with minute leaves and tiny flowers so numerous that the bush in bloom looks like a pink mist. At the other end of the scale the Loderi hybrids have done well, so have the old 'hardy' hybrids. Some of the tree-like species have also done quite well, including *R. macabeanum* and, surprisingly, *R. sinograde*. But after the latest flowers in early July most rhododendrons are a painful spectacle, and every autumn, alas, several will be material for the shredding machine.

The unqualified success of the rhododendron family has been the azaleas. Both evergreen and deciduous azaleas seem to be perfectly adapted to our conditions. A planting of deciduous Exbury hybrids stands twelve feet high, deliciously fragrant and requiring no attention. And then there are the deciduous hybrids of *R. occidentale*. These Americans have a powerful and quite different fragrance and flower a little later than the Exburys. They are exceedingly floriferous and only somewhat lacking in range of colours.

A couple of hundred different Japanese and American evergreen azaleas are a successful ecosystem all on their own. Many came as tiny plants from Tsuneshige Rokujo. In recent years I have added many satsuki azaleas, so valuable because they flower three weeks later than all the other evergreen hybrids, and are in my opinion more beautiful: large flowers, lots of them, marvellous new and subtle colours, colour combinations and flower forms. The blooms are often edged with a second colour or prettily striped or flecked with red or purple on a white ground. Dozens of these plants are available from Nuccio in California who has been breeding on from the Japanese hybrids. They are very inexpensive and jet-lag means nothing to them: they are excellent travellers, even on bare root which is required for import from the USA into Switzerland. There are even some tiny miniatures, on the same relative scale as miniature roses, of which 'Kokonoe' is an outstanding example. Too small to be grown in the open ground, the miniatures are plants for a trough or a pot or perhaps for the rock garden if one possessed so labour-intensive a luxury.

In the early years of bare earth and hot sun, the buddlejas were an obvious choice: quick growing, beautiful, fragrant and a magnet for butterflies for which the Italian Lakes were famous. Readers of Trollope will recall that the Reverend Dr Vesey Stanhope neglected his duties as a Prebend of Barchester Cathedral and lived instead on Lake Como, collecting butterflies. Como is just over the mountain from Vico Morcote. Trollope evidently knew his Italian Lakes. Besides clouds of peacocks and red admirals, I frequently saw two species of swallowtail, several fritillaries and occasionally that gem of the family, the Camberwell Beauty. No more. Now all that I see are cabbage whites. I provide the buddlejas in a number of colours but in vain. Perhaps the host plants which these insects require have been destroyed as building has gradually covered the neighbourhood. But the buddlejas are very well worthwhile even without the butterflies.

Bamboos had always fascinated me, particularly in the tropics where they assume gigantic proportions. The dwarf ground-covering varieties are perilous weeds which should never under any circumstances be admitted to a garden. They are as dangerous as ground elder. But the giant ones? Some of them are even more dangerous, because of the power of their invading forces. But grandeur they certainly possess. I planted the beautiful yellow-caned and giant *Phyllostachys sulphurea* and surrounded it with a concrete Maginot Line. Taking a lesson from the Germans it managed to get round the ends of it. As a matter of fact this was my second attempt to grow this bamboo. I had received a tiny plant of it from Treseder early on in the making of the garden. Thinking that it would perhaps grow eventually to twenty-five feet I planted it at the foot of the house where it would not reach the main level thirty feet above. The plant grew slowly for several years but was suspiciously green. Then it suddenly erupted. Giant, magnificent and beautiful canes rose to a full sixty feet. Sometimes growing eighteen inches in twenty-four hours, they would complete the whole length from ground to tip in seven weeks before beginning to open the lateral branches which in turn would bear the leaves. The beautiful feathery green foliage completely blocked part of the main windows of the living room. (PLATE 22)

Wolfgang Eberts, the president of the Bamboo Society, with a nursery in Baden-Oos, was consulted. My bamboo was *Phyllostachys pubescens*, the bamboo which is used instead of steel as scaffolding to construct the sky-scrapers in Hong Kong. It is also the bamboo which is widely cultivated in the Orient for cooking. So the problem of invasiveness was solved. In the month of May as soon as the new shoots break ground – off with them to the kitchen. After boiling in salt water for half an hour they can be converted into almost anything for the table.

Of course, for better or for worse, the bamboo is there for ever and has even become a notable specimen visited by enthusiasts. It has provoked some unusual reactions. The late Ken Scott, a famous designer from Milan, had a minute Chihuahua dog. We were going round the garden with his camera, with which he would record images to be used later in his fabrics. When we got to the giant bamboo, a new shoot was growing fast out of the ground.

The little dog was terrified and absolutely refused to pass by. It had to be carried. No doubt a plant which puts on eighteen inches in a day in a folded structure of leaves must make a certain creaking noise, audible to a little dog if not to a slightly deaf old gent. "A plant that talks? No! No! Something terribly wrong here," thought little Jicky.

I am apprehensive not only about bamboos in the garden but about the entire family of the *Gramineae*. Too many of the grasses, great and small, are impudent weeds. But an exception is *Hakonechloa macra*, a clump-forming elegant grass which in this garden grows about a foot high and spreads very slowly. It has never seeded. My plant is the colour variant 'Urahajusa zuku' which has been renamed 'Aureola' for the benefit of those who find Japanese names difficult. It has green stripes on a gold background. In case it should get out of hand, which seems most improbable, it is easily controlled by an unlikely predator: our long-haired blond dachshund. Tatsu – 'Dragon Boy' – browses regularly on the young shoots of this grass which he much prefers to any other. I have tried them myself but cannot share his enthusiasm. To my palate they taste very much like lawn grass. This plant was a present from Prince Wolkonsky. A particular pleasure of a garden tour is the fact that large numbers of our best plants bring back the memory of the friend who gave them to us.

Paulownia tomentosa is a prominent tree throughout the Italian lakes, beautiful both in flower and in leaf. A paulownia would certainly be included in the garden. But no ordinary paulownia for me! It would be *P. fargesii* (PLATE 23), which received the highest award of the Royal Horticultural Society, a First Class Certificate, when shown by Lionel de Rothschild in 1944. Planted as a stick three feet high, the trunk of this tree, clear of branches up to twenty feet, is now over eighteen inches in diameter. There is a rounded head of huge green leaves, which I estimate has now reached nearly sixty feet in height and is still going up fast. In spring it is full of pale blue flowers – but though the camera sees them I seldom do so. Pale blue flowers against a blue sky? My neighbours in the village above us enjoy them against the rich green of the garden below. I should have planted this tree at the bottom of the garden – or perhaps not at all. For it has a sex problem. An immense quantity of large seed pods are produced – a veritable orgy. And they persist, shamelessly flaunted on the tree right round the year and into the next flowering season, hideous in winter when the leaves have fallen and untidy next spring when the new flower crop comes. But the tree is magnificent and beautiful in spite of all, and I am curious to see just how large it will grow. Bean says seventy feet tall.* It will soon be there and shows no sign of stopping.

A seed from this tree lodged itself in a rock face near the road, where there seemed to be no soil at all, though there must have been something. For the seedling took root and grew a single shoot about five feet high in the first year. It could not be permitted to continue, so it was cut down. Next year it shot up in a single unbranched growth about nine feet high with gigantic leaves, perhaps twice the size of those on the parent tree. Now every year it is cut down and once again it performs this extraordinary and rather beautiful high jump. And if there are, naturally, no flowers, there are also no hideous seed pods.

Chinese friends tell me that the paulownia occupies a special place in family life. When a girl is born a paulownia is planted. When she is married the tree is cut down to make the furniture for the matrimonial dwelling.

Mahonias have always been favourites of mine. Several species and hybrids of this genus, including the elegant *M. lomariifolia*, have worked themselves into the vegetation and now sow themselves. Some stand fifteen feet high and are beauties of the garden. They provide flower and fragrance from Christmas until Easter according to the species. Through great heat, heavy snow, drought and torrential rains they have never complained. There is also much satisfaction in seeing in the garden a plant which one has also met in the wild, and in finding that it still seems to fancy itself in Asia.

However my enthusiasm for these berberids does not extend to the genus *Berberis*. I always disliked them, probably because they were often so prickly – but then I love my cacti – well, I just disliked them anyway. Why I decided to plant a large collection of them on a steep slope I cannot now imagine. Perhaps it was because of the glowing descriptions and immense number of kinds listed in Hillier's catalogue. The brutes grew with the greatest vigour and within three years I had a planting which equalled the Mexican cactus desert in ferocity. They did not even control the weeds, and getting in there to weed was unthinkable. Removing the whole collection was literally a bloody awful operation, but not one remains. They have been replaced throughout the area which they occupied by more friendly plants, the Japanese evergreen azaleas.

Though I am suitably humble about my own gardening errors, I am comforted to know that others, of great distinction, also sometimes err.

---

* *Trees and Shrubs Hardy in the British Isles*, Vol. 4.

When a schoolboy I used to visit Hillier's West Hill Nursery, always a great treat. I was usually turned over to the care of 'Mister Arold', as the gardeners called the future Sir Harold Hillier, then aged eighteen, as an escort. Four decades later, when this garden was being planted, I naturally asked Harold Hillier for some suggestions for tender plants which should thrive in our milder climate. He came up with an excellent list, including such gems as *Ceanothus arboreus* 'Trewithen Blue' which grows into a treelet in three or four years and which in its third generation of propagations delights me to this day.

Less fortunate was Harold's suggestion of *Viburnum odoratissimum*. A promising name. I consulted the catalogue. After commending its fragrance and other virtues in a quite exceptionally long description, it concluded, "A magnificent species for gardens in mild areas". Just the thing for Vico Morcote. In a genus containing so many wonderful and fragrant species this 'most fragrant' would certainly be a marvel. I consulted the entry in Bean,★ where it was described but with no syllable of praise. My suspicions should have been aroused. The brute has never given me even an instant of pleasure or a whiff of fragrance. Every time I look at it I wonder what Harold and the compiler of the catalogue were dreaming of. The rather insignificant flower panicles have a slight odour which is hardly a pleasure and they are of very short duration. This leaves the foliage. It is a rampant grower with plenty of shiny leaves. If one needed to fill a gap with such, there are more rewarding plants. Well, it is said that Homer sometimes nods. It is comforting to know that sometimes Harold did the same. Or did he? It may be that this plant, like some other fragrant species, comes in clones which are less fragrant than others, and that I was just out of luck.

Before building of the house had begun, before work on the garden had even started, 'Shu' Hirao, author of the illustrated monograph on *Iris kaempferi*, the Japanese iris, had sent me a collection of over a hundred different plants. Treasured in pots until their place was ready, they grew and flowered magnificently. Since a child I have been captivated by the elegance of these iris, particularly by their provocative carriage and by the form of the flowers. Though the colour range is limited they have a quite extraordinary elegance. These are geishas of the garden, bred to give delight. No gardening lifetime is complete if it has not included growing these seductive plants.

The idea that *I. kaempferi* hybrids must grow in water is a misconception.

★ *Trees and Shrubs Hardy in the British Isles*, Vol. 4.

In the Meiji temple they are flooded when in bloom, but this is for purely aesthetic reasons. They do not mind this but neither do they need it. Strangely, the priests of the Meiji temple have insisted on restricting the planting there to the varieties grown and loved by the great Emperor. But since his time, innumerable magnificent new hybrids have been raised in Japan and some in the United States. These have greatly improved upon the Emperor Meiji's plants. I fear that he must look down in wrath, denied access to these splendid new varieties which he would be the first to appreciate. However, the philosophy of the temple priests is logical if, in my view, mistaken.

All that these plants ask is an acid or at least neutral soil, plenty of water in the growing season and plenty of sun. The magnolias began to shade the beds where the iris grew and I knew that they were doomed by the planned evolution of the garden. Rather than see them die, the whole collection, which included many fine American varieties raised in Kalamazoo, was bundled off to Mount Congreve in Ireland, where they lived happily ever after.

A large collection of American hybrid herbaceous peonies was planted, flowered, and was left to dwindle away in the deepening shade. Even today one or two surprise us with a flower, just as a reminder of past splendours. I miss them more than anything else which has perished. They were magnificent cut flowers both at Itchen Stoke and at Colebrook. My wife is a talented flower arranger and with the progress of the ecosystem some valuable cut flowers have been lost.

Collections of *Dianthus*, which grew surprisingly well in our slightly acid soil, of *Lithospermum*, of *Campanula*, of coloured variants of *Vinca minor* were used as ground cover where needed. Very many delightful small plants, individuals rather than plantations, were included in the ground flora. Then an unforeseen problem arose.

Growing up in Hampshire, leaf fall had meant the falling of beech leaves in Selborne Hanger or of oak leaves in Plash Wood on Ovington Down. These were small leaves which decomposed easily: benevolent things in an ecosystem. The magnolia leaves were very large and with the rapid growth there was an immense quantity of them. Though they decomposed easily enough into a rich humus layer, before doing so they began to smother many small plants. (PLATE 16) This has been one of the prices to be paid in order to have my particular ecosystem. The alternative which could have been adopted as planting choices arose was to proceed with the magnolias and abandon principle, sweeping up the leaves, or to use trees with smaller foliage. Now it was too late, and the loss of innumerable delightful terrestrials had to be accepted.

On the bare rock face exposed by the explosions which carved out space for the dining-room, a very large collection of *Sempervivum* was established. Planting sempervivums is like stamp collecting: there is no end in sight. They thrived on the bare rock as few other plants would have done. When a little humus began to accumulate lewisias were added to them. Above the rock face in the thin layer of soil *Cotoneaster dammeri* was given a place. This is one of the garden eccentrics, which much prefers to grow downwards rather than upwards. It did so splendidly, covering a great deal of the rock, flowering and berrying freely, and capturing falling leaves to add to the growing detritus on the rock face. Then my part-time gardener, working at the top of the rock, noticed a bare trunk descending the rock face. He sawed it through and dug it out. Too late, he discovered his mistake when he went to throw away the 'dead' trunk. Too late? Not at all. By then the cotoneaster had rooted throughout its growth. It did not appear to notice the insult to which it had been subjected and it grows on merrily to this day. It? Perhaps I should say 'they' for there must be dozens of plants.

Cotoneasters are not my favourite plants, but if a garden is troubled with wasps a plant of *Cotoneaster horizontalis* is a useful antidote. This unexciting plant flowers at about the time in spring when the queen wasps appear. One grew on the west front at Itchen Stoke. My father noticed that the queens were attracted to the open flowers in considerable numbers. He would sit on his shooting stick in front of the plant with a butterfly net, waiting. He had also noticed that when disturbed the queen would not fly straight out from the plant, or up from it. Instead she would drop vertically for six or eight inches before flying away. Perhaps this had something to do with aerodynamics, or it may have been an instinctive evasion tactic. However that may be, it played straight into father's hands, or rather into his net. All he needed to do was to hold the net beneath the queen before alarming her, and when she dropped into the net, turn it over sharply, capturing the unfortunate monarch. Only queens behave in this manner: the fruit wasps which appear later in the year do not usually visit flowers and cannot be taken thus easily.

In various exposures according to their needs many species of terrestrial orchid were given a trial at Vico Morcote and quite a few succeeded, some brilliantly. (PLATE 23) So successful was a clump of *Cypripedium macranthum var. speciosum* carrying nine blooms that when I returned after a short winter absence there was a hole where the clump had been the previous summer. I never succeeded in securing it again. This was the only theft of a plant ever to occur inside the garden, and I must admit that the thief was a connoisseur of plants.

Several kinds of *Convallaria* including the pink one were set out in already shady places and they have become part of the system. Surprisingly the alpine *Gentiana acaulis* established so well that it attempted seeding itself in the lawn. It also makes a welcome second flowering in November and December if the weather is at all favourable. Several cyclamen species were planted in quantity and established themselves, seeding quite freely, sometimes in improbable places: *C. hederifolium* and its white variant for the autumn, *C. coum* in many shades for the winter, *C. europaeum* in spring and my favourite, the bright clear pink *C. pseudibericum* which holds its flowers up well above the foliage. *C. graecum* and *C. cilicium* have settled down nicely in full sun at the foot of a wall. Other species come and go and some are exciting plants for pots in the cold house which contains the nerines. I speak of them in a later chapter.

With the increasing shade, hepaticas in various colours have been added to the mix but they take a long time to multiply, though being natives they survive without problems. Many hellebores including Miss Ballard's elegant hybrids of *Helleborus orientalis* thrive and increase from year to year. (PLATE 24) Good forms of *H. niger* sow themselves, for this plant is a local native. Three kinds of another native, *Anemone nemorosa*, are established in the garden and multiply: two are blue and one is an elegant double white. All three appear to be permanent. Of erythroniums, the Californians have settled down and multiplied, but the European *E. dens-canis* for some reason refuses to be established.

Except for primroses, which are everywhere, primulas have been a notable failure. Many have been tried but after a brief flush of bloom, even the easiest such as the beautiful colour selections of *P. denticulata* have gradually dwindled and disappeared. We are too hot in summer for this genus. The primroses have invaded the garden from the neighbouring woods, which are fast disappearing, and now put on an excellent show in early spring. Surprisingly they seem just as much at home here as in a copse in Hampshire. It was therefore logical to suppose that the English bluebell, *Scilla nonscripta*, its companion plant from Hampshire, would also succeed. It resolutely refused to do so. This means that for a similar effect we must fall back on growing the fine coloured varieties of *Scilla hispanica*. But no! These scilla friends have been chased all around the book by the taxonomists. Now they are no longer scillas, they are hyacinthoides. Annoyingly, when planted here, the blue, white and pink forms of this plant, after an initial polychrome flowering, seem to end up all blue. They are very handsome, but they do not equal the display or the elegance of the Bluebell, *Scilla . . .* No! No! *Hyacinthoides non-scripta*.

Many different *Galanthus* were planted. Their performance has been erratic. Perhaps we are too hot for some of them. The big *G. nivalis* ssp. *Elwesii* from southern Europe, with broad glaucous leaves, has flourished, multiplied and seeded itself. But others of the *nivalis* group, which contains so many beauties such as the green-tipped 'Viridapicis', after doing well for some years, are dwindling away in our increasingly hot and dry summers. However I felt sure that the autumn flowering *G. corcyrensis*, which we have in both its Sicilian and its Greek forms, would flourish here. This proved correct and it multiplied so well that I was able to give away clumps of bulbs. Visitors to the garden, astonished at the display in late October, used to say "But . . but . . . snowdrops don't come till January." "Not in this garden," I would say smugly. Well, I cannot be smug any more. The planting suddenly disappeared leaving only a few isolated specimens. The reason is an unsolved mystery. It has been replaced by some of the beautiful coloured forms of *Ipheion uniflorum*, which multiplies so well that I am able to give away clumps of bulbs . . . so far.

In a garden in which plants are supposed to do most of the work, climbing plants must not expect to be tied up and trained. Only wistarias are exempt from the rule, though even they will climb happily into a tree and look after themselves. The handsome *Vitis coignetiae* will do the same. But I do not intend visiting the walls at regular intervals with hammer and nails, so on them climbers must either be self-clingers, such as *Schizophragma*, *Trachelospermum* or *Pileostegia* which will attach themselves to a wall, or twiner-scramblers such as *Lapageria*.

Lapageria rosea is one of the most beautiful of all climbers, and is named for one of the romantic figures of history, Josephine de la Pagerie, wife of Napoleon Bonaparte. It is also the national flower of Chile. Perhaps this has something to do with the name, for France was the origin of most of the original unworkable constitutions of Latin America which have since passed through many revolutions and are preserved only in the history books. In the earliest stages of this garden the fine darkest pink *L. rosea* 'Nashcourt' was planted on a north wall to scramble over camellias, along with a pure white variant. Another plant of 'Nashcourt' was planted in the greenhouse on that half of the back wall not occupied by *Passiflora edulis*. Both 'Nashcourts' have survived and flourished, flowering continuously through the summer and early autumn. I notice that the flower colour is darkest in cool weather and correspondingly paler in the hot months. The white variant died out after flowering for a year or two. Relatively few people have seen these very beautiful plants in bloom in Europe and a visiting Chilean Ambassador was startled to be greeted by his national flower on the lunch table.

It was hard to believe that there were not superior selections of *Lapageria* cultivated in Chile but I had never been able to obtain information on this point, let alone plants. Then in 1993 Swiss friends were visiting Limache in southern Chile and they made inquiries for me. There is indeed a nursery specialising in the national flower. Ten selections with most seductive descriptions of their variant flowers were obtained and dispatched in late winter, that is to say Chilean early autumn. Swiss regulations prescribed that they must come on bare root after root washing. Lapagerias are not easy to transplant in the best of circumstances. And then they would have to overcome a six-month jet-lag to adapt to the new growth cycle. All would probably have been fairly well if the plants had not been delayed for three weeks on the way by air to Europe. However, on arrival they looked very healthy – deceptively healthy. They were potted up and put into intensive care in the cold greenhouse. These are plants which relish cool, moist but not extremely cold conditions. The struggle began.

A year later it was still going on. Seven of the ten were definitely alive and growing with varying degrees of enthusiasm. One of them, a very large white, 'Toqui', had flowered. (PLATE 46) I hoped that the rhythm of the remainder would settle down into that of the northern hemisphere in time for blooming next year. The condition of two had seemed hopeless. No green of any kind had graced the pots for the past seven months. In the month of September, the beginning of spring in southern Chile, in one of the 'hopeless' pots, a vigorous shoot suddenly sprang from the bare earth and grew an inch every day. Apparently this plant, 'El Vergel', described as an exceptionally fine flesh pink, and thus much paler than 'Nash Court', was still under the impression that the Chilean summer was just around the corner. It had a nasty surprise in store! Taking the hint I removed the other bare pot into the house where the temperature is much higher than in the greenhouse. 'Rayèn', described as a very large pink, sprang into growth. But even if only the beautiful 'Toqui' had survived it would have been well worth the trouble. Now four more named clones have arrived from Chile and are growing here and one more is expected.

Perhaps a reader of this book will have received the impression that for me gardening is a matter of obtaining and growing flowering plants, neither more nor less. This is far from the truth. Anybody inspecting an old stone wall in Cumbria may examine the beauties of the mosses and ferns, which fruit without 'flowering'. Alas, our climate in Vico Morcote is now too hot and dry to permit a growth of mosses such as one may see in Japan – or Cumbria. But some ferns are more tolerant of our conditions. At the outset we planted a couple of hundred different ferns, from Mr Kaye's nursery in Cumbria. Some settled down here and indeed interbred amongst themselves, while others died out. In the shade at the bottom of the ravine ferns still luxuriate. An essay in form and texture in shades of green can be a beautiful element in a garden. But, like a Corot landscape, it needs the slightest touch of bright colour so that the greens may be thrown into relief. For the past twenty years Backhouse hybrid lilies have provided just that. (PLATE 29)

Plants which flower towards the end of the summer and in early autumn are particularly valuable. The nerines, of which I speak elsewhere in this book, and which flower from the end of September until December, are immediately preceded by their distant relatives, the various clones of *Amaryllis belladonna*, flowering in early September. All have a delicious fruity fragrance, something rarely noticed in nerine. It is also an unusual fragrance, which I have not detected in any other flower. But the common variety of *A. belladonna* is a poor thing compared to the selections made in California by Mr Hannibal and to those made in South Africa, the latter bearing the names of various cities in that country.

I had admired the splendid planting of *A. belladonna* in one of the few good private gardens in Mexico belonging to Mexicans, at the village of Banderilla, in the Sierra de Agua descending towards Jalapa, the capital of the State of Veracruz. Again I had seen it luxuriating in the beautiful garden of Sir William Walton on the Island of Ischia. Both were far sunnier than my garden in Winchester. However, for the garden at Colebrook House I had obtained bulbs from Mr Hannibal. My garden register tells me that I received eight named clones from him in August 1961. I planted them at the foot of a south-facing wall along with some South African named clones. They grew and flowered quite well until I left for Strasbourg in 1964. In

1970 Hillier's kindly visited the garden, dug up the bulbs, and shipped them to me in Switzerland. Inevitably the names were divorced from the bulbs, so what I have here is a mixture of fine clones, but mostly Hannibals. For contrast I added to them the beautiful pure white *A. belladonna* 'Parkeri Alba'. (PLATE 49) I expected them to like conditions at the foot of a south wall in Vico Morcote, and so they did. After a year to settle in they flowered with abandon. Since then the shade has closed in upon them to some extent, but wherever they can see the sun they flower prodigiously, filling the area with perfume. Beautiful cut flowers, they will scent a room with their fragrance. (PLATE 49)

Amaryllis belladonna flowers without leaves, hence the name, also applied to *Colchicum*, of 'naked ladies'. It then produces foliage which persists through winter and into early summer when it disappears and nothing remains of the plant above ground. It therefore needs companion planting for the summer. In this garden selected new American hybrid daylilies, splendid things, provide just this and so do various selected *Agapanthus*. Both bloom in the green month of July and then the foliage of the daylilies begins to die down in time for the parade of the naked ladies. Seed is set by the said ladies in great quantity and is easily grown on if you have patience, and room for more belladonnas.

Towards the end of the belladonnas comes the other troop of naked ladies: the colchicums. This, that is to say the colchicum, is the ideal plant to give to a child. When one is very young a month is a very long time. The six-month wait from the planting of a daffodil to the appearance of the bloom is an eternity. My mother sent me back to Hawtrey's School in late September with some colchicum bulbs, probably *C. autumnale*, with instructions to leave them just as they were on the table in my bedroom. Sure enough, a couple of weeks after the beginning of term the flowers began to emerge, one after the other. Ever since, these members of the lily family, whose flowers mimic the crocuses from the iris family, have had a special place in my gardener's heart.

A lasting memory from 1937 is of a visit to Manderston House in the Scottish Borders. There Hugh and Nancy Bailie had a beautiful display of colchicums. Huge flowers, and – no pink woman flesh here – they were pure white. It was *C. speciosum* 'album', in my opinion the most magnificent of all the many colchicums and one of the finest of garden plants. They were planted at Vico Morcote in the very first season: not many of them because it is a most expensive bulb. Over the years they have flourished and multiplied.

At the same time typical *C. speciosum* was planted. This wild plant seems to me to be the most elegant of the pink colchicums, surpassing the more brightly coloured garden hybrids. Both these plants are late bloomers, an advantage. 'Violet Queen' is a splendidly dark early bloomer and a good companion for them. All make long-lasting cut flowers which open well in water, provided that the slugs have not got them first.

Another plant which mimics the crocuses is an amaryllid, *Sternbergia lutea*. In the month of October it produces masses of very large golden 'crocuses' of beautiful form. Like the colchicums they make excellent cut flowers. This lovely plant revels in a sunny but moist situation, but will also do quite well on a hot slope. It is one of several candidates suggested as the plant referred to in Holy Writ as the 'Lilies of the field'.

The true autumn crocuses, which I had grown in my house master's garden frame at Harrow, are a seductive lot. My pick from them all is the Greek *Crocus niveus*, one bulb of which I had grown at Harrow: a pure white beauty with contrasting scarlet anthers. Next comes another Greek *C. goulimyi*, a late-flowering prolifically-increasing blue with a splendid honey fragrance. But unlike the colchicums, the true crocus are palatable to field mice. We have plenty of the latter and never many autumn crocuses the second season after planting, although the rapidly increasing Goulimy crocus manages to keep up with the demand.

Crocus corms must be exceptionally good eating. My father planted hundreds of spring flowering crocuses in the park at Itchen Stoke House, using a bulb planter which removed a small circular divot of turf. He would then put the crocus corm into the hole and replace the divot, firming it with his foot. Meanwhile the cock pheasants, which were plentiful in that sporting neighbourhood, had been watching patiently from the shelter of the thicket of the old churchyard. As soon as father returned to the house, out would come the pheasants. They would work the area, pulling out the divots and eating the corms. They did not bother to replace the divots. The problem was that father really admired the pheasants more than the crocuses.

So it was decided to plant colchicums, which the pheasants would leave alone. This plan worked quite well in spite of the large persistent leaves which appear in spring, until my parents went to Zürich to consult a famous eye doctor. By misfortune it was the month of September when the train passed through Swiss meadows full of wild *C. autumnale* in full bloom, a pretty spectacle. Father did not think so. "My dear, do you see that? Just look! Why, those things are weeds, nothing but damned weeds growing wild!" He never felt quite the same again about his work planting them at home in Hampshire.

At the end of the autumn-blooming as the frosts approach, a spectacular parade is drawn up on the dining-room terrace at the end of the small central lawn: five trees of different varieties of Japanese persimmon, *Diospyros kaki*. (PLATE 25) The lavish display of orange fruits lights up the leafless winter landscape, and for full measure it is floodlit at night. There are many theories as to the proper method of ripening 'Kaki' for the table, but the blackbirds just eat them off the tree. There are more than enough for all of us.

A former gardener seemed to have rather frequent visitors who would take away bottles of some liquid. "Where do you get all this stuff?" I asked him. "What do you imagine that green barrel in the garage is for?" was the reply. I find grappa from grapes much too ferocious: that made from persimmon is altogether outrageous.

I omitted to say in the chapter which describes the designing of the garden that boundaries are a great blessing. Their discipline inhibits the tendency of the plantsman to expand 'just a little more' every year to accommodate the fascinating plants about which he has read in a catalogue. In fact, the smaller the garden the greater the artist must be to make a success of it and the more fastidious must be his choice of plants. This chapter could go on more or less indefinitely describing the many plants which have given me delight – or sorrow – in my garden. But perhaps I have reached the boundary.

CHAPTER 9

Wistarias: A Scene of the Greatest Confusion

BUT THEY ARE AMONGST THE MOST REWARDING OF ALL PLANTS AND THEY LIVE FOR CENTURIES

This chapter begins with a warning. Early in the last century this genus of climbing plants of cascading beauty was named to honour Professor Caspar Wistar of the University of Pennsylvania. He must have been delighted at the bestowal of so great an honour and at the establishment of so durable and lovely a memorial. His pleasure may have been slightly diminished by the carelessness of the botanist who described the genus. The latter misspelled the professor's name, writing the name of the genus as 'Wisteria'. The International Code of Botanical Nomenclature decrees that the name should be so spelled.

If the authorities who interpret the code were lawyers, they would follow the sound principle of trying to give effect to the intentions of the authors of the document. This was to clarify botanical nomenclature and to avoid misleading names. The name 'Wisteria' is misleading. But the authorities of the code are botanists, not lawyers, rightly interested in the minutiae of plants. Unfortunately the same rigidity is applied to the interpretation of the code. Many absurdities result. There is something highly personal about a name, and something irritating to the person concerned when that name is misspelled. Whatever the authorities of the code may decree I decline to disturb the shade of the good Professor, at rest for so many years, by misspelling his name. So for me these plants are and will remain 'Wistarias'.

An abiding memory from a holiday in Florence is of a wistaria. Italy is packed with them, some of such poor colour that they approach being grey rather than blue. Others are the delightful lavender shade, falling short of true blue, with which we are familiar. On the way up the hillside to Fiesole, at a bend in the road, on the right hand side, there was a gazebo: a square wrought iron structure. It was intended no doubt that the family would sit there on a fine evening, watching the horse traffic going up and down the hill, saluting their friends and enjoying the blooms of a truly magnificent dark purple wistaria which would provide them with shade. But now it was the decade of the Vespa, an extremely noisy but convenient motorised scooter, on which young Italians travelled with a girl on pillion. I doubt that the family ever sat in the gazebo. But the wistaria still grew there, magnificent in purple. Unforgettable.

The terrace on which our house is built at Vico Morcote has a balustrade fifty-four metres long. The change from the delightful eccentricity of inches, feet, yards, furlongs, rods, perches and poles had been a disaster for me. My shod foot is exactly a foot long, a measure ready to hand, or rather, ready to foot. But the house was built on a module of fifty centimetres, so all dimensions were metric. Fifty-four metres was the length of the balustrade. Just the place for a collection of wistarias. They would be in full view and also readily accessible for pruning.

The Treseder nursery, now defunct, which figures prominently in my chapter on magnolias, listed a very dark-coloured wistaria as 'Black Dragon'. Possibly it resembled the plant in Fiesole. I ordered 'Black Dragon'. Hopefully it was a lively dragon, because to arrive at the balustrade it would have to climb twenty feet vertically from the ground below before it started out on its long horizontal journey. A well fed dragon, it reached the balustrade in three years and in the fourth started out horizontally. Perhaps because of the heavy feeding it had never flowered. Now no doubt the horizontal growth had the effect of arresting the sap and it burst into flower. It was pure glistening white.

Mr Andrew Treseder was the nicest of men and could hardly be expected to check everything which his nursery staff did. Nevertheless the letter was rather a stiff one: it asked him to send me a black not a white dragon, and to include four lost years in the consignment. It might have been rather less caustic if I had known what the outcome would be. The wistaria turned out to be, in Japanese terms, 'Shiro Naga Fuji', the 'White Snake'. A long inflorescence, of purest white, a very vigorous grower, profuse bloomer, exceptionally fragrant and – and this made it a garden treasure – the latest of my fifteen wistarias to flower. Today this wistaria covers a twenty-four metre run of the balustrade, and it would have covered the whole length if given the chance: but others had to have a look-in.

It was in August two years afterwards that the late Shuichi Hirao – 'Shu' to his innumerable gardening friends round the world and surely one of the most judicious and generous plantsmen of all time – arrived at Milan Airport from Japan. Looking somewhat furtively in every direction he hastily handed me a plastic carrier bag. It contained seven wistaria plants on bare root. On bare root! In August! What a hope, I thought. Shu assured me that all would be well. All was well, though it took a long time in intensive care for each of the seven to decide that life, after all, was worthwhile.

'Fuji' in the highly ambiguous Japanese language means at least two things: wistaria, or a colour similar to that of wistaria. It is both a noun and an adjective. So Fuji Yama is either the wistaria mountain because the plant grows there, or the mountain which is the colour of wistaria. The language gives you no guide as to which it is. You must go there and find out. Shu named his plants and gave me his translation of the names, as follows:-

Murasaki naga fuji	= Purple Snake Wistaria
Showa beni fuji	= Red Wistaria of the Present Emperor's Reign.
Shiro capitan fuji	= White Captain's Wistaria
Honko fuji	= True Crimson Wistaria
Kuchi beni fuji	= Girl's Red Lips Wistaria
Shiro noda fuji	= Common White Wistaria
Kokkuryu fuji	= Black Dragon Wistaria

"But Shu, a red wistaria? Surely it is pink?" "No, red." "But then, Honko fuji, crimson?" "Yes, crimson." In the event, 'Showa beni fuji' turned out to be a bright deep pink with a short truss and large florets in the style of some plants of *Wistaria sinensis* while 'Honko fuji' was a clear paler pink with longer narrower trusses which in English garden parlance might have been called *Wistaria floribunda rosea*. 'Shiro capitan fuji' was the white counterpart of 'Showa beni fuji'. 'shiro' = white: 'capitan' = came from overseas (China) in a boat.

'Kuchi beni fuji', Shu explained, meant 'Girl's red lips'. When it flowered it was a very pale shade of blush but the tips of the flower parts were lined in pale mauve. These were the lips. The flower is beautiful in the Japanese taste for delicate pale colours, particularly on close inspection. But it seems to me that a girl with lips that colour would be near to death. The Japanese perception or naming of colours is baffling indeed. I still do not know if the difference is really one of perception or only one of linguistics.

'Murasaki naga fuji', the 'Purple Snake', was one of the group which we call *macrobotrys*: a very long narrow inflorescence, about two and a half feet; some Japanese forms are much longer.

'Kokkuryu fuji', the 'Black Dragon', (PLATE 31) was a dragon indeed. The very large broad trusses of large deep-purple florets are always the earliest to open, about a week before all others. Their colour was similar to that of the plant on the gazebo on the way up to Fiesole. There is a fine perfume. The young growths appear about halfway through the flowering and are golden, making a beautiful contrast with the masses of purple flowers. In my opinion this is the finest wistaria in my garden: at least it is my favourite. But then the trouble began.

It turned out that the trade is full of black dragons, not all the same. Was there a true black dragon? Who could tell? At this point I made a decision. I would not attempt to give 'true' names to my wistarias, but would keep them under the names with which they came, excepting only the false 'Black Dragon' which turned out to be 'Shiro naga fuji', the 'White Snake'. Under these names they have been propagated by the Eisenhut nursery.

I have never been able to find a specialist Japanese nursery dealing in wistarias, though no doubt there are several. In a genus which grows so readily from seed the market is full of seedlings on offer to the public. There is no way of identifying any wistaria as 'true to name' unless it has been grafted from a particular plant. The name of that plant may mean nothing, but at least if it has been seen in flower the result of the planting is predictable. These are very long-lived climbers surviving for centuries and eventually making immense trunks of venerable appearance. If such a thing is to be planted, it is worth taking pains to make sure that it is what you want.

The 'White Snake', in its journey along the balustrade, had an adventure. When the house was designed I asked Architetto Bossi to try to preserve a large walnut tree which stood immediately in front of it. To do this he modified the structure of the building so that the trunk might pass up in front of the house. The head of the tree would then shade the terrace. When the 'White Snake' encountered the tree trunk on its journey along the balustrade, it climbed the tree, quite of its own volition. In a couple of years it had filled the head of the tree and at flowering time the whole was a cascade of white snakes: beautiful. (PLATE 30) Then the tree died, killed not by the wistaria but probably by a combination of building work, the poplar moth borer and old age. It had to be removed and the 'White Snake' had to be content with the balustrade. But I strongly commend the idea of planting

a wistaria, preferably one with long inflorescences, to clamber over an old –
but not too old – tree.

Several other wistarias have come into the garden, the most notable of
which is 'Caroline', an unusual shade of reddish mauve and a good grower
and bloomer. Another, received from a nursery in England as *macrobotrys*
turned out to be nothing of the kind, but was a very handsome red-purple
with an inflorescence of good form and medium length. The so-called
yellow wistaria, 'Hichirimen', does not belong in the genus, or in my garden,
for it proved disappointing.

An experiment, the result of which pleased me, was the mixing of
varieties. For example the bright pink 'Showa beni fuji' and the pure white
'Shiro capitan fuji', have been trained into the same space. (PLATE 30) The
flower form of the two is identical, and the resulting pink-and-white colour
contrast is unusual and rather dramatic. I do not think that this would be
successful unless the trusses of the two wistarias mixed were of approximately
the same form.

The two main groups of wistaria, the floribundas from Japan and the
sinensis from China, climb in different modes. The Japanese, as might be
expected, twine the same way as the sun: the Chinese twine in a contrary
direction. Any attempt to make either go in a different direction is doomed
to failure. Hybrids between the two – and I suspect that my 'Black Dragon'
is a hybrid – do not as might be expected, seem confused: they opt for one
or other of the modes. 'Black Dragon' opted for the Chinese mode.

In this warm climate wistarias set a lot of seed. The rows of pods hanging
downwards resemble broad beans. On a sunny day in late autumn we are
disturbed by pistol shots on the terrace, the sound of the exploding seed
pods. This is a spectacular distribution mechanism which throws the seed
quite a long distance and ensures that the seedlings will be some way from
the mother plant. It is also a nuisance. It may be that that self-sown seedling
would turn out to be the greatest wistaria of all time, but it is unlikely. So
seedlings are pulled up and I resist requests from people wishing to give them
a good home. If they go to the trouble of training a wistaria they should buy
a named plant of proven colour and form so that their labour will not be
wasted on a weed.

Our wistarias disappear annually under the cascade of bloom (PLATE 32)
and I am often asked how to train them so that they will flower with such
abandon. It is simplicity itself. After they have occupied the space desired,
the surplus long growths should be cut back each year to about a foot in

length. This will be in July in most climates. In late autumn when all the leaves are off and you can see what you are doing, shorten each of the growths to three or four buds. The whole thing takes very little time. The result looks rather like a well-pruned apple tree with many fruiting spurs. But of course, you must grow your wistaria so that it is readily accessible for pruning. At Colebrook House I planted wistarias on the three-storey west facade of the building. It was a bad idea. After nearly falling out of a window in an attempt to carry out the pruning, a long ladder was purchased. In a labour-saving garden wistarias must either go where they are easily accessible for pruning or they must clamber over a tree as they might in nature. Then, as in nature, they will get no pruning at all and will still flower well on the outside of the tree.

Wistaria belong to the great family of the Leguminosae, the peas and vetches. At school at Harrow I 'took' Botany for my school certificate. The botany teacher, Duggie Reid, was an engaging Glasgow Scot. In a school of six hundred young men I was one of his two pupils. Duggie Reid's teaching methods were unorthodox but sound, I suppose. To this day I remember that the family of carnations and pinks, the Caryophyllaceae, is the 'Carry off a Lassie': the Leguminosae are the 'Let go me nosie'.

PLATE 25 *Diospyros kaki* 'Tanenashi' and several others decorate the terrace in late autumn and are floodlit at night.

PLATE 26 *Allium giganteum*. Each plant needs different photographic treatment to draw out its beauty.

PLATE 27 *Lapageria rosea* 'Toqui' from El Vergel nursery in southern Chile.

PLATE 28 *Garrya elliptica* 'James Roof'. The power of macro-photography used to reveal hidden beauty.

PLATE 29 *opposite*
In the valley the sombre greens of many species of fern are illuminated by the flowers of Backhouse hybrid lilies.

PLATE 30 Wistaria 'Shiro naga fuji', the 'White Snake', decided to climb a tree.

Wistaria 'Showa beni fuji' (pink) and 'Shiro capitan fuji' (white) trained into the same area for contrast.

PLATE 31 Wistaria 'Kokkuryo fuji', the 'Black Dragon', is the earliest of the family to bloom at Vico Morcote, with golden young foliage.

Wistaria 'Honko fuji'.

Dojean, Peter, Tigur with wistaria and *Embothrium coccineum* 'Norquinco Valley'.

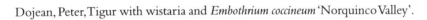

OVERLEAF: PLATE 32 Plenty of sun and correct pruning wistaria 'Kuchi beni fuji'.

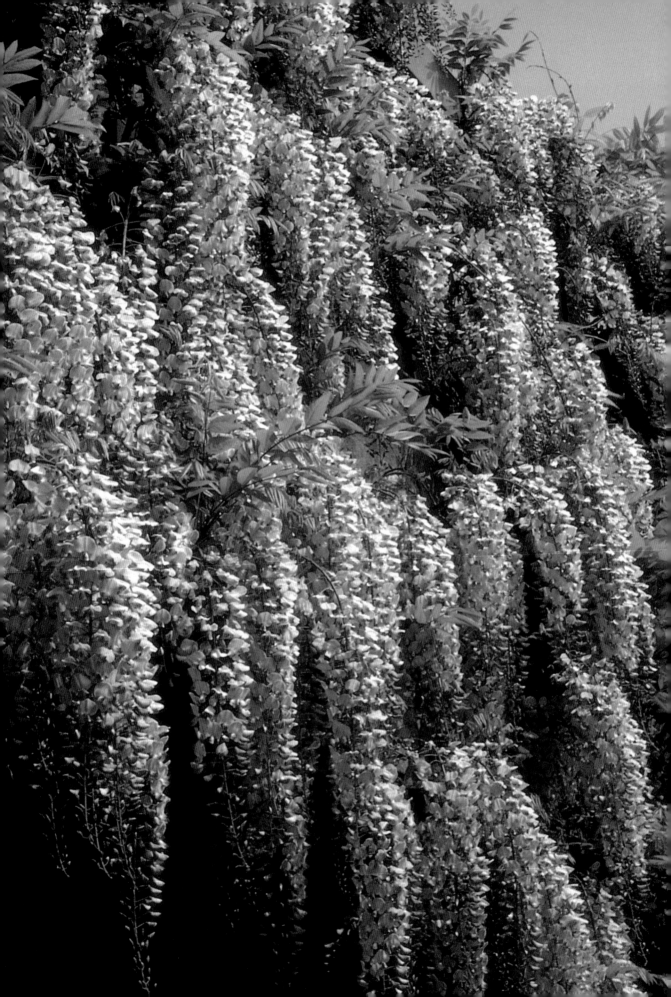

CHAPTER 10

Lilies, a Lifelong Love Affair

BUT THEY SOMETIMES BREAK
YOUR HEART IN THE END

It must have been in 1927, when I was fourteen years old, that the Lily Catalogue of R. Wallace & Co. of Tunbridge Wells fell into my hands. It was devoted mainly to wild species of *Lilium*, the real thing. There were few hybrids in those days. It was an informative document written for the owners of innumerable gardens throughout Britain who employed from one to three gardeners. I was fascinated, dazzled. That catalogue fired my first romance with a genus of plants. It was quite unlike modern nurserymen's brochures, in which the harsh colours of the illustrations often conceal the subtle beauty of the living plant. It did not attempt colour. It was the text that mattered. I read it cover to cover.

One plant stood out. Surely *Lilium sulphureum* must be one of the most elegant and beautiful of all Lilies: its imposing stature of six feet or so, taller than I was at that time, the great sulphur-coloured fragrant trumpets and its romantic origin on the Burma-China frontier. I ordered a bulb at the then high price of five shillings. It was the Easter holidays and late to plant. I potted the dark purple scaly object as soon as it arrived, taking care to allow depth for the stem roots to develop, and returned to school at Harrow. Back at half-term weekend the first thing I did was to look for the six or seven foot stem. It was in fact about eight inches high, and that was all that happened in 1927. I reported my disappointment to R. Wallace & Co. Next spring they sent me another bulb, free of charge, an act of comprehension which gives me pleasure to this day. In 1928 both bulbs grew to six feet and at the end of the summer holidays in September both flowered magnificently. I was transported by their beauty and fragrance. But I felt badly about my complaint to R. Wallace & Co. and said so. They responded by sending me seven seeds of *L. langkongense*, evidently a great rarity.

119

Next year in June, back at Harrow and on my way to a class, I was arrested by something growing in a bed of azaleas at the entrance to the Science Laboratories: a clump of yellow Turk's-cap lilies with black spots, contrasting red anthers and narrow bright green leaves, standing about four feet high. It was *L. pyrenaicum* in its yellow form: extremely elegant. How it got there I cannot imagine, unless Sir Arthur Hort, the authority on iris, who had been a house master at Harrow some years before, had planted it. I had already discovered some unusual species of iris which he had planted round the lake at the foot of the hill and which held their own with the native plants. The school garden took on a new allure.

At this time I had just won an English essay prize at Harrow, and to the indignation of my form master who considered that I should spend the credit at the school book shop on Shakespeare or some such worthy, I had ordered E. H. Wilson's *Lilies of Eastern Asia*. There was *L. langkongense* fully described: an elegant modest beauty, at the opposite pole of the genus from *L. sulphureum*.

In Wilson's book I noticed frequent mention of one W. W. Smith at Edinburgh Botanic Garden. Having no friend in the lily world other than R. Wallace & Co. I wrote to W. W. Smith about my lilies and received a delightful reply from Sir William Wright Smith, Regius Keeper of the Garden. He regretted that he seldom visited London, but his friend A. Grove had a house near Marble Arch besides his garden in Berkshire. He had promised to look me up. One day in late June A. Grove, the most eminent horticulturist working on lilies at that time, the continuator of Elwes's magnificent seven-volume folio *Monograph on the Genus Lilium* and himself the author of *Lilies* in the 'Present Day Gardening' series, arrived at Harrow to 'take me out'. He brought me a copy of his book, with a preface by the great Elwes himself and a description of the magnificent *L. sulphureum*. One of the few coloured plates was dedicated to that lily. Yet more gratifying, there was a mention of *L. langkongense* but only in the table of species at the end of the book with the note 'Not in cultivation'. Well, it was in cultivation in the garden at Itchen Stoke House: just to the extent that all seven seeds had germinated.

We left Harrow Hill and drove to a Georgian red-brick house somewhere out on the Harrow Weald. I see it today in my mind's eye along with the kind elderly lady – at least she seemed elderly to me at that stage of my life – who was its owner. There was a magnificent lawn, irrigated by subterraneous ceramic drainpipes laid without cement, so that when water was hosed in at one end, it seeped out at the joints. I was to copy this ingenious and simple device with success later on in my own garden. But the unforgettable spectacle was a clump of *L. monadelphum* in full bloom. I looked up – yes, up – into the large yellow Turk's-cap flowers. I could hardly believe my eyes: it was like some wonderful dream. But the garden was real enough, made on the stiff clay of the Harrow Weald. Fortunately, I could not know that throughout my gardening life I would try to grow that beautiful lily as well as my hostess had done, and that I would never succeed. But then, I have never gardened on Wealden clay.

Arthur Grove gardened on Berkshire chalk and my parents, no mean gardeners, did so on Hampshire chalk. He understood my limitations with lilies. A friend and benefactor for some years he brought me a large packet of seed of *Cyclamen hederifolium* from his own garden. He felt sure that it would naturalise at Itchen Stoke House. He was right. When I was last there thirty years later the huge corms were still happy beneath a very ancient apple tree, a 'Hambleden Deuxans'. He also brought me a large packet of seed of *Fritillaria meleagris*, in my opinion the most elegant wild flower growing in Britain, though admittedly it is only a 'native' by adoption. He hoped that it might naturalise in the park. In this he was wrong. I was to admire it every year growing by the hundred thousand in the Water Walks of Magdalen College. They were flooded every year and wet for all of it. The park was dry in summer and grazed by cattle. Nevertheless, so far as I was concerned this beautiful flower would always remain connected with the memory of my kind and much admired friend. Several gardens and many years later in life, I have never failed to respond to a request for help by young and aspiring gardeners. I now understand the pleasure which A. Grove derived from encouraging and helping my enthusiasm.

The war came and I was away from the garden at Itchen Stoke for five years. When I returned, almost all my lilies including *L. sulphureum* had died. It was a lesson learned. Grow the plants which like your conditions and will look after themselves if required to do so. Why spend time struggling to make unwilling plants survive in conditions which they plainly dislike? For their beauty? Perhaps. For the challenge to your skill? I prefer to avoid challenges whenever possible both in and outside of the garden, and as for beauty, there are enough beautiful plants with an obliging temperament to fill any but the very largest of gardens.

When I began to make the garden at Vico Morcote in 1970 I was working for the first time in conditions which most lilies would appreciate. A light well-drained slightly acid soil, plenty of sun – 2001 hours the statistics said – and 70 inches of rain, mostly in spring and summer. I bought what lilies I could find and thought would grow well and sowed seed. In his preface to A. Grove's book, Elwes had written, "Hybridisation has done less for this Genus than for many . . . whilst some of those which have been raised are distinctly inferior to both their parents in beauty, and do not seem to have gained vigour of constitution from crossing, as happens in so many other plants." Since that time innumerable hybrids have been raised and widely distributed in gardens, and in the end the desired vigour of constitution was achieved. But in spite of their number and commercial success, I did not myself think that there was a single hybrid lily which exceeded its parents in grace and beauty. However, like Elwes, I made an exception for the reputed natural hybrid between *L.candidum* and *L.chalcedonicum*, the nankeen yellow *L.testaceum*. This lily equals but does not surpass its two alleged parents. But then, its hybrid nature is only conjecture. So I would plant species not hybrids at Vico Morcote.

In the 'thirties I had visited the wonderful lily garden of Professor Lyttel in the pine woods north of Southampton: the English seaport not the American resort. It was a marvel, dedicated entirely to his splendid collection of lilies. But the lilies dictated what plants might and might not be planted as their companions. My garden was to be an ecosystem in which it was hoped that lilies would find a place and survive: it was not to be a 'lily garden'.

An obvious first choice for such a system was *L. martagon*. The literature sometimes decries this lily, apparently on account of its colour. So often in gardening books one writer simply repeats what some other writer said before, without ever having grown and contemplated the plant. But if the colour of the type plant is modest, it is also charming, and that of its varieties is downright beautiful. The form and habit of the plant is superbly elegant. The whorls of leaves, and the form of the numerous Turk's-cap flowers and their poise and disposal on the inflorescence are of sculptural beauty. The colour variants from the albino 'album' through the bright pink 'Inshriach Rose' to the glossy maroon 'Cattanae' are all of exceptional loveliness. It may be that in a blazing herbaceous border this lily would be outfaced, but in the subdued greens and half-shade of my magnolia woodland one comes upon it as a gem in its own setting. As a component in the ecosystem it has proved a good choice, having settled down and survived in several forms for many years without any attention being paid to it other than my affectionate admiration.

An early and truly exciting event was a brilliant success with one of the most spectacularly beautiful of all lilies, *L. chalcedonicum*. I managed to obtain ten bulbs, planted them in full sun and in three years had perhaps thirty spikes of the dazzling scarlet Turk's-cap flowers. I even gave away a few bulbs, it being a self-serving principle to distribute any particularly precious plant. If mine dies, then perhaps . . . Mine did die. The whole planting disappeared. There had been no sign of disease. Perhaps it was inadvertently given fertiliser, always dangerous for lilies. Perhaps the field-mice dined off it. And none of those to whom I gave bulbs had succeeded with them. I have never been able to find it since that time and my attempts to raise it from seed have failed.

Lilies win your love with their beauty and grace and a certain indefinable allure: and then they break your heart in the end. It is a very old story. But then, the stages which precede a broken heart are rather delightful.

Of course my first search for a lily for the garden at Vico Morcote had been for *L. sulphureum*. This plant from the Shan States of Upper Burma, which liked to grow at a depth of nine inches or so and revelled in hot sun, would surely grow at Vico Morcote where day temperatures reached the nineties although the nights were cool. The trouble was, that after having been used quite extensively in hybridisation it had been lost to cultivation. It had apparently been grown by Captain MacEacharn at the Villa Taranto on Lago Maggiore which enjoys a similar climate to Vico Morcote. In literature it is stated that this lily grew well at the Villa in ground "frozen a foot deep for several weeks".* Such conditions never occurred nor could they occur on the Italian Lakes and this dangerous mis-statement should be corrected. But *L. sulphureum* was no longer to be found there anyway. I advertised for bulbs, I inquired of breeders in Oregon, in Australia, indeed wherever it might be found, but without success. Then a kind friend in South Africa sent me a dozen bulbs. Somehow, the young growths did not look right, but they grew and flowered freely, with quite nice yellow trumpets. It was certainly not *L. sulphureum*, but probably 'Sulphur Queen', one of several crosses raised from that lily.

In spite of these disappointments I felt sure that so splendid a plant must be in cultivation in gardens in the Shan States of Upper Burma, but that unhappy country was practically inaccessible except for a few tourist locations. However, a member of my family had connections in Rangoon

* P. M. Synge, *Lilies*, Batsford 1980.

and through a nurse in a hospital in Taunggyi he succeeded in obtaining a bulb which looked, and indeed proved to be, the right thing. Encouraged, my wife and I flew to Rangoon the following year. The train from Rangoon to Mandalay took about twelve hours and all too frequently seemed to be on the point of leaving the rails. It broke down twice but got going again and discharged us in Mandalay. I remember it with affection and gratitude for a fascinating journey. Burma has every source of natural wealth imaginable: oil, minerals, rice, timber, gems and a charming and industrious population. But we rode up the fertile valley of the Sittang through a countryside in which the inhabitants had been reduced by an incompetent government to a level of life only just above that of their cattle. Incongruously, on offer at wayside railway stations were delicious hard-boiled quails eggs, regarded as a luxury in most countries.

In Mandalay we hired a taxi of doubtful mechanical health for the drive north into the mountains and on to Maymiu, headquarters in happier years gone by of the Burma Forest Service. There in the early 'twenties the British had laid out a great Botanic Garden. Perhaps something of it still existed.

Maymiu at that time was strictly out of bounds, and our taxi driver resolutely refused to go further north on the road to Lashio, saying that it was far too dangerous. So we halted at Maymiu and put up at a new, small and comfortable hotel called Nan Myang, managed by a Burmese woman of memorable beauty, Yee Mun Oo. It seemed that she had never received foreign visitors before and she made us very welcome. Yes, she said, the Botanic Garden existed and we should ask for its Director, Aung Swe. We set off in one of the small horse-drawn closed carriages which were then the normal form of transport in Maymiu. These were highly decorated miniature stage-coaches straight out of a comic opera. We imagined that they must be for tourists – but there were no tourists. In fact they were used for every kind of transport including firewood. In stark contrast, all around were the houses built by the former British Government for the staff of the Burma Forest Service headquarters, incongruous echoes of what might have been built in a Surrey suburb of London in the 'twenties.

Aung Swe also was unused to foreign visitors. He had had one such visit before, he said. We began to walk round the garden, which seemed to be very large, perhaps a hundred acres, and which was immaculately maintained by a staff of fifty. There was a fine collection of *Michelia* species, a *Caryota* species, possibly *C. no* though I never saw even that giant palm grow to such dimensions. It was the largest and tallest palm that I have seen, not exceeded by anything at Bogor or at Peradeniya. There was also a tree of *Eucalyptus citriodora* of titanic proportions, no doubt brought by the Forest Service from Australia. Clearly it was a climate which combined hot sun, plenty of rain and a good slightly acid soil. A splendid climate for sun-lovers. In winter there was even a salutary light nip of frost at night. It was rather like the climate of Vico Morcote but in the tropics at high altitude. There were no labels on any of the plants.

I brought up the subject of *Lilium sulphureum*. Aung Swe, a friendly man, had seemed uncomfortable when discussing the plants in his garden. He now confessed. "I am," he said, "just an old forester, a former member of the Forest Service. I know all about cutting down trees but nothing about plants." He added, however, that one of his gardeners grew what he thought were lilies: he would ask him to come next day.

When we met the gardener I explained what we were looking for. He did not understand any English and translation was difficult so I took pencil and paper and began to draw. First the large trumpet flower, then the numerous long recurved linear leaves. When finally I sketched in the bulbils at the leaf axils which are a conspicuous feature of *L. sulphureum* the man's face brightened and he nodded vigorously. Next day he came with twenty nice bulbs which looked right to me. The price for the lot was the equivalent of five US dollars. After expostulation with Aung Swe I managed to raise it to ten but he would go no higher. Perhaps the Shans are not a race of business men.

Back at Vico Morcote in February the bulbs were potted up at once and grew with great vigour. By late August this latest of all lilies to flower was already in bloom, the magnificent fragrant trumpets seen for the first time since my youth. Returning from a dinner party one night at the full moon my wife and I walked out on to the terrace, where the lilies stood, to enjoy their fragrance. We were assaulted by a large flying creature, perhaps a bat. Then it made for the lilies and hovered there darting from trumpet to trumpet. I ran for a camera and captured its image, the flash reflected in the eyes of *Sphinx ligustri*, the giant Privet Hawk Moth. (PLATE 33)

But I had been there before the moth, and the wet stigmata of the lilies were already thickly covered with the pollen of *L.* 'Royal Gold' and *L.* 'African Queen', purchased and grown for that purpose. I had come to the conclusion that *L. sulphureum* had died out in cultivation because of its susceptibility to virus in damp mild climates. Perhaps some of its beauty could be perpetuated in a hybrid which might prove resistant. A mass of seed was set which germinated rapidly and grew vigorously. After a couple of years virus reduced the wild species to almost nothing and it finally disappeared both in pots and in the open ground.

The hybrids confirmed my hopes by proving vigorous, virus-resistant, floriferous, beautiful and fragrant. Wherever they are in full sun they have grown into clumps six or seven feet tall without any attention and where they are in shade they have dwindled away. The hybrids with 'Royal Gold' are of a brighter though not a subtler yellow colour than *L. sulphureum*. Of those from 'African Queen' only one or two had an acceptable form. One registered as '*L.* × 'Vico Queen', has a fine apricot orange colour, deeper in the throat, and carries seven or more large flowers with a splendid sulphureum fragrance. (PLATE 33) Some but not all of these hybrids carry bulbils though these are smaller than the large ones borne by *L. sulphureum*. Seed from them has been widely distributed through the Lily Group of the Royal Horticultural Society. I am afraid that Elwes would have agreed with me that in beauty and elegance they all fall short of *L. sulphureum*. But they do grow well in full sun and give no trouble.

There was a follow-through to our visit to Maymiu. Aung Swe had pleaded with me to send him literature about plants: anything which would enable him to learn something beyond felling trees. *Exotica* seemed to be the answer since there was substantial coverage of tropical plants in the massive illustrated work. I procured a copy, and knowing that it was unlikely to reach Aung Swe if sent by post I asked if the British Embassy in Rangoon could arrange for its delivery next time somebody was in the Shan States. It was not a matter of urgency. The Agricultural Attaché informed me that the Embassy could not become involved in private transactions of that kind. Ah, well! So through the American side of my family the United States Embassy was approached. No problem, I was told. One of their people would drop off the book, and so they did.

The letter from Aung Swe was touching in its gratitude. I suspect that *Exotica* lay by his bedside for some years and probably still does so. The letter ended with the phrase "please give my best wishes to your old woman". As may be imagined, this did not at first produce the response which the writer had intended. But then we reflected that in the Orient it is thought an honour to be old and that what was offered was an expression of esteem and respect. Perhaps this seems strange in Anglo-Saxondom. I recently rode in a London taxi which carried an advertisement for computer software "so user-friendly that even somebody over 40 can understand it".

It will by now be apparent that my garden is a personal one. Plants find
a place in it if I like them and judge that they will grow for me. Collecting
complete collections of genera is no part of the philosophy. In lilies my taste,
or some would say prejudice, is in favour of the dainty Turk's-cap lilies and
the magnificent trumpets. In spite of memories of thriving clumps of *L.
croceum* var. *bulbiferum* in my aunt's garden at Pelham Place on the chalk, I
do not much like lilies which look up at me. So trumpets and Turk's-caps
have been given a trial here. *L. candidum* has been no particular problem and
its marvellous scent, redolent of honey and unlike that of any other lily that
I know of, is an annual delight recalling childhood memories. *L. formosanum*
is not very permanent but is very beautiful and easy to raise from seed. Other
Asiatic trumpets such as *L. sargentianum* have proved difficult. Both 'Royal
Gold' and 'African Queen' have dwindled away, perhaps because shade from
the magnolias has overtaken them. I do not really mourn their decease. On
the other hand a grex of pint trumpets raised here grows to six feet and
carries a dozen flowers. They seem to flourish in full sun and increase at the
root. Several variants of *L. regale*, some perhaps of hybrid origin, have settled
down well and are appreciated if fragrant, which some are not.

Lilium auratum in its various forms is *sui generis*: not a trumpet, not a
Turk's-cap, not an upward looker. Perhaps in modern terms it should be
called a 'dish'. A couple of variants of this lily settled down amongst tree
peonies and were a delight every year until I inadvertently over-watered one
of them in very hot weather. But they do not multiply at the root. I was told
in my early gardening years that this lily, once very common in its native
Japan, was cultivated there for food, and rumour had it that a pre-war dinner
of the Lily Committee of the Royal Horticultural Society was served with
the bulbs cooked somewhat like potatoes. However the bulbs may have
smelled in the kitchen, the flowers of this lily, which neither hang down nor
look up at you but look you in the eye, have a superb perfume.

I classify fragrance in a rough and ready manner. First-class scents which
are pure and delicious: memorable for a lifetime and indispensable in the
garden. *L. candidum* is one of these. Second-class scents are entirely pleasur-
able, but somewhere on analysis there is an underlying hint of coarseness: *L.
sulphureum* and most of my sulphureum hybrids fall into this category though
one of the latter just rises to the first class. A third-class scent is worth a
passing sniff while touring the garden. Anything below that is best avoided.

After gardening in the Itchen Valley, in Strasbourg and then here, I am
impressed with the fact that so many lilies appreciate a continental climate

with very hot sun and quite a cold winter. Tree peonies have the same taste in climate and the two plants, lilies and tree peonies, associate well together. Moreover, the resting period of the tree peonies begins in late August and lasts through September, just the time when lilies also need relatively little water and are thinking of dying back for winter. The English and Scottish climates, so favourable for *Rhododendron, Meconopsis* and the lily cousins *Nomocharis*, lack the hot summer sun and the snap of a cold dry winter which some lilies seem to relish and all tree peonies certainly need. The baking which they get seems to strengthen their constitution and they are spared a chilly but wet winter. This is particularly true of *L. sulphureum* and its hybrids, which vegetate later in spring than all lilies that I know of, which flower here in July and which remain green up to November.

Slugs used to be a very serious danger to the lilies and to many other plants. Of course we still have them and they do some damage. But as the ecosystem has settled down they seem to be less of a menace. No doubt several slug predators are now living happily in the dense vegetation. But, alas, the lily beetle, so elegant in its bright scarlet casing, has arrived in Vico Morcote. An exotic, it has no controlling enemies in our ecosystem. The situation is one of great simplicity. If I did not attack it with insecticides I would have no lilies: another instance of what the late Nikita Khruschev used to call 'Life Itself', though not in connection with lilies.

CHAPTER 11

Some Plants which Have Won My Award of Merit

WITH SO MANY BEAUTIFUL PLANTS
FROM WHICH TO CHOOSE
THE GARDENER MUST DISTRIBUTE
HIS AFFECTION SELECTIVELY

The Royal Horticultural Society's system of awards to plants has served gardeners well for many years. The First Class Certificate for the quite exceptional plant, the Award of Merit for an outstandingly good plant and the Certificate of Preliminary Commendation, an invitation to an aspiring plant to try again. These three awards have now been superseded by the Award of Garden Merit conferred on plants which are of exceptional all-round merit in the garden. Confronted with the vast range of planting material, one could not go far wrong by choosing awarded plants.

But in recent years this system has become difficult to administer. No longer does Britain have a near monopoly of the growing and breeding of ornamental plants. The Americans have taken over the lead in iris, orchids, magnolias, rhododendrons and several other important genera. New Zealand is breeding magnolias, camellias and rhododendrons. It is therefore increasingly difficult to evaluate a new plant before the Committee in Westminster against a competition with which the committee members may not be acquainted.

I am not inhibited by any such responsibilities, yet I am sometimes in difficulty in replying to visitors to the garden who often ask me, 'What is your favourite plant?' Unreasonably, I always find this irritating. In a garden with so many plants, none of which would be here if I did not like them, it is impossible to choose one above all others. This is not matrimony, it is gardening. Nevertheless, as this is a matter so often raised, I will select a few plants which have a particular appeal for me. Amongst them I have no 'favourite'.

Magnolias, wistarias, tree peonies, lilies and other genera which have a chapter in this book to themselves are disqualified from competition for a place in the following list. The order in which the selected plants appear is of no significance. I love them all. Ah, well! In my youth it was said of some young man whose name I forget, that he had a heart like a hotel. That is how it is with plants, and the hotel should really have a very large number of rooms.

I. *Sambucus canadensis* 'Maxima' (PLATE 38)

I saw this plant in full bloom for the first time in Princess Sturdza's wonderful garden in Normandy, Le Vasterival. It was lucky that it was in flower, otherwise I would certainly have overlooked it: just a common elder.

A common elder? It is a much underrated plant. It is indeed common, perhaps sometimes too common, but that does not detract from its beauty, or from its delightful fragrance, or from its utility, or from its traditional duty as the guardian of the house. For centuries innumerable products have been made from both the flowers and the fruit. Not all are for the kitchen. The fresh open flowers will perfume a hot bath on a cold spring day. My mother used to make elder flower Champagne. It was a pleasant drink in hot weather, until one such day, sitting in the shade of the great Lebanon cedar on the terrace at Itchen Stoke House, we were startled by a loud explosion within the building. It came from the direction of the larder, the cool room which was the precursor of the modern deep freeze and refrigerator. They have by no means replaced it. We rushed to the scene. Of the very large earthenware vessel in which my mother, unwisely it seems, matured her elder flower Champagne, not a single piece larger than a child's hand remained. It had exploded with the force of fermentation within.

In the Italianate world in which I now live, the 'Sambuco' has many uses, two of which have become a part of our daily life. The fresh flower panicles are cut, just before the opening of the florets, and by mysterious processes in the kitchen are made into a syrup for serving with fresh strawberries. The marriage is a perfect one. The rather simple flavour of strawberry is much enhanced by the subtlety of the elder flower.

Our other use of the common elder, also of the flower panicles just before the opening of the florets, is as a vegetable. With a little batter they are converted into elder flower fritters, to be served hot with whatever meat, game or fish you please, or perhaps as a delicacy by themselves. Delicious! And in the age of refrigeration they may be deep-frozen for use out of season. Italian country folk have many other ways of presenting the flowers and fruit at table. But all of this has to do with the common elder, *Sambucus nigra*, which has a number of uncommon and beautiful forms with golden or variegated leaves, now growing in my garden.

Sambucus canadensis 'Maxima' appears to be a much larger version of the common elder, flowering three weeks later. Not for nothing is it called 'maxima'. The flower panicles, carried in profusion, average more than a foot in diameter. They have a delicious scent which reminds me of the meadow sweet of the Itchen Valley bottom. As it is never possible to make a direct comparison with the scent of the common elder because they flower three weeks apart, I cannot confirm my suspicion that the two fragrances are slightly different. The display and the perfume of a large specimen in full flower are nothing short of spectacular. This is what I had the good luck to see in Princess Sturdza's garden.

I must also confess to a perverse reason why this plant gives me pleasure. It has a very special place in the garden right in front of the dining-room terrace where its display and its perfume may be enjoyed. Of course, when it is out of bloom, it might well be a common elder. What a place to permit a great big weed to grow! The words are unspoken but the visitor's face suggests them. Then the plant is introduced as one of the choice inhabitants of the garden. This produces either a look of puzzlement or incredulity or even of scorn which will fade as the explanation follows. It is one of the booby-traps constructed for the skeptics. There is another nearby. It is *Osmanthus heterophyllus* 'Gulftide', which when not carrying its very fragrant white flowers in the early autumn, looks deceptively like a holly. It rarely happens that a visitor falls into both of my booby-traps: in fact I think it only happened once. A red letter day!

The fact that *S. canadensis* 'Maxima' flowers three weeks later than *S. nigra* is useful, because it does so when the garden is about to enter the green period. But would the flowers be safe, let alone palatable, as fritters, or for syrup? If so, we would have a second crop of fresh fritters three weeks after the first one, without drawing on our frozen reserves. I asked my gardener whether he thought the flowers were edible? "I suppose so," he replied, "because you and Lady Smithers have been eating them for the past two seasons and are still alive."

2. *Daphne bholua,* Daman form (PLATE 38)

It was the winter of 1970 and my wife and I booked into a tour of Nepal. It was no ordinary tour, because it was led by Tony Schilling, later of Wakehurst fame and formerly the Director of the Botanic Garden at Kathmandhu. He knew his Nepalese plants and knew where they were to be found without undue discomfort. He took us to the Daman Ridge, at about 9,000 feet altitude. The bus halted, the distinguished, rather elderly gardeners which it contained got out and walked fifty yards, and there on a hillside in light woodland were the plants of *Daphne bholua* scattered across a wide area. I make no claim to be an intrepid plant-hunter. This was a most comfortable expedition.

What we saw was an evergreen plant, ranging from tiny seedlings obviously only one year old to shrubs about eight or ten feet tall. They were in full bloom. The scent was glorious. I set to work and lifted fourteen of the seedlings and carried them back to Vico Morcote in my sponge bag, an excellent container for plant collection. On return I sent seven of the plants to Hillier's and potted the remainder. After the first winter all were large enough to plant out but one was kept in the cold greenhouse. During the growing season and the following winter the plants out of doors were notably happier than the one coddled in the greenhouse. I should have known. The foothills of the Himalaya at 9,000 feet accustom plants to plenty of air.

The accepted wisdom on *Daphne bholua* said that evergreen forms were less hardy than deciduous ones. The logic of this was that they were more vulnerable to winter cold and were evergreen because, allegedly, they came from lower altitudes. In my garden the Daman plants grew alongside the deciduous form 'Gurkha'. I have been unable to detect any difference in their reaction to cold weather, but the evergreen forms are certainly longer lived. This may be because they are on their own roots while my 'Gurkhas' have all been grafted. In any case, both plants were put to a severe test in 1985. By then the Daman plants had grown to a height of ten or twelve feet and a second and third generation of seedlings had appeared, many of them self-sown in natural regeneration. Clearly the plant was settling down in Vico Morcote. Then the frost came. That night it was −17 degrees Centigrade, or approximately 2 degrees Fahrenheit: thirty degrees of frost. Next morning I expected to see the daphnes, then in full bloom, stone dead. It was a sunny morning and when I went out on to the terrace I was greeted by a familiar perfume, borne up on the rising air current: the scent of the daphnes. They were absolutely unharmed: not a leaf scorched, not a flower blemished. And it must be borne in mind that this was the frost which killed all my eucalyptus as well as ancient olive trees in Italy nearby.

I suspect that the reason for this surprising behaviour is that here on our mountain-side, as in the middle ranges of the Himalaya, there is a large differential between day and night temperatures. The daphnes were perfectly accustomed to very cold nights provided that next morning the temperature would rise sharply. The roots of these deep-rooting plants were never frozen. But what would happen if there were a frost of, say, five degrees but which continued for a week in damp conditions? I suspect that it would be the end of the daphnes.

They seed very freely here, and the juicy deep brown, almost black seeds are enjoyed by blackbirds. They consume the pulp and regurgitate the seeds. As a result, colonies of the daphne have sprung up under some of my magnolias where the blackbirds evidently roost. The mechanically very delicate seeds which only remain viable for a couple of weeks, seem unmoved by this surprising treatment.

As *Daphne bholua* is a plant much coveted by enterprising gardeners, I have distributed seed of the Daman form from this garden to Japan, Australia, New Zealand, the USA and other countries nearer at hand. The sowing instructions are few and simple. First remove the soft outer coating. It is not necessary to do this by the same process as the blackbirds: you can use your fingers, with care because the seed within is fragile and bearing in mind that the abundant juice stains the skin an ugly dark grey colour. Sow immediately. A temperature of about 65–70° Fahrenheit, not more, will be right. Do not over-water. Germination should take about three weeks and after six weeks it is probable that nothing more is coming.

As the seed is always ripe just about the time of the Chelsea Flower Show in late May I have made it a practice to take a quantity for distribution on that occasion. A bag of seed sent to Tony Schilling at Wakehurst Place seems to have resulted in a couple of hundred plants in the valley in that wonderful garden. I was less successful with Wisley. I suggested that the seed be sown immediately, but this treasure was kept for the seed distribution. Not a single plant could have resulted. For this is a monsoon daphne. Unlike its relatives whose seed must be frozen or at least heavily chilled before it will germinate the following spring, the seed of *D. bholua* germinates when it falls to the ground and grows through the monsoon. By winter it has already made a sturdy small plant. But I understand that in England seeding is rare. This may have something to do with the strain, for in my garden 'Gurkha' is a reluctant setter of seed.

The Daman form is extremely variable both on the Daman Ridge and in my garden. It varies in colour from almost white to a good dark pink and it varies in habit from fastigiate to a small rigid tree-like shrub twelve feet high or to a large floppy bush.* I read in literature that *D. bholua* is a suckering plant both in nature and in the garden. In this garden in twenty-four years and with hundreds of plants I have never seen a single sucker on this form. This seems to me to be an advantage, particularly as propagation from seed is so easy. I do not really like suckering plants though I have to put up with some of them. Could it be that some observers have mistaken seedlings growing around the foot of the wild plants where the seeds fall, for suckers?

In my garden, where this plant is naturalized and now sometimes has to be pulled up, it scents the whole of the hillside on any sunny day from early January until the end of March. In some years, notably 1994, it will start to bloom in late November and will scent the garden on a fine Christmas Day. Quite unexpectedly, it has become one of the principal features of the garden and has achieved a certain international notoriety – and all out of my sponge bag.

Most daphnes grow well in our slightly acid soil. Only the coveted yellow *D. jezoensis* has proved difficult and the chalk-loving *D. mezereum* and its attractive white form, impossible. So it seemed unlikely that the very beautiful 'blue' species, *D. genkwa* would be happy here. It luxuriates on the limestone cliffs of the Ichang Gorge on the Yangtse River. But all surprises in the garden are not unpleasant. This daphne grew away into a bush about five feet in diameter and four feet high and was a lavender coloured cloud of bloom every year. I say 'was', for daphnes are not long-lived. '*Daphne genkwa*, much beloved by all, R.I.P., suddenly, in the seventeenth year of its age.' But it propagates from cuttings under a bell jar, and the cuttings will flower as tiny plants in their first full year of growth (PLATE 38).

This beautiful daphne, alas, has no scent. A daphne without fragrance, like a rose in the same plight, is in some measure a reproach to the family. In this garden the finest daphne fragrance is that of *D. odora*. It differs from the fragrance of *D. bholua* in that it has an element of fruity sharpness behind the sweetness which both exhale. Both are first-class fragrances. But in plants

---

* Mr. Peter Cave has sent me from New Zealand plants from seed of *D. bholua* collected on the Milke Dande Ridge in Nepal at an altitude of about 8,202 feet. One of these evergreen plants seems to be a pure white clone.

PLATE 33 The giant flower of *Lilium sulphureum*, ten inches long, pollinated at midnight by the Privet Hawk Moth, *Sphinx ligustri*. The camera flash is reflected in the eyes of the insect.

Lilium × 'Vico Queen' (*L. sulphureum* pollinated by *L.* 'African Queen'). The large flowers have inherited the powerful sulphureum fragrance and will scent a room particularly in the evening.

Lilium × 'Vico Gold' grex (*L. sulphureum* pollinated by *L.* 'Royal Gold'). Not as beautiful as *L. sulphureum* but easier to grow and more flowers. Height six to seven feet.

PLATE 34 *Brugmansia × candida* 'Grand Marnier' fills one end of the greenhouse from May to October and flowers several times. The huge apricot-coloured trumpets are beautifully fragrant.

Kalmia latifolia 'Ostbo Red'. To perform the act of sexual intercourse in an efficient manner, and thus to secure their survival, plants have evolved devices, more numerous, varied, ingenious and surprising even than those which are described in the *Kama Sutra*. Kalmia is in the vanguard of this movement.

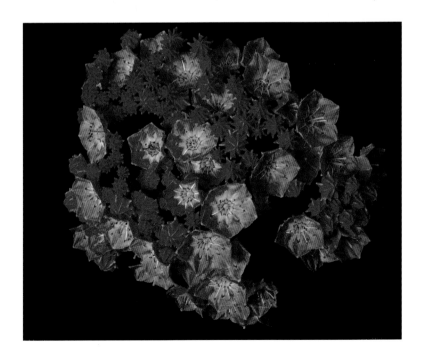

Rhododendron 'Europa'. Its parents are from Burma and from Western Asia. It thrives in the hot summer at Vico Morcote and flowers in late June.

PLATE 35 An open-pollinated seedling from *Rhododendron nuttallii* raised at Vico Morcote from the Royal Horticultural Society's seed distribution.

OVERLEAF LEFT: PLATE 36 *Arisaema candidissimum* has delighted me for fifteen years at the foot of a north-west wall. The flower is followed by spectacular trefoil leaves.

OVERLEAF RIGHT: PLATE 37 *Dracunculus vulgaris*. A magnificent beauty – with an appalling smell.

PLATE 38 *Sambucus canadensis* 'Maxima'. No 'common elder' this, with panicles a foot in diameter and plenty of them, a fine scent and flowering three weeks later.

Daphne bholua Daman form. Brought back from Nepal in my sponge-bag in 1970, it varies from almost white to very dark pink and is now naturalised throughout my garden, sowing itself freely. It grows to about twelve feet and lives for about twenty years.

Daphne genkwa from the Ichang Gorge on the Yangtse River. It is the nearest approach to blue in daphnes and makes a bush four feet across.

PLATE 39 *Edgeworthia* 'Mitsu mata', received from Japan, makes a shrub seven feet high and is covered with flowers from mid-February to mid-April.

Lathyrus odorata 'Matucana'. A rich perfume and a romantic travelogue distinguish the only annual flower in my garden. It is becoming naturalised so it has joined the ecosystem.

Muscari muscarimi flavum. One of the finest fragrances in the garden but inconveniently near ground level for the nose.

園芸文化'85冬号（通巻第89号）季刊　　　　昭和60年2月20日発行

園芸文化

Journal of The Japan Horticultural Society

特集・君子蘭のすべて

1985 冬 No.89

社団法人 園芸文化協会 発行
The Japan Horticultural Society

PLATE 40 *Clivia* × *Kewensis* 'Vico Yellow'. "World's best yellow clivia, the one to beat," said the Japanese. I was astonished!

this is a capricious business. *D. bholua* is extremely variable in colour and growth. There is also a slight variation in its fragrance, though I have never nosed a bholua of which the scent was not first class.

When this garden was planted I received *D. odora alba* from Hillier's. It was persistently fasciated in growth but it flowered profusely and grew reasonably well until it died of old age. The plant carried a fragrance so marvellous that in my opinion it exceeded even that of the type. The search for a replacement began. Finally visiting friends sent me two plants from a Swiss nursery. They were planted in a prominent place where they could be easily nosed. They grew as expected but without fasciation, and flowered freely in pure white. The first blooms opened and I went to nose them. Alas! The fragrance was deplorable: not even third class, not even a pleasure. It would be nice if the men of science would tell us something about the genetics and chemistry of fragrance. Or perhaps it is better that so marvellous a pleasure – or disappointment – should remain mysterious.

3. *Cornus florida* 'Double White'

I had returned from Nepal with the tiny plants of *Daphne bholua* in 1970. Seven of them were growing on here. One day in the summer of 1972, a young man walked into my garden saying, "I hear you have *Daphne bholua*: I would like a plant to take back to my nursery in Belgium." I suggested as kindly as I could that he was perhaps asking something not quite reasonable, so the conversation turned to general gardening topics and to the planting of my garden, full at that time with innumerable small plants, many of them of exceptional interest. But the young man turned out to be so extremely knowledgeable about garden plants that finally I relented. I handed him a very small pot which contained one of my seven plants. Silly fool, I thought to myself as I parted with my plant: "and then there were six". How wrong I was!

The young man went to his car outside the gate and came back with an old terracotta pot containing a very small plant, evidently a cornus. "You will like this," he said. "I found it in an old Italian garden." He got into his car and drove away. I planted the plant in none too good a location thinking that it was probably just another colour form of *C. florida*. Wrong again! It flowered after a year or two. It was indeed *C. florida*, and white, but the 'flowers' were double. The tips of the multiple 'petals' of what one miscalls the flowers remain attached at the centre. The effect is one of little white balloons: quite delightful. Everybody who sees the plant falls instantly in love with it, as I did at its very first flowering. It is floriferous and has grown into a small tree twelve feet high and fifteen feet wide. The branches are carried horizontally until the flowers mature, when they droop in an attractive manner.

Neither Bean⋆ nor the *New RHS Dictionary* seem to know about this plant, but as it was a propagation and not a seedling, clearly there was a mother plant somewhere in Italy. Perhaps there is one in the USA? Having no information about this I have called it *Cornus florida* 'Double White'. And perhaps you are wondering why I have not asked the young man who gave it to me where he got it? The reason is a sad one. On returning to his nursery I am told that he was arrested. A splendid plantsman, he was a poor businessman. He ended in prison, and was last heard of, so far as I know, in Brazil. So when I look at my much-loved tree in full bloom, there is a disconcerting image of iron-barred windows.

4. *Lathyrus odorata* 'Matucana' (PLATE 39)

This is the only annual plant which I grow, in clean contradiction of the principles of the garden. My excuse is that I hope that it will settle down and sow itself, becoming part of the ecosystem. There is some evidence that this is happening.

It is not a rampant grower. Five or six feet is its maximum height, clambering over shrubs and other plants. It carries two or three flowers on a stem, violet and bright pink in nice contrast, but it is not spectacularly beautiful: just a nice modest flower. However, there are two reasons why it is favoured above all other annuals. First, its superb scent: the richest though not the subtlest sweet-pea perfume that I know; and second, its romantic history.

The seeds came to me from an eminent plantsman, Mr E. F. Allen. I looked it up in the reference books but could find no mention of it by name, neither did any of the descriptions in the *New RHS Dictionary* seem to fit it. The name 'Matucana' I recognised at once, from cactus nomenclature, as being Peruvian. The plot thickened.

The story accompanying the seeds was something as follows. The plant was thought to be originally native to North Africa, where it is now extinct.

⋆ *Trees and Shrubs Hardy in the British Isles.*

However, when the Moors conquered Andalusia they took it with them. How right they were! When they were driven out of Spain the beautiful fragrant pea lingered on for a time before becoming extinct there also. But before this occurred, one of the Conquistadores, or perhaps a priest accompanying an expedition, had packed some of the hard durable seeds in his baggage as he sailed for Peru. In Peru the plant flourished exceedingly and received its name. Inevitably it was spotted by a British gardener and carried back across the Atlantic to England, whence the seeds came to Vico Morcote. This is a remarkable and romantic vegetable travelogue which, along with the superb scent, endears the plant to me. But is it a cock-and-bull story? I consulted Sylvia Norton, the reigning authority on *Lathyrus* in cultivation.

Typical *L. odoratus* is a Linnean plant, originating in Sicily. Where this colour form originated seems not to be clear, but that it was taken to Peru and Ecuador is well established and when brought back from those countries two forms were named 'Matucana' and 'Quito' respectively.

I have made a practice of raising a considerable number of seedlings in thumb pots to give away to visitors to the garden. My own plants have been planted out individually to clamber over tree peonies or any other handy small shrub. They flower and set seed freely but unless the flowers are picked they end their blooming rather early in the season. Because of the truly delicious fragrance it is advisable to pick most of the flowers for the house anyway, leaving one or two plants to seed. Miss Norton, however, has a superior cultivation plan. She sows ten seeds in a pot and then plants it by her fruit cage. "The blaze of colour and cloud of scent is overwhelming as one walks past." I have no fruit cage but the plan will be tried in modified form next year.

5. *Muscari muscarimi flavum* (PLATE 39)

The Musk Hyacinths were well named '*moschatum*' for their delicious fragrance. But now the taxonomists have got hold of them, and I am now supposed to call this old friend by a new name: *Muscari muscarimi flavum*. It is difficult to find in commerce and when found it is expensive to buy. It is slow to increase, but when established in full sun it survives from year to year and multiplies slowly. Its small yellow flowers in March are a cheerful spot in the garden provided that they are not overshadowed in that yellow season by the display of much larger more spectacular plants. In the small company of the purest and most delicious scents of the year, *Lilium candidum*, *Chimonanthus fragrans*, some sweet peas and the gardenias, it easily holds a place.

How does one describe a scent? Now that commercial fragrances can be produced synthetically by placing a flower in a gas chromatograph, analysing the scent and recording the results, no doubt a scent can be reduced to a formula. But one cannot smell a formula, at least not yet. Visitors to the garden when given a fragrant flower will often try to describe its fragrance by likening it to some other better known scent: but this gets us no further than the name of the better known. I always find this irritating, an attempt to demystify one of the delights of life, which should remain mysterious.

A problem with *M. muscarimi flavum* is that it is a very small plant with its blooms at most six inches above the ground. To savour the mystery one must descend to all fours and, like a truffle dog, nose the earth. This is an undignified posture to impose on visiting plantsmen. Or else the flower must be picked, something I am reluctant to do. But there are three solutions to this problem. First, the very powerful fragrance persists for several days and reaches its maximum after the flower begins to fade. So one may pick and enjoy the scent of the fading flower. The second solution is to plant *Muscari ambrosiacum*, which is in commerce and is not unduly expensive, in company with *M. muscarimi flavum*. *M. ambrosiacum* is hardly noticeable in the garden: a bluish greenish flower shading to cream, somewhat larger than *M. muscarimi flavum*. It is visually uninspiring. But the fragrance, which also reaches its maximum when the flower fades, is indistinguishable from that of the lemon-yellow beauty and it is far less expensive. But why not plant typical *M. muscarimi* for this purpose? You could do so, for the fragrance is identical with that of its yellow variant; but though not as scarce or quite as expensive, it is still hard to find, and visually no improvement over the ambrosiac.

There is a third and radical solution to a problem which occurs with all small plants which are better viewed or nosed at very close quarters. My mother adopted it at Itchen Stoke House. She made a short sunk walk, with the pathway perhaps eighteen inches below ground level. Either side of it she planted anything which she liked to see at close range. Because of the heavy rainfall and consequent drainage problems, and lack of soil depth, this solution would be difficult to employ here. The alternative of a raised bed would dry out too quickly. All in all the answer is to combine planting of scarce and expensive *M. muscarimi flavum* with that of the relatively inexpensive *M. ambrosiacum*, and to avoid undignified acrobatics by picking the latter for sampling.

6.   *Edgeworthia* 'Mitsumata' (PLATE 39)

Edgeworthia chrysantha is a small clump-forming shrub sometimes to be found in gardens on the Italian Lakes. It is a daphne cousin, and in late winter it carries parchment coloured flowers with a fine fragrance. It is well worth a place in any garden where it is hardy. In Japan it is used for the manufacture of fine papers, and it sometimes passes under the name of *E. papyrifera*.

A small padded envelope arrived from Tsuneshige Rokujo. Anything which this fine Japanese plantsman sent me was sure to be outstanding. Packed with Japanese expertise, the tiny plant was in excellent condition and it settled into a small pot without any problems. It seemed to be an *Edgeworthia*, under the Japanese name of 'Mitsumata', translated as 'Three Branches'.

As the plant grew the meaning of the name became apparent. At each terminal bud the growth would divide into three: trifurcation is the botanical term according to Professor Asa Gray. In a couple of years the plant flowered, in late January, with flower clusters shading from red in the centre through orange to yellow at the periphery. I was astonished. The books gave no hint of its existence. It was fragrant, though as is so often the case with brightly coloured flowers, it was less so than its parchment coloured relative. Even when small it immediately attracted the attention of every visitor, and was coveted. Otto Eisenhut propagated it. It sold on sight. Now my plant is about eight feet high and as much through, and each year it puts on a splendid show. It remains in bloom for a very long time, because the circles of florets open in succession beginning at the outside and ending at the centre. But it is in an inadequate location. I never suspected that it would be so beautiful or that it would grow so vigorously.

The hardiness of 'Mitsumata' is not established. Like *Daphne bholua* it passed through the heavy frost of 1985 without the least damage. I cannot guess how it would fare in prolonged frost in damp conditions. It 'looks' to me like a plant which enjoys a very thorough ripening. It gets that here. It is so handsome that it is worth a try in any relatively mild garden. I hope one day to discover its botanical co-ordinates. I am not entirely convinced that it is in fact an *Edgeworthia*.

7. *Arisaema sikokianum*

The arisaemas have become rather fashionable in gardens, and as a result somebody must needs coin a 'popular' name for them. 'Cobra Lilies'! Lilies, forsooth! An insult both to the Liliaceae of which it is not a member and to the Araceae of which it is, as well as to the intelligence of any serious gardener. However that may be, the genus *Arisaema* contains some real beauties. For fifteen years *Arisaema candidissimum* (PLATE 36) has delighted me annually with its flowers, of palest blush beautifully striped as are so many of the genus, and followed by spectacular trefoil leaves. In many parts of the garden other less spectacular members of the genus are established and one notices these elegant eccentrics with amused surprise. But surely *Arisaema sikokianum* is the most striking: I think that is the word for a plant which once seen it is impossible to forget. It has indeed a 'cobra' hood, and then those extraordinarily beautiful white flower structures. It seems to have settled down in a half-shaded spot in the garden here. The flower and leaf are now much larger than they were at first planting, it sets seed and I am hoping for increase at the root.

8. *Dracunculus vulgaris* (PLATE 37)

I suppose that a literal translation of the botanical Latin might be 'Vulgar Little Dragon'. The name would not be inappropriate. But the beauty of the plant and the fidelity with which it flowers and fruits every year compels me to overlook what would otherwise be its unpardonable lack of manners. It has been established for many years at the foot of a wall which supports the road. The vulgar little plant is not visible to passers-by who have been heard to pause, sniff, and say, "Must be something dead," before hurrying on. This is the signature of this aroid which stands about five feet in height. Its huge red-chocolate flower spathe, like a purple cloak, is followed by brilliant orange seeds – which do not stink. (PLATE 45)

I was not looking forward to photographing the Vulgar Little Dragon in the studio, and after providing all available ventilation, steeled myself for the ordeal. To my surprise, when the flower was cut and put in a vase the stink vanished. Possibly it was due to do so anyway, its purpose of attracting flies to pollinate the flower having been fulfilled. I have not risked repeating the experiment.

Visitors often imagine that this and other similar plants are carnivores.

To attract flies they do indeed mimic the odour of rotten meat, but the purpose, as almost always in the insect-flower relationship, is sexual not gastronomic. The fly is often trapped and expires at the base of the flower, but I doubt that its remains are a significant source of nourishment in so large and vigorous a plant which has made all of its growth previous to flowering and which dies down as soon as the seed is set.

9.   *Brugmansia × candida* 'Grand Marnier' (PLATE 34)

My greenhouse is now dedicated almost entirely to the breeding of hybrids of *Nerine sarniensis*. They must have a cool winter, and in summer they are dormant, and in any case they are out of the greenhouse from April to August. The plant of *Brugmansia × candida* 'Grand Marnier' is planted in the greenhouse bed and grows up through the staging to fill the whole of one end of the house during the months of May to October. During that period it flowers several times, the huge apricot trumpets hanging down in great quantity, sometimes a couple of hundred open at the same time. They are extremely fragrant at night and if the door to my study and bedroom is left open the whole room is scented. When the nerines begin to grow in October the plant is cut right down to stage level, and in the cold winter which the nerines demand, it remains dormant, so that the nerines get all the light they need.

We also grow another apricot coloured brugmansia which came to me without a name as a present from a visitor. The trumpets are slightly smaller than those of 'Grand Marnier' but instead of hanging directly downwards they have a jaunty poise looking outwards. This plant is probably one of many seedlings in circulation, though I have never seen another similar. It seems to be part of a group which passes under the specific of *aurea*. Both plants are exceptionally beautiful and fragrant, hardy to a light frost, quick and easy to grow and simple to strike from cuttings.

10.   *Iris japonica* 'Bourne Graceful'

The work of the specialist societies is a wonderful help to gardeners. In the early days of this garden, when it was a sun-drenched slope, many iris were planted and enjoyed. As it gradually became a magnolia woodland, inevitably the sun-lovers disappeared. In those sunny days I belonged to the British Iris Society and a legacy from them is still flourishing in my garden.

Iris japonica is by any measure a delightful plant. Perhaps its hardiness is questionable, but it has survived all the heavy overnight frosts which from time to time have tested my garden. Its branching flower spike goes on producing flowers for a long time in early summer. It has also become a highly satisfactory ground cover on the steep western slope of the ravine through which our stream runs. It puts on a remarkable display and its flowers of unique form and elegant beauty are much admired by visitors. The uninitiated ask, "Is it an orchid?" This is the typical form in cultivation, known as 'Ledger's Variety'. For foliage contrast we also grow a few plants of *I. japonica* 'variegata', which has striking white-striped leaves but is rather a shy bloomer.

The annual volume published by the British Iris Society for the year 1975 carried as its frontispiece a picture of *I. japonica* 'Bourne Graceful'. From the illustration and from the description it seemed to be a substantial advance upon 'Ledger's Variety'. Its raiser, Dr J. R. Ellis of Bourne End, kindly sent me a piece of it. He raised this splendid plant by pollinating 'Ledger's Variety' with pollen from the 'Capri form' of *I. japonica*. The latter was described in the *Iris Yearbook* for 1966. He notes that both the parents of 'Bourne Graceful' are hybrids, and that their offspring has approximately 61 chromosomes.

'Bourne Graceful' now grows freely over a partly shaded bank which it shares with *I. wattii*. It grows to a height of about four feet in a favourable location, it is larger in all its parts than 'Ledger's Variety', more flowers are carried on the spike and the flower colours are darker. It is a first-class acquisition to the garden. Like the parent plant it has the amiable habit of forming running rhizomes which can be pulled up without ceremony and given to visitors. They root immediately with no trouble. Dozens of such pieces have been given to friends who have admired 'Bourne Graceful' in the garden. In view of the splendour of this plant I can forgive Dr Ellis for perpetrating a pun in naming it, and I think of him with gratitude every time I see it.

11.   *Rhododendron* 'Tyermanni'

In the Easter holidays from school I lunched with a friend and contemporary, 'Bunny' Cayzer, now Lord Rotherwick, at his family home Tylney Hall. He was interested in plants and after lunch we set off round his father's large and magnificent garden. In the greenhouse was an extraordinary plant, never to be forgotten: *Rhododendron nuttallii* in a large pot in full bloom. I was already lily-mad, and the great lily-like trumpets of the rhododendron and their delicious scent are fresh with me to this day.

R. nuttallii is not reliably hardy here, though some of its relatives in the Maddenii Series certainly are. The hybrid *R.* 'Fragrantissimum' has been long established at the Villa Carlotta on Lake Como, and thrives in my garden, along with one or two others of the group. However, the wonderful Rhododendron catalogue of G. Reuthe Ltd., for about the year 1972, listed *R.* 'Tyermanni' First Class Certificate, a hybrid between *R. nuttallii* and *R. formosum*, the latter another member of the Maddenii series somewhat hardier than *R. nuttallii*. "Apricot trumpets flushed pink, scented. Very scarce," said the catalogue. It was rated 'H1', suitable only for greenhouse cultivation. But that was for Britain where the wood is less hardened by the sun. And 'Fragrantissimum' was rated H1–2, and was happy on Lake Como. It was worth a try.

It was planted in the patio, a cool sheltered situation. It grew magnificently, running up to a height of ten feet in a few years, and it covered itself with extremely large trumpet flowers looking one directly in the eye, until little foliage was visible. Not, indeed, the even larger lily-like flowers of *R. nuttallii* but splendid none the less, and whereas the latter plant would carry but a few blooms, this one was deluged with them. I thought it the finest rhododendron I had ever seen. I still think so. If I could not have *R. nuttallii* this was indeed a delightful substitute. Writing in *Rhododendrons of the World* David Leach says of this plant:

> "Its enormous flaring white trumpets, exquisitely ruffled and
> fluted around the edges and suffused with yellow in the throats,
> are a startling spectacle. The opulent effect of the outward-facing
> clusters is further enhanced by the stately poise of their carriage,
> making this one of the finest of all flowers, theatrical in size and
> extraordinarily beautiful in form and colouring."

I agree with every word of that description, but unfortunately my plant collapsed and died in the tenth year of its age. The cause could not be established, but something had displeased the roots, possibly overwatering in hot weather from the municipal water supply. The death of a beautiful plant after ten years of love is a painful thing. Should I start all over again? Time was getting short. The plant could not be obtained in Britain. But Peter Cave in New Zealand located a couple of propagations for me and dispatched them. They have settled in well. Perhaps I shall see once again 'one of the finest of all flowers'.

Meanwhile there has been compensation, though to a very limited degree. I received seed of *Rhododendron nuttallii* from Wisley and grew several plants. After a number of years they flowered. The list did not say that it was open pollinated seed, but when the seedlings bloomed this was clearly the case. The seedlings were beautiful (PLATE 35) but it was not the overwhelming splendour of my dead favourite or the elegant magnificence of *R. nuttallii*.

12.   *Rhododendron* × 'Europa' (PLATE 35)

It is not because I was joint-secretary of the Brussels Conference of the European Movement in 1949, and later Secretary-General of the Council of Europe in Strasbourg, that this is a favourite plant. In fact the name is singularly unfortunate and misleading. The plant has nothing at all to do with Europe, except for the fact that it was raised by Lionel de Rothschild at Exbury. But then, malicious foreigners sometimes infer that Britain is not a part of Europe at all.

Ever since my early adventures with *Lilium sulphureum*, Burma and Burmese plants have had a particular fascination for me. It was always my ambition to succeed in growing *R. rhododendrum kyawi*, a lovely Burmese tree-like species. But I could not find it. Along the way, however, that alluring rhododendron had contracted a number of liaisons. Of these, that with the West Asiatic *R. ungernii* was available, named 'Europa'. It was a member of a grex, that is to say a family of seedlings from the same cross which might vary considerably in their characteristics. I planted it in a hot sunny part of the garden.

There have been many problems with rhododendrons at Vico Morcote. *Armillaria mellea*, honey fungus, ravaged the early plantations. For many rhododendrons the summer is tryingly hot, though relieved by the cool nights. But 'Europa', half from Burma and half from western Asia, seems perfectly content here from the time of planting down to today. Of course, there is still tomorrow! The plant is now about fourteen feet high and the same through, scrambling around in full sun amongst a thicket of self-sown *Daphne bholua* and the remains of two or three other less happy rhododendrons. Better still, its flowers appear in latest June or early July, when their great pink trusses with a suspicion of orange and raspberry in the mix, and carried with aplomb, make a beautiful contrast with the vigorous silvery new growths. They are a splash of colour in the green season.

13. *Kalmia latifolia*: The Mountain Laurel and its Hybrids (PLATE 34)

Of course it is not a laurel. Americans have taken unkindly to botanical Latin. *Kalmia*, along with *Rhododendron*, is a member of the great family of the Ericaceae, the heathers. It was my misfortune that the new hybrids of this plant raised in the United States became available just too late to be included in the main planting of the garden. Had this not been the case they would have assumed a prominent place in it. Beautiful and floriferous, native of the north-eastern States, they are tolerant both of extreme cold and of great heat. In the garden here they flower profusely, grow well, have dense attractive foliage when out of flower and, in short, are desirable and trouble free.

The new hybrids come in a range of colours from brilliant reddish pink to pure glistening white. There are also forms with rings of one colour upon another. Some are dwarf and some are strong growers. All are worth a place in full sun in mildly acid to fully acid soil.

But there is an additional attraction. This book recognises, if the general public does not always admit the fact, that a flower is a sex mechanism and, in the laws of nature, neither more nor less than that. My photography was once described by an American lady as floral pornography. I trust that it will not be censored by our contemporary prudes on that account. But the fact is that to perform the act of sexual intercourse in an efficient manner, and thus to secure their survival, plants have evolved devices more numerous, varied, ingenious and surprising even than those which are described in the *Kama Sutra*. Kalmia is in the vanguard of this movement.

It is a romantic-seeming procedure. In the centre of the flower stands a solitary girl, the pistil. True, she has ten lovers, no mean feat, but unhappily all ten are in prison, no mean misfortune. For the ten anthers, the aspiring suitors, are all held captive in pouches in the petal structure of the flower. They await a touch from a visiting insect which will release them. Then the filaments, each with an anther attached to its tip and which are springs under tension, will project each suitor in the twinkling of an eye into the arms of the girl. Soon she will be lonely no longer: all ten lovers will be with her. Anybody who has the curiosity to do so may verify this spectacular mechanism by assuming the part of the insect, using the tip of a penknife or a toothpick to touch the filaments one by one and thus to release the anthers and distribute the pollen.

14. *Clivia miniata* × *kewensis* 'Vico Yellow' (PLATE 40)

This plant finds a place here not because it is of my own raising but because of the curious and instructive story of its origin. This in addition to its undoubted beauty.

Clivias have suffered from being distributed commercially in a very indifferent form and also because of one of their great merits. They are amongst the most long-suffering of pot plants which, like the aspidistra, will put up with almost anything except over attention. Just so! They are bracketed with the aspidistra as inhabitants of lodging-house parlours.

I did not feel any of these inhibitions with a very handsome plant. From Mr Russell at Castle Howard I obtained three forms of *C. miniata* under the name of 'Kewensis'. One was yellow, though called 'cream'. All had been bred by Charles Raffill at Kew, selecting back to recover a lost South African yellow.

In one of my few idle moments in the early days of planting this garden I crossed the orange and yellow clones. After the necessary five or six years there were flowers: no yellows though some worthy orange plants. However, I had had too many seedlings to be able to keep them all and had discarded a number under the greenhouse stage. Then 'Kewensis Cream' died, mysteriously, just as the South African yellow had done at Kew many years before.

It was some years later that to my astonishment a yellow Clivia bloomed under the stage. It seemed to me good, perhaps an improvement on 'Kewensis Cream'. I rescued it, potted it, and in due course sent an offset to my friend Dr Shuichi Hirao in Japan. I thought no more about it. After a couple of years Shu sent me *Japan Horticulture*, No. 89 for 1985. My yellow clivia was the cover picture and there was an article about it inside. Inexcusably, for the Japanese are consummate plantsmen, I did not take this event too seriously. Then 'Shu' Hirao died, sadly and prematurely.

It was a couple of years after his death that I had a letter from Yoshikazu Nakamura, at Clivia Breeding Plantation, Mobara, Japan, to say that Shu's widow had sent the yellow clivia to him. He would like permission to breed from 'Smithers Yellow', "world's best yellow Clivia, the one to beat". I was astonished! Of course he was perfectly free to make any use of the plant which he liked, but might it be called 'Vico Yellow'? Perhaps it was too late: 'Smithers Yellow' was already in the trade in Japan.

Subsequently another yellow flowered amongst my seedlings. It was very similar to the first but in my opinion slightly superior in form. Only time would tell. It was of course a separate clone. No 'Smithers Gold' this time: it is named *Clivia × kewensis* 'Vico Gold'.

The latest development in this story of entirely unmerited success, is that the *C. miniata × kewensis* 'Vico Yellow' is now to be registered in Japan and will be micro-propagated by Miyoshi & Co. of Yamanashi, for mass distribution.

15. *Clivia miniata* 'Albomarginata'

This astonishing plant was sent to me by Yoshikazu Nakamura to express his satisfaction with 'Vico Yellow'. It came with several other attractive seedlings with leaves variegated in different degrees. In this case there are broad cream margins running the length of the leaves, that is to say almost exactly two feet in a well grown plant. But the leaves do not stand up, they arch over gracefully and hang down around the pot. To grow the plant, therefore, you must stand it on top of another tall pot otherwise its leaves will touch the ground long before they are mature. The effect is dramatic.

The modern improved clivias are spectacular plants when in flower, but it must be admitted that when out of flower they are inconspicuous to the point of boredom. That is to say, inconspicuous for eleven months and two weeks of the year. This extraordinary variegated plant is conspicuous and dramatically beautiful for all 365 days. The flower, were it needed, is a pretty apricot, a good colour, of modest size. But it is not the flower which counts in the case of this foliage plant.

Some people dislike variegated plants but I am not amongst them. True there is always the suspicion that virus is at work in variegation. In this case, however, no virus is involved. Most surprisingly the characteristic of variegation is transmitted by seed. We may expect a race of variegated clivia from Japan in the years ahead. This and the new hybrids being raised in Australia, notably the Cowlishaw strain, will probably rescue the genus from its present condition of neglect and will divorce it at last from the aspidistra.

16. *Moraea polystachya*

Moraeas, beautiful South African irids, were an irresistible temptation in the relatively mild and sunny climate of my garden. As with another genus of South African irids, the watsonias, a number of species have come – and gone. Some lingered for many years. But one has remained with me for nearly twenty years and flowers unfailingly through the months of November and early December. *Moraea polystachya* is a slender branching plant growing from a small corm to a height of about two feet. Some of the long thin leaves lie prostrate on the ground. A succession of small bright lavender blue flowers with the conspicuous yellow peacock-feather eye which characterises the genus, follow one another in long succession. The plant has settled down at the foot of a south wall and it sets plenty of seed which germinates readily. I suspect that it is very hardy in this rather tender genus, provided that it gets plenty of sun. There are certain small plants in the garden the annual return of which is always a particular delight because they show up when relatively few flowers are available. This is one of them.

17.   *Cucurbita maxima* 'Atlantic Giant'

Pumpkin pie seems to me barely edible, but pumpkin soup is surely one of the very best beginnings to an Italian meal. However, one may make excellent soup from a modest sized pumpkin, readily obtainable in the market. It is because of the temptations of Thompson & Morgan's Seed Catalogue, a standby of mine for over sixty years, that this plant finds a place here. The picture in the catalogue shows the proud grower of a plant of 'Atlantic Giant', standing behind his champion fruit and practically hidden by it. Surely enough pumpkin to provide soup for the winter, but until this year

Pumpkin 'Atlantic Giant'. Decorated by our cook, Elena, and photographed by our part-time gardener, Antonio.

I had resisted the temptation to undertake such a frivolous eccentricity.

In spring my neighbour had felled some tall trees which formerly shaded the bottom of my garden. I waved goodbye with some satisfaction as one by one they rose up from the ground into the sky, trunks, leaves and all, and flew away at 100 kilometres per hour transported by a powerful helicopter. But the absence of the trees left what had formerly been a shady corner exposed as a sun-blasted steep slope. It was March, late to get plants, and I did not have much on hand. Now was the time to try out 'Atlantic Giant'. I received eight seeds from Thompson & Morgan: one would have been enough.

My part-time gardener, Antonio, a good vegetable grower who lacked scope in this garden, was delighted. He knew all about pumpkins, that is to say normal pumpkins. But it was a disastrously hot and dry summer, disastrous for practically everything – except the pumpkin. As the four fruits developed on two plants I became more and more delighted but Antonio became more and more concerned. Down to the bottom of the garden where the pumpkins grow are many flights of wooden steps. I had not really expected the pumpkin to succeed to the extent to which it was clearly doing and I had not considered how to get it up the steps. A neighbouring construction crane which might have helped had just gone away. I wanted my soup. Meanwhile the pumpkin had become something of a local celebrity particularly amusing to children. Considerations of 'face' were now involved. I could not walk away from my pumpkins.

It had not occurred to me that they might walk away from me yet this is what one of them did. This pumpkin must have weighed about a hundred pounds: it was the smallest but one of the four. One day it was no longer there. Surely it was too heavy to have been stolen. A search cleared up the mystery of the missing cucurbit. By its own weight it had broken away, rolled down the hill, crashed through the fence which it smashed, and fallen into the next property where it broke up. The pieces were retrieved for the kitchen.

The largest pumpkin, weighing over two hundred pounds, was too much for us to carry. It was carved up on the spot and taken to the kitchen for deep freezing. The second largest, which weighed one hundred and thirty-two pounds, was wrapped in a double hammock, slung on a pole and carried by two strong men up to the house. In spite of the great size of these pumpkins, the flavour of the soup is excellent.

If life itself is a mixture of tragedy and comedy, so sometimes is gardening.

CHAPTER 12

Cacti Wet and Dry

THE SPLENDOURS, PERFUMES
AND FEROCITY
OF THE FLOWERING CACTI
BY DAY AND BY NIGHT

In Mexico and Central America where so many of the large family of the Cactaceae have their home, they grow at sea level and at every altitude up to the deserts of the high plateau. Some are epiphytes, clambering over the trees on which they lodge. Most are terrestrials living in a semi-arid desert. They are cultivated in almost every garden. The fruits are eaten, the young leaves are a substitute for green beans, the pith is used as a substitute for crystallised pineapple in a country where there are plenty of pineapples anyway, and cacti are made into a truly forbidding hedge. They are a part of life in most villages.

It has always been so. On 9th December 1531 the Virgin of Guadalupe, 'Patroness of New Spain' (1745) and 'Empress of the Americas' (1945) made her first apparition. According to legend she did so in a cactus bush or a maguey (*Agave*). But did she? I am informed on good authority that in fact the first apparition of the Virgin was on a bare hillside. At the time, so soon after the destruction of Tenochtitlán, Mexicans were understandably reluctant to adopt the new religion. To make the Virgin of Guadalupe a more credible part of the Mexican scene the early Spanish painters showed her surrounded by cacti or maguey. Thus did Mary become and remain to this day truly Mexican.

Some desert cacti

Beyond the ranks of dedicated cactus fans, schoolchildren and the literature of Travel Agents, the day-blooming terrestrial cacti seem to me to be a most underrated family of plants. I admit to a prejudice in their favour: five

PLATES 42 Hybrid epiphyllums: *above* 'Celestial Snow'; *below* 'Witching Hour'.

PRECEDING PAGE: PLATE 41 *Epiphyllum oxypetalum* is one of the 'Queens of the Night'.
The giant flowers unfold at dusk releasing a powerful fragrance. At dawn they collapse, never to revive.

PLATES 43   Hybrid epiphyllums: *above* 'Copper Horn';   *below* 'Macho Beauty'.

PLATE 44 *Echinocereus palmeri* pollinated by *Syrphus ribesii*, a hover-fly pretending to be a wasp to protect himself from insect–eating birds.

Echinopsis are cushion cacti with very large trumpet flowers in colours from pure white through lemon yellow to apricot, pink and scarlet. This is *E. eyriesii*, a species from Argentina.

years in Mexico showed me the beauty of the cactus desert in flower: unforgettable in its combination of beauty and hostility. There is a wonderful diversity of forms as well as of flowers and also of the varied savageries of the spines. Some of the latter will penetrate the leather sole of a shoe, let alone a rubber one: some were hard enough for use as needles in the gramophones of days gone by: others with hooked spines capture the flesh in a grasp impossible to disengage without bloodshed. But the wonderful geometry of many species, surely designed upon some celestial computer set up with a mathematical formula, the beauty and variety of form and texture, the savagery of the armament carried and the venerable dignity of an 'organ' perhaps twenty feet high and of immemorial age, or of an ancient 'barrel' three feet in diameter – these are things which remain with me and which excuse the sun-starved soft little buttons which it pains me to see in the supermarket.

Part of the problem with the desert cacti is that it takes several years for the most magnificent of them to get into good flowering form. In spite of the fact that they are so little trouble – they can be put into a store in low light and forgotten without a drop of water for five months of the year – there are not many people who will derive enough pleasure during the long wait to make it worthwhile holding out for the great reward at its end. Spectacular hybrid *Echinopsis*, which I purchased as buttons in 1985, flowered now and then in recent years, but are only getting into top flowering gear nine years later.

There is a means of compensating for this. The rebutias, sulcorebutias, lobivias and parodias are small cacti which flower at a very early stage in their lives and later form cushions covered with bloom. They flower early in the year when they will not be outshone by later splendours. Being so small they can be collected like postage stamps and occupy little space. Their brilliant oranges, reds and yellows with a few whites, are the most cheerful of flowers and the pots can be assembled into nice table decoration at lunch-time; but not for dinner, when, like all cacti except for the nocturnals, the flowers will be closed against the evening rains which are common in their native habitats.

Cactus specialists will reproach me for not mentioning several other genera which flower early and as young plants, but these four are my personal choice. Now throughout the period mid-May to late July I have a magnificent succession of flowers. As the early bloomers are coming to a close the *Echinopsis* take over. These are cushion cacti with very large spectacular trumpet flowers in colours from pure white through lemon yellow to pinks, apricots and scarlet. (PLATE 44) Many of the hybrids have been raised in England. In the United States several other genera have been introduced into the breeding of *Trichocereus*. These are much stronger growers and very free flowering with suggestive American names: 'Mad Scarlet', 'Oh! Wow!' and even a very large pink and white trumpet called 'Stars and Stripes' which I commend to anybody looking for a fine plant. These American hybrids grow fast and flower young and rather early, putting the rebutias out of countenance.

I must not give the impression that the finest large-flowered desert cacti are all hybrids. Many of the species of *Echinocactus, Notocactus, Echinocereus* and other genera have magnificent flowers. The choice is so wide that, as with postage stamps, if one is afflicted with the disease of collecting, specialisation is essential. To me the concept of collecting is in itself unacceptable: for a place on my cactus table there are only two criteria, beauty and fragrance. A few of the day bloomers have a nice perfume.

Out on my terrace in the months of May and June there is a fresh display of beautiful cactus flowers every morning, often pollinated by a wasp. But no, on inspection it is not a wasp at all, but *Syrphus ribesii*, a hover-fly pretending to be a wasp by his black and yellow stripes. (PLATE 44) A stationery target, he hopes to fool insect-hunting birds so that he may hover with impunity. He probably succeeds, for birds are not too bright. How many millennia did it take him to evolve that device? Certainly since long before *Homo sapiens* was quarrelling around the world. So a fragment of the procession of the seasons in my garden is the annual return of the cactus flowers and with them the handsome hover-fly. His great-grandfather was a friend of mine.

In the late afternoon the flowers will be closed and the hover fly will be gone. In the native habitat of many cacti during summer time it tends to be fine in the morning and to rain in the afternoon. I therefore make a point of watering my cacti, when in growth, in the evening after the flowers have closed. Back home in the Americas they would be expecting the evening rain and a consequent drop in temperature. The accepted wisdom suggests watering all plants in the early morning: but then, the accepted wisdom is so often behind the game.

Perhaps they are not for everybody, but I enjoy those cacti which are conspicuous for their ferocious armament: the aptly named ferocacti, and, supreme amongst them, *Echinocactus grusonii*, named by some embittered husband 'Mother-in-law's Cushion'. They have a year-round beauty, but it increases in the summer when they are in obvious active growth and the textures are lively. In winter they are equally obviously in a deep sleep.

Some jungle cacti

For the gardener the epiphytic cacti, scrambling over trees in the tropical forest, have little other than structural similarities in the flowers to relate them to the dry cacti of the cactus desert. They comprise some of the most spectacular of all flowering plants, in so far as the flower itself is concerned. In my greenhouse *Epiphyllum anguliger* and *Selenicereus grandiflorus* scramble about over the back wall amongst the growths of *Passiflora edulis*, our source of passion fruit ice-cream. *Epiphyllum oxypetalum* (PLATE 41) is not really a climber, perhaps only a clamberer. It stands about six feet high in a large pot.

The arrival in Europe of the giant flowered epiphytic cacti from the American tropics was one of the horticultural sensations of the last century. They captured the imagination of the botanical illustrators. Amongst them were one or two nocturnal species, highly perfumed, usually white, inevitably called Queen of the Night. There are several rival Queens, two of them in my greenhouse. It is a somewhat unqueenly performance. The whole spectacular operation begins at about eight in the evening. The numerous tightly packed petals of the very large flower bud of *Epiphyllum oxypetalum* begin to stir and gradually open in a process which is visible from minute to minute. In about half an hour the flower is open sufficiently to reveal the numerous stamens and the stigma. It will be another hour before the petals have recurved to their final posture and the flower is fully developed. Its extraordinary elegance and beauty is accompanied by a release of a powerful fragrance. At dawn the flower will collapse and hang downwards, never to re-open. The whole elaborate performance is designed to attract an insect. The purpose of the queen, though not of the insect, is sex.

My plant of *Epiphyllum oxypetalum* has grown from a 'leaf' which I collected, intrepid, not in the jungles where it grows but from a plant by the swimming pool of a friend in St Louis, Missouri. This native of Central America blooms twice or with luck three times during the summer. The heavy flowers with a long pink tube hang down from the plant but then turn up to a horizontal position to look at you: but it is not you they are looking for, but the wished-for pollinating insect. It is a most elegant yet voluptuous balancing act. During that one night an insect must find and pollinate the flower. Perhaps for this reason I notice that blooming usually takes place within a few days of the full moon, making things easier for nocturnal navigators. So size, colour, perfume and moonlight ensure the perpetuation of the race.

There will be several flowers at each blooming: perhaps seven or eight, occasionally ten or twelve. They open over a period of three evenings. It is a spectacular event for which we sometimes invite friends to dinner and the subsequent 'floor show' which perfumes a whole room. If anybody doubts that sex can be elegant, the floor show put on by *E. oxypetalum* in order to complete the act of procreation should surely convince them.

A quite different plant, the hybrid 'Epiphyllum', is not really an epi-phyllum at all. It is a plant which arose from breeding in England at the beginning of the nineteenth century and subsequently in France and Germany. Day blooming *Heliocereus speciosus* and *Nopalxochia phyllanthoides* were amongst the first species used in evolving the modern hybrids. In the middle of the century *Epiphyllum crenatum* was added to the mix which was further extended by Kurt Knebel in Germany at the end of the century. The work of breeding was then taken up in California where it continues with great success until today.

The hybrids range from pure white through every shade of purple and pink to crimson and scarlet. Some of the scarlets are shot with what can only be described as electric blue: a stunning combination. There was no true yellow though some of the species had a few yellow outer petals. After many years of work two old California Irishmen, Fortt and O'Barr, achieved the goal: a splendid golden yellow *Epiphyllum*. They called their plant 'Reward' and I remember them with gratitude every year when the flowers open.

The hybrid epiphyllum is a diurnal bloomer. Its flowers are large and brilliantly coloured. Perhaps for this reason it does not need fragrance to draw attention to itself and few of them have any scent. There are innumer-able named varieties available in California, of which I grow about forty.

When out of flower for ten months of the year the plant could not possibly be described as beautiful or, except to the specialist, even interesting. It is not quite frost-hardy so it must have frost-free space in which to grow. The flowers are of relatively short duration, and they arrive at a time of year when there is a profusion of bloom in the garden. These are all good reasons not to grow a hybrid epiphyllum. But the individual flowers are of such spectacular colouring, of such grace of form and carriage and so large and impressive that I am willing to overlook all faults in the name of impact and, yes, of beauty. Besides, they are easily propagated from a 'leaf' sent through the post and they are of simple cultivation. I shall not describe the flowers: colour and form are best shown in illustration. (PLATES 42 and 43)

Though not frost tolerant, hybrid epiphyllum are safe down to a couple of degrees above freezing. Being mainly epiphytic in origin, they can be grown in small containers with mildly acid compost such as would suit many terrestrial orchids, and very sharp drainage. An occasional whiff of rhododendron or orchid fertiliser will make them happy. Unlike the desert cacti which revel in full blazing sun, they like half shade. During the resting period in autumn they can do with very little light and can be more or less forgotten, though a spray overhead now and then will be appreciated. I suspect that like some epiphytic orchids such as *Dendrobium nobile* and its hybrids, they need a nip of cool weather in the resting season to ensure prolific blooming.

Little trouble that they are, during the ten months of the year when the plants are indeed unattractive I have sometimes felt tempted to discard them. Then the flowers come and they seduce me all over again with their beauty, elegance and allure. It is another very old story but this time with a happy ending.

The least conspicuous or decorative cactus on my table, a desert cactus, the tiny *Lophophora williamsii*, has a different fascination. I seldom pass it without an exciting shudder. For the little buttons, which after many years of growth are still only two inches in diameter and which have an insignificant pink flower, are stuffed with alkaloids. Amongst them is mescalin, one of the most terrible of all hallucinogens. It brings on the phenomenon of split consciousness – or so I read. For this reason it has been used by Indians in North Mexico for prophecy. Although it grows wild in southern Texas the mere possession of the plant is an offence in certain of the United States. As though to draw you into trouble, the little plant sports not a single spine to come between you and visions of horror. Well, as I pass by ... I do wonder ...

CHAPTER 13

Adventures in Pots

SO MANY FASCINATING PLANTS
ARE BEST ENJOYED IN A POT

No gardener should be content to forgo the pleasure of growing in pots a few of the plants which cannot be left to fend for themselves in the garden. In a system which seeks to reduce labour to the absolute minimum, this urge needs the discipline of careful planning if it is not to get out of hand. There are so many delightful plants which one would like to grow in pots. The classic Chinese garden was filled with pots; also of course with gardeners. The pots themselves were ornamental. But the western equivalent, the large terracotta pot, is not for me. It is far too heavy when it comes to moving. All pots in my garden, except for one or two decorative miniatures, are in plastic. They are cheap, light, easy to handle, hygienic and some of them are not ugly. For all sizes I much prefer square to round. Not only do they occupy less space on the bench, but when it comes to potting on to a larger size the old square of earth is placed diagonally in the new pot so that the angles of the old compost now touch the sides of the new pot leaving spaces for new compost in the corners. Filling these angles is much easier than tucking the compost in all around the rim of a round pot. The plant is happier too: once the roots have reached the side of the pot the whole system inside it works better. In a square pot this happens almost at once after repotting.

Without a troop of gardeners, watering must be carefully provided for. At Vico Morcote the position was fairly easily dealt with. Beneath the greenhouse is a tank of 20,000 litres capacity supplied with rainwater from the roof. It is large enough to outlast even a prolonged drought. An electric pump brings water up to wherever it is required. Plants prefer rainwater to the municipal water supply, particularly plants in pots. On the terrace, where most of the pots stand and where they can be enjoyed from the living rooms, is a large dipping tank. So many of the books advocate watering in the early morning. Nature does not always do this. Many of the plants in pots will be tender, coming from the sub-tropics: otherwise they would be planted out in the garden. The routine of nature in the sub-tropics during the rainy season is almost always a fine sunny morning with rain beginning in the early evening. The plants absorb the water during the cool hours of darkness.

The correct watering of plants in pots is one of the most taxing of all garden operations. The multiplication of electronic devices which the gardener can insert into the pot to show the humidity of the soil testifies to this fact. Old Lonsdale, my Aunt Evelyn's head gardener, the master grower of potted plants, was referred to in an earlier chapter. I never saw him test the dampness of a pot by feeling the surface of the soil. And of course in those days there were no electronic devices. If there had been he certainly would never have condescended to use them. To find out if a pot needed water, he would merely lift it slightly from the bench. With practice this is the surest test. It is dangerous to water a 'heavy' pot and dangerous to neglect to water a 'light' one. This is not a skill to be acquired over long years of practice, though with the years it becomes instinctive. A run through the pots in the greenhouse will be quite sufficient to give one a sense of what 'heavy' and 'light' really mean.

The next most important element in watering pots is that the soil mix for a particular type of plant should be the same for each one of them. Here I must confess to having failed. Every year some hundreds of seedling nerines will be repotted by me. If I had made my compost exactly the same every year, then perhaps all could be watered together. But I have modified the makeup of my compost in the light of experience, so my nerines are growing in a variety of soils. This would be a nurseryman's nightmare, to be avoided at all cost in cultivating thousands of plants to be turned out and sold as a batch. In a greenhouse such as mine where each plant must be an individual, it is inevitable. Besides, with the passage of a year or so some elements in the compost, such as peat, disintegrate. Before flooding the trays in which my nerines stand, I must therefore go over them to pick out any plants which are still wet before the rest get watered. Only at the height of the foliage growth when it is difficult to overwater a nerine is the situation eased. If I were sure that I had found the best compost in which to grow these plants, then in the course of say three years I could probably get the whole collection growing in a standard mix. Alas! I am far from sure that I have yet arrived at the best possible of all soil mixes.

Fancy soil mixes, John Innes and so forth, are no doubt admirable

157

where they can be obtained and afforded and they would go some way to solving the problem. But personally I find that a mix of good garden soil, peat and fertiliser in proportion to the needs of the particular plant and a very generous helping of perlite or some such absorber-lightener, will serve perfectly well. An electric soil steriliser saves the work expended in sterilising many times over by reason of the resulting absence of weeds and pests in the pots.

Most of my pots when out of doors stand on the terrace of the house. Our architect in this Italianate world did not expect his clients to do anything so eccentric as living largely out of doors. The sun beat down pitilessly on the slate paving in front of the dining-room which was to be our preferred sitting area. The local expert in sun blinds was called in. Yes, large blinds would extend on metal arms carrying the canvas far out over the slates to provide shade in an area large enough for dining and sitting. Did I want them electrically operated? It seemed to me an extravagance. The Swiss are a direct people. "What about your wife if she wants to run down the canopy?" and with a look at me, "And you, you are not getting any younger, are you?" Electric they are, and it was a good if expensive decision, for in this summer climate the canopies are running in and out all the time.

But the sun still beat in beneath the canvas, heating the slates. My mind went back to the Boulevards of Paris and those discreet nondescript green plants on the pavements which separate the diners from the passers by. The answer became a kind of vegetable quadrille. As spring began, Japanese maples in pots would stand along the terrace at the extremity of the blinds. They would remain there to display the beauty of their spring colours. (PLATE 47) and to extend their shade under the canopy. As they began to turn green and the danger of cold weather receded, they would retreat to the relative shade of the patio and would be replaced by citrus in pots: a Ponderosa lemon, a Nagami kumquat, a Meyer lemon, a Lisbon lemon, a Key lime, a Persian lime, a Valencia orange and a Trovita orange.

This arrangement has been highly successful. The citrus delight us first with their very fragrant flowers and then with their decorative fruit which hangs a long time on the tree. I say 'decorative' because with the exception of the limes and the kumquats, the former used for jelly and ices and the latter eaten from the tree, the fruit in the supermarket has, alas, a better flavour.

The fruiting cycle of citrus is an extremely long one: about a year from flowering to maturity. Valencia and Trovita are our preferred oranges because they tend to ripen in summer when they can be admired, instead of when crowded into a corner of the greenhouse in winter.

As the nights get cooler in autumn the second figure of the dance is performed. The citrus retreat to a corner of the greenhouse, where they are huddled together in close quarters, and the Japanese maples come back to the terrace to display their magnificent autumn colours. These are answered by one or two maples in the garden nearby. 'Shishigashira', the latest to give an autumn display of brilliant gold and the red-twigged 'Senkaki' are now big specimen plants: small trees, in fact.

Hybrid hibiscus from Florida (PLATE 48) astonish all beholders and delight me. They seem to be unknown in Europe. The gigantic flowers up to ten inches in diameter and their fantastic colours place them amongst the most spectacular of all garden plants. Furthermore in a climate to their liking they flower continuously for most of the year. The winter climate of Vico Morcote is not to their liking, so in this garden they must retreat to the greenhouse. Fortunately they do not object to a cold winter rest and they are therefore compatible with the nerines. As soon as the weather warms up and the danger of frost is passed they go out on to the terrace in the full sun, of which they cannot ever have too much.

Unlike their hardy relative, *Hibiscus sinosyriacus*, the hybrids of *Hibiscus rosa-sinensis* must be grafted in order to grow satisfactorily. This is not an operation easily performed here, so they must be imported. They come from Florida on bare root, and the roots are extremely delicate. However, the plants are surprisingly inexpensive considering their novelty and magnificence – less than the cost of a plate of fish in their Florida home. The success rate in establishing them has been about eighty per cent. This has only been achieved when the plants are imported at the beginning of the warm weather in May. The fine white roots, which have been washed in Florida to comply with Swiss regulations, demand the smallest pot into which they will fit until the plants are established. During that period they require careful nursing. First they must stand in warmth and shade with spraying overhead with lukewarm water. As soon as they seem to have taken hold of life they must go out into the sun. They will probably need potting on for the next season and they will continue to grow and flower well for many years with a minimum of attention. Only beware of pruning severely in spring. The first flowers of the new season will come from last year's wood and it will be some weeks before new growth is ready to produce blooms.

Bonsai were an obvious choice for our terrace but were rejected. I once saw the Imperial Collection of Bonsai in Tokyo, awe-inspiring vegetable monuments dating back to the Tokugawa Shoguns. But bonsai are an infinity of labour and more responsibility than a dog. When the owner is away the latter can be fed, and if his dinner is forgotten he will complain loudly. If the bonsai are not watered, and correctly watered, they will not complain: they will just die and countless years of labour will be lost.

The answer, surprisingly neglected by gardeners, is natural dwarves. From my Japanese friends came three pines, naturally dwarf, which have never been pruned of so much as a needle. After twenty years they are still delightful individuals in small pots. They are very hardy. Visitors usually mistake them for bonsai.

Most remarkable of all my dwarves is the vine, 'Riyu shin'. The Linnean name of this plant is *Vitis japonica* 'Pygmaea Conglomerata' which in any normal printing font is about half the width of the plant itself after its sojourn with me for twenty-one years. How long Shuichi Hirao had it before he sent it to me I do not know. It is indeed a vine; each year it adds a few millimetres of growth and produces fine autumn colours. Shown on local television, I promised the viewers of this wine-growing region where wine is a part of diet that all would be welcome at the first vintage. However the significance of this plant is spiritual not vinous. In Shinto every plant is inhabited by a spirit, a dragon. Not the unpleasant kind of dragon which St George most obligingly slew, but a nice protective one. But it is not a dragon which resides in 'Riyu Shin' but the 'God of the Dragons'. This is the meaning of its name. It is a plant to be treated with circumspection.

Other natural dwarves of great beauty which we use as bonsai-substitutes in small ornamental pots are the satsuki Azalea 'Kokonoe', a tiny gem; *Cryptomeria* 'Tenzan', just as good as the pines; and the Japanese maples 'Wozishi', 'Tatsugashira' and 'O Jisi'. Japanese plant names are fascinating. The name of the tiny 'O Jisi' means BIG LION!

Sadly we have no pond. The ground is too steep to permit of that delightful adjunct of a garden, and particularly of its marshy edges in which so many fine plants delight to grow. Thus *Calla aethiopica* cannot grow in its favourite location, in shallow water. So on the terrace is a large plastic pot standing in a deep saucer which is kept filled with water. In this it will flower through the summer and when it retreats to the greenhouse it will flower much of the winter. *Iris laevigata* in its variegated leaf, blue and pink variants is treated the same way but must have a cold winter rest.

At the opposite end of the iris spectrum the minute gem, *Iris mellita*, would get lost in the open garden, but it covers itself with cheerful yellow flowers over a long period and is easy to grow in a pot.

Amorphophallus rivieri (PLATE 50) is established in the garden and multiplies, but seldom flowers. When it does so inspection is a doubtful pleasure because of the appalling smell. In a large plastic pot it is manageable and blooms every year. The magnificent flower of this aroid, of sculptural beauty, has an evil mystery about it which captivates the imagination. In its large pot it can be placed on the terrace outside the closed living-room window and can be admired without our being exposed to the aroma. The giant flower then dies down completely and is followed by an immense and elegant compound leaf on a single stalk which is most decorative and persists for the rest of the summer. The corm of this plant, which with time grows very large, is said to be edible. I succeeded in obtaining *Amorphophallus saraburiensis* but it did not survive, and I have been unable to obtain any other species of this extraordinary genus.

The idea of passifloras in pots was provoked by Mr John Vanderplank's splendid book on that genus in cultivation. The illustration of the new hybrid from Miami, 'Incense', was too much to resist. Mr Vanderplank sent me plants. Grown in a pot, 'Incense' more than lives up to its name and its portrait. The large violet self flowers are spectacular and freely produced and the perfume is excellent. It also fruits but I cannot yet report upon its gastronomic merits. It looks as if this *Passiflora* will also establish itself in the garden at the foot of the Japanese Maple 'Senkaki'. One of its parents, *P. incarnata*, is extremely ground hardy. If this characteristic has been transmitted in a reasonable measure the pot may not be necessary.

The common passion flower of commerce, *P. caerulea* is hardy here, and so is the beautiful pure white variant 'Constance Elliott'. But unhappily *P. edulis*, with its deliciously flavoured fruit, will not stand any appreciable frost. If it is to attain the dimensions needed to provide an acceptable crop it will be much too large for a pot. So desirable is it in the kitchen that it is given half of the back wall of the greenhouse. It bears twice yearly and produces a hundred or so of its purple fruit. These are converted into passion fruit ice cream to my great satisfaction. The purple form has a better flavour than the larger apricot coloured 'Granadilla' of the sub-tropics and tropics, though both deserve a place in the appropriate climate. To obtain this desirable plant is easy. The shrivelled fruits appear sometimes in the fruiterers' shop. Half of one fruit will provide enough seed, sown immediately, to plant an orchard with this rampant climber.

Worsleya rayneri is not a pot plant for the terrace, at least not in winter. The famous fragrant blue amaryllis is not in fact an amaryllis though it is a member of the family Amaryllidaceae. Neither am I yet convinced that it is blue. The type description reproduced in the *New RHS Dictionary of Gardening* hedges its bets on colour: 'lilac to heliotrope to opalescent blue'. What is opalescent blue I wonder? Will I ever know? It says nothing about fragrance.

I obtained four seeds of this exceedingly rare plant from Thompson & Morgan in 1971. From them I obtained one plant which grew well. After ten years and no flowers I wrote to Marcia Stewart, a great connoisseur of Amaryllidaceae and a most generous plantswoman, in Brownsville, Texas, asking her what I should do to produce blooms. She replied by congratulating me on having kept the plant alive for so long. Alas, Marcia is dead and there is nobody quite like her. But the *Worsleya* is still alive, and fourteen years later has still not produced a bloom.

Almost the only source of information and help in dealing with Amaryllids other than daffodils, is the International Bulb Society, headquartered at the University of California at Irvine, and publishers of *Herbertia*, an annual volume dealing with lesser known bulbous plants. Worsleya was the cover flower of *Herbertia* in 1991. The colour, if correctly shown, is mauve and certainly pretty. Mr D. V. Rix writing from Australia describes it as 'pale blue edged with deeper blue'. I shall not know what the colour of this flower really is until I am able to see one. That prospect still seems far off.

The *Dictionary* referred to above advises growing this plant, 'a challenging species with a reputation for being short lived and difficult to flower', in a loam-based mix. Mr Rix suggests growing *Worsleya* in a 24-inch pot – they do things in a big way in Australia – in something resembling an orchid mix. He advises that it be 'grown hard' in full sun. The article ends with a cautionary note that bulbs are not available from Mr Rix and seed only rarely. I might as well add that neither is available from me. How happy I would be if they were, but perhaps one day . . .

I recently read an article which was scathing on the subject of plantsmen who like to say that they possess certain very desirable but exceedingly rare plants. It cited *Worsleya rayneri* and *Paramongaia weberbaueri* as the prime examples of this eccentricity. I recognised myself at once in the description.

Of my few amaryllids in pots which are not nerines, the *Paramongaia* is also one. Of course it has never bloomed for me in several years. At the greenhouses of the University of California at Irvine, where I bought my plant at an auction, I saw it flowering. What a golden-yellow gem! I do not really expect it to flower for me, but what a delight it would be if it did! The sensation of owning this plant and *Worsleya rayneri* is akin to the pleasure of holding tickets in a multi-million lottery. The latter pleasure terminates with the draw, or it just might not do so. The former terminates with the final death of the plant, or it just might not do so. I have discovered the trick of growing the *Paramongaia*. It is dormant and must be quite dry for the summer. But when in early autumn it begins to grow it does so with astonishing speed and immediately requires a great deal of water. After going slowly downhill for several years, it is now going quite quickly uphill. Then I have to find out how to flower it. There must be a trick to flowering the *Worsleya* but what it is I have yet to discover.

One other amaryllid in a pot is permitted greenhouse space at the expense of a number of nerines, for it is very large. It is *Hippeastrum fragrantissima*. It astonishes me that the horticultural industry consistently underrates the value of fragrance in a plant. I cannot imagine anybody in their right mind buying a rose without fragrance. It is something which instantly commends itself to the public, even in an ugly plant. The *Hippeastrum* hybrids which have been bred to such magnificent size and colour over many years do not have even a whiff of fragrance: a most serious defect. Here then is a pure white hippeastrum which is a large and vigorous grower with a delicious scent. The Japanese are apparently working with it, but I have yet to see any results. I would certainly do so myself, but such a plant requires at least four square feet of staging, and to have any chance of getting a good first result one would have to grow rather a lot of them.

One of my favourite pot plants is a scilla. The Linnean system of classification which has done such yeoman service to generations of botanists and gardeners, places great emphasis upon the number, shape and disposition of the sexual organs of the flower. I cannot think of a better approach to taxonomy than that of the great man over two centuries ago, and yet his system sometimes leads to disconcerting results. Some taxonomists have recently been engaged in splitting up the vast and diverse family of the Liliaceae into a number of new families, thus doing some violence to the Linnean principle, for the structure of the sexual parts of all members of the Liliaceae is similar. I would have preferred that the new families remained as sections of the Liliaceae. The genus *Scilla* is now placed by the reformers in the new family of the Hyacinthaceae, but this has not eliminated seeming incongruities. Most of the scillas remain together in the same genus, with startling results.

To European gardeners a scilla is a pretty little plant three or four inches high, most welcome as it emerges from below ground with three to five flowers in late winter. But *Scilla natalensis* (PLATE 24) is a stately creature sometimes two feet high, with a fountain of large broad beautifully sculptured leaves from the centre of which arises a spike of uncountable tiny blue flowers. Leaves and then flowers emerge in early autumn. At their base is a large fat bulb sitting on top of the earth in the manner of a hippeastrum. And it comes from South Africa. In every respect this plant is the exact opposite of what we think of as a scilla, except that if you take a glass you may see that the minute sexual organs are indeed similar in structure to those of the European scillas and, for that matter, to all of the vast family of the Liliaceae. We have Linnaeus to thank for this, but I do not think that anybody has yet thought of a better foundation for taxonomy. As is evident from the case of the scillas, if the Linnean principle is to be modified by splitting up the Liliaceae, that will not give us a neat and tidy system of similar plants unless reforms are carried much further even than those already proposed. I fear that this would create rather than reduce confusion.

Heedless of the controversies raging around its family relationships, *S. natalensis* is a reliable as well as an elegant pot plant which can be depended upon to flower every autumn. It must have a complete rest after the foliage dies down in summer, and the protection of a frost-free place during its season of growth in autumn and winter. To my eye it is beautiful and it lasts in flower for a considerable time.

The choice of what to grow in pots is obviously a personal one. 'Bushu-kan', which being translated means Buddha's Hand, is a raging eccentric but I think it interesting and beautiful. It came to me from Tsuneshige Rokujo, and it has been dignified with the name of *Citrus medica* var. *sarcodactyloides*.

It is well known that the Buddha was endowed with ten fingers on his hand. This very ancient citrus is illustrated in Chinese manuscripts for centuries past and has been reproduced in jade sculptures for a like period. In origin it is probably a mutation from a citron. It produces fruits which are better illustrated than described. (PLATE 46) The oil of the peel has the characteristic aroma of citron. Within the fruit is nothing but pith. The number of 'fingers' is variable but certainly never so few as five. The plant is grafted, I think on *Poncirus*, and is of irregular growth. It is exceedingly difficult to propagate and attempts by specialists to do so from my plant have all failed.

While I enjoy this strange plant the impression which it invariably makes upon visitors is astonishing. Returning to the garden after some years they often remember the Bushukan and ask to see it.

I suppose that at some time or other any serious gardener has toyed with the idea of growing Oncocyclus Iris. But except for those who live in semi-desert climates, few are rash enough to make the attempt. But the arilbreds, crosses between Oncocyclus species and tall bearded iris, are quite easily manageable. I grew an early model arilbred, 'Lady Mohr', in the open border at Colebrook House. The huge flowers in sombre colours were impressive. At Vico Morcote in the early years of the garden I grew twenty or so arilbreds. In spite of seventy inches of rain, they flourished without any attention wherever there was full sun. Very beautiful they were, and one was deliciously scented. Not the coarse scent of the tall bearded iris, but a sharp fruity perfume. Most of them came from the annual plant sale of the Aril Society.

But pure Oncocyclus? Not for me the feats of engineering described by members of the Society in their attempts to grow these plants on a more or less permanent basis in climates not really to their liking. Principle No. VII of this garden reads, "Difficult plants, if not successful after a fair trial, are abandoned: there are plenty of easier subjects." But – I was getting rather old, and it would be a pity to depart this life without ever having flowered some of these extraordinary plants. I did the obvious thing. I wrote to the great hybridist at Tirat Tsvi in Israel and asked him to send me a selection, including some yellows. I like yellow iris.

It was late in the year to do this. The plants arrived from Mr Shahak on the very day that war broke out in the Persian Gulf. I looked with misgiving at the news, at the very dead-seeming rhizomes and at the chill winter weather. But still no engineering for me. They were potted at once in black plastic pots to give maximum heat in what sun there was: 5 inches square and 6 inches deep. Our own local soil just on the acid side of neutral, with the addition of some ground limestone, some perlite and a little general fertiliser, would have to suffice. The pots were watered and stood in the open air but under cover to take the winter's cold. They must root down before they grew up.

It was quite an array of pots. For what might have been the price of dinner and a half-bottle of wine at a fashionable hotel if I had been foolish enough to spend my money that way, Mr Shahak had sent me twenty-two crosses and named hybrids, several plants of each: a most generous and exciting collection. For good measure he added several packets of seed, including some of yellow crosses. But would I ever see the rhizomes bloom or germinate the seed? I watched the pots and was gratified after about ten days to see signs of movement. Inquiry beneath indicated vigorous plunging root growth in the January weather. In plastic pots one can always look to see what is going on without insulting the plant since the roots do not cling tenaciously to the plastic as they do to terracotta.

As soon as there was enough leaf to profit from the late winter's sun the plants were put upon a slatted stage on wheels on the terrace outside the living-room windows, the sunniest exposure in this shaded garden. When we had some late snowstorms the stage was wheeled under the eaves of the house. Perhaps it was not necessary. I felt that they would take the spring rains and they were allowed to do so but about snow I was not sure. They probably got it at home, but then, they were not at home now and they were not fully established as yet. Growth continued but I doubted there could be any bloom that season. The plants were given liquid feed several times. They seemed to like it.

As for the seeds, I had read somewhere that they must be chipped and soaked and have all manner of indignities performed upon them. I soaked them indeed, and then sowed them, and by mid-April they were germinating nicely. What future did these displaced persons have, I wondered? The answer turned out to be 'not much'.

By late April some of the growths on the big plants were swelling in a promising manner. The first flower opened on 14th May, an immense bloom with towering standards in lavender and brown-netted falls with marvellous dark 'eyes'. (PLATE 87) A procession of flowers followed: notable greys with black netting: white standards and palest green falls with dark brown 'eyes'; a couple with blood from a species in the regelia section carrying two flowers; a couple with tall bearded blood also carrying two flowers; two or three nice yellows. Each was more astonishing than the last. I felt like an oriental potentate opening and exulting over a casket of extraordinary jewels. All were photographed and some of the pictures were shown at the Royal Horticultural Society the following winter.

Have I indeed grown Oncocyclus iris at last? Certainly not. Mr Shahak grew them: I just flowered them. In summer they were dried off in the pots,

PLATE 45 *Dracunculis vulgaris*, the fruit.

PLATE 46 'Bushukan', ('Buddha's Hand'). The Buddha had ten fingers on each hand.
This centuries-old plant, *Citrus medica sarcodactylis*, never has so few as five.

PLATE 47 *Acer palmatum* 'Matsu kaze': spring colour.

PLATE 48 Hybrid hibiscus 'All Aglow'.

The hedychiums, relatives of the ginger of commerce, include some plants with a delicious fragrance. Several species and hybrids grow in the garden and bloom in late summer. *Hedychium flavescens* grows at the back of the greenhouse, attaining a height of about eight feet. Its deliciously scented flowers are picked for the house in the autumn.

PLATE 49 *Amaryllis belladonna*, 'Parkeri alba' provides good contrast in a planting of pink selections.

Amaryllis belladonna Hannibal hybrids from California are a great improvement on the typical plant. All 'belladonnas' are excellent cut-flowers which will perfume a room.

PLATE 50 *Amorphophallus rivieri* keeps the gardener at a respectful distance from its sinister beauty with an appalling smell.

PLATE 51 An Oncocyclus hybrid iris from Mr Shahak at Tirat Tsvi, Israel.

PLATE 52 Hybrids of *Nerine samiensis* raised at Vico Morcote.

ripened in the sun and started again next autumn. But they gradually declined from year to year. One of the arilbreds still survives and flowers in the garden. But for the rest of life the pure Oncocyclus will remain in memory, mysterious and beautiful: unforgettable. And then, there are the photographs.

Those species of cyclamen which are not fully hardy are an open invitation to growing in pots or pans. The foliage alone is often worth the trouble. They lend themselves to decorative oriental pots and are best watered from below by dipping. Most of the delicate species must be given an entirely dry rest during summer but will spring into growth after the first 'dip' in early autumn. They are delightful plants with which to decorate the outdoor dining table. I shall not repeat the descriptions given in the literature of that admirable body, the Cyclamen Society. I only mention them here to allude to the annual delight which they give me, together with a smug satisfaction at having succeeded with what are in some cases slightly miffy plants. My choice of three relatively tender species would be *C. rohlfsianum* for its marvellous foliage as well as a nice pink flower, *C. graecum album* for its beautiful white flowers and fine foliage and *C. libanoticum* in pale pink for elegant large flowers. Authority says that this cyclamen has an unpleasant scent. I find it unusual and curious and not unpleasing.

Rhododendrons of the Maddenii series are excellent subjects for pots if one has greenhouse room in winter. We grew a number of them until the nerines drove most of them out into the open garden. There only a few survived. But in pots they make splendid plants to carry into the house when in bloom. For in late winter and early spring they cover themselves with flowers, almost always white though in some species with an attractive yellow throat, and at least one, *R. rhabdotum*, is a spectacular beauty, boldly striped with red on a white ground. As so many of these plants are epiphytes, growing upon the branches of host trees or upon rocks, they are quite happy in a relatively small pot.

It was in January 1973 that we were in Chiangmai in the far north of Thailand with an introduction to Ruang and Buppan Nimannahaeminda. Ruang owned the market, a hotel and much besides; Buppan, amongst many other activities, was President of the Chiangmai Orchid Society. It was the flowering season of *Vanda caerulea*, the famous blue orchid which really is blue. I had grown it in my garden in Cuernavaca, far from home. Here was where it lived. The Chiangmai Orchid Society was holding its annual show, which consisted mainly of numerous variants of the blue vanda collected in the wild. There were also some of the hybrids from it which have produced larger flowers, but at least at that time had never quite equalled the intense blue of the best forms of the wild plant. It was a unique display which I doubt could be staged in any other place.

Ruang suggested a day up in the mountains north of Chiangmai, which could be reached comfortably by a road running towards the Burmese frontier at Mae Hong Son. From Doi Sothep, a mountain not far from Chiangmai, we looked down on the poppy fields far below, and I looked up into a large tree which was filled with white blossoms in its upper branches. The flowers did not seem to fit the tree. I suddenly realised that for the first time I was looking at an epiphytic rhododendron in its natural habitat and in full bloom. Amused at my extreme excitement, Buppan spoke to a boy in the local language. He ran off towards the tree and in no time was in the upper branches. He returned with two sprays of a white rhododendron with a yellow blotch and a delicious fragrance. But he had cut them off! Buppan spoke to him again and he shook his head vigorously. "He says it is part of the tree: he cannot bring roots." Buppan, who knew all about epiphytes, persuaded him to go up again, which he did. He returned with two small plants of the rhododendron, perhaps nine inches high, complete with their roots which he had detached from the tree.

The first thing which struck me was that one of the plants had a pronounced 'pseudobulb', like an orchid: a thickening at the base of the stem. No doubt this was a reserve of resources for the dry season. It gave a broad hint as to the cultural requirement of the plants. I subsequently noticed plants of this same rhododendron in gardens near Chiangmai growing as terrestrials. They were much larger than anything in the tree tops. Back in Vico Morcote with my books, the rhododendron was easily identified as *R. veitchianum*. Today, twenty-one years later, the pseudobulb and the plant in a pot in my greenhouse are quite large, but not excessively so. It has been 'grown hard' as is the case in nature.

I would not advise anybody to grow *R. veitchianum* 'Doi Sothep' although it has the merit of being the first of the Maddenii series to flower. *R. veitchianum* 'Walder', from the rich resources of the Glendoick Nursery, is a far superior clone flowering a couple of weeks later. But gardening, unlike botany, is more than a science. For me the Doi Sothep plant recalls delightful memories of friends and of an adventure. These make it no ordinary plant but a part of life.

Nelumbo nucifera, the Sacred Lotus (PLATE 60) is not really in a pot. Perhaps 'basin' would be the proper word. It has earth and vegetable detritus in the bottom and water to the brim. It is a Thai Lotus Tank. We have several items of this ware, brown and yellow with designs of dragons and suchlike things upon them. They are very large handsome objects used also as household water reservoirs in Thailand. Visitors sometimes mistake them for antiques – until they notice, amongst the dragons of the decoration, the image of a telephone and a telephone number, in case one might wish to order another. This particular basin has a design of sacred lotus instead of dragons, and we use it to grow that mysteriously beautiful plant.

It is unfortunate for us in the West that Linnaeus, the human pillar which supports the whole vast modern structure of taxonomy, should have used the name Lotus for a family which belongs to the Leguminosae, the peas and vetches. No doubt he did so because Dioscorides and Theophrastus had already done just this many centuries before. So the lotus of the Temples became *Nelumbo nucifera*, the name under which it is grown in Sri Lanka. Such it will remain for botanists while much of the rest of the world will continue to call it 'Lotus'.

The flower is indeed mysterious and very beautiful. So it should be, for it is the abode of Bodhisattvas, and notably of the Bodhisattva of compassion, Kwannon. She – or perhaps I should say 'it' when speaking of a being which has passed far beyond the joys and travails of the flesh – stands or sits in a lotus flower. It might be more comfortable sitting upon one of the immense circular peltate leaves of the lotus. These attain a diameter of over two feet and are held like pedestals, three or four feet above the water. The flowers join them in due course at that level or perhaps higher.

A plant loved and cultivated since time immemorial, the seed of which is edible, and for which girl babies are named in the hope that they may grow up beautiful and gracious, has given rise to many varieties. They differ in colour, quality of flower, size and hardiness. I grew mine from seed. This must be sown under water. In nature the seeds fall into shallow water and germinate there.

Some hardy kinds of *Nelumbo* survive all year round in tanks in our climate. I have not tested mine in this way, partly because I have no pond in which to do so. The ceramic tank in which my lotus grows sits on a wooden platform on wheels. When the leaves show signs of dying down, it is wheeled into the shelter of the patio, along with any Bodhisattvas which might be resident. Most of the water is drained off and the tank is covered up and stays thus until it is wheeled out again next spring. With advancing years there is much to be said in favour of mounting heavy pots on wheels.

169

Every year before the autumn retreat into the greenhouse and the winter storage, the battle against the pots begins. They multiply over the spring and summer as plants arriving or raised from seed get potted up. Space is very limited indeed and the annual give-away or throw-away is a difficult and sometimes painful but essential part of the growing of plants in pots.

CHAPTER 14

An Adventure in Breeding Nerines

THE EXCITEMENT OF CREATING
EVER GREATER BEAUTY

The purpose of establishing an ecosystem in the greater part of the garden was, amongst other things, to reduce the workload. Not only would this save labour: it would free time and thought for other gardening projects such as plant breeding. The planned creation of new forms of life is a godlike pleasure known only to those who have experienced it.

Nerine sarniensis is not to be confused with the pink *N. bowdenii* of the florists shops, which is an excellent garden plant for a sunny place in southern England and in similar climates. *N. sarniensis* will not tolerate a wet summer, and as it carries its foliage through the winter it will not tolerate frost. But its colour range, from brilliant scarlet through all shades of orange, red and pink to magenta, mauve, purple and white, is spectacular. (PLATES 52–56) The petals have a unique scintillation in direct light, gold flecks in the scarlet flowers and silver ones in the pinks and whites. I have not seen this in any other plant. The phenomenon, caused by the crystalline structure of the petals, makes them interesting cut flowers under artificial light. It also poses technical problems for the photographer. (PLATE 52)

In 1928 according to my garden register, I bought three bulbs of *N. sarniensis* 'Fothergilli Major' at Hillier's garden shop on Winchester High Street. I thought it beautiful and elegant, exciting in fact. The magic of a bulb, a packet of stored life from which a gorgeous scarlet flower followed by green leaves would explode. This is probably a clone of a wild plant, and has been much surpassed by later hybrids. But as it was and is still the earliest of all sarniensis nerines to flower, it would bloom just before I went back to Harrow for the autumn term.

Aged fourteen at the time, I did not know that I was in good company.

N. sarniensis had captured the imagination of that great connoisseur of plants H. J. Elwes, who was the most important breeder of its hybrids in the 'nineties of the last century and in the first decade of this one. The work had been taken over later on by Lionel de Rothschild at Exbury. At the time when I bought my bulbs at Hillier's shop he was beginning the most important breeding programme in *N. sarniensis* up to that time. It was to last for forty years and to exceed even the performance of Elwes in advancing the quality of the hybrids. I could not know that fifty years on I would be running a breeding programme based upon his work.

After I moved from Itchen Stoke House to Colebrook House in Winchester, I no longer had a greenhouse suitable for nerines. The one which I attached to the dining-room was used for growing hybrids of *Dendrobium nobile*. The dendrobiums and the nerines shared a liking for a cold autumn and for all the air they could get at all times, but their similarity of taste ended with that. Nevertheless I began to grow a few Exbury hybrids on the windowsills of the dining-room overlooking the river and facing east, and in an electrically heated frame in the garden. They flowered well, and I made one or two crosses before departing for Strasbourg for nearly six years as Secretary-General. The Official Residence on the main square of the city was a stately affair but it had no greenhouse, neither was there room for one in the formal town plot which contained it. So my nerines were fortunate in being able to enjoy the hospitality of the Royal Horticultural Society's greenhouses at Wisley. In 1970 the Society kindly handed them back, including some hybrids of my own crossing which were now of flowering size. They were welcome to retain stock of any which they wanted. Now I could set about breeding in earnest in the new greenhouse at Vico Morcote.

The first task was to survey the available material. Exbury had stopped breeding and had sold their collection, or so they thought. The purchasers, finding that they could not run it as a commercial proposition, had dispersed it. Or so they thought. While the nerines were at Exbury it had been the custom to send a bouquet of the flowers every autumn to the Queen Mother, renowned for her love of gardens. Apparently an old gardener at Exbury, heartbroken at the loss of his treasures and remembering his favourite Royalty, had secretly retained some nerines in a little-visited greenhouse. He had continued to arrange for a bouquet to go to the Queen Mother every year.

With Exbury no longer breeding, the field seemed to be clear for me to begin from where they had left off. I managed to obtain almost all of the best of their hybrids. Sadly, one or two of the stars of the programme had disappeared. Borde Hill had also bred some nerines and I obtained one or two from that source. Also included were the older hybrids of Elwes and his contemporaries. Often all that I could get were very small offsets which would not flower for several years. The only other breeding seemed to have been in New Zealand, where the late Mr Harrison had raised a number of hybrids. But he had kept no breeding records and, though vigorous, his plants were inferior in form to the later Exbury breeding and more limited in range of colours. They appeared to originate from one or two parent plants of Exbury origin. Nevertheless there were two amongst them which had interesting breeding qualities.

The Dutch commercial growers seemed to be concentrating their work upon crossing *N. bowdenii* with hybrids of *N. sarniensis*, hoping to combine the ease of cultivation and hardiness of the former with the magnificent colours of the latter. They did not seem to have made any progress. Altogether I bought about 300 'names', some of them probably not true to type. With the aid of my computer a very large number of crosses have been made at Vico Morcote, at first using this collection as a breeding base and now working mainly with my own selected hybrids.

From the time of making a cross it takes at least four years and sometimes six or more to obtain a good flower. This idea frightens off some who might otherwise undertake breeding. But the process is like a water-pipe: once the pipe is filled it keeps on running at the outlet. After the initial wait, which is enlivened by the flowering of the purchased breeding stocks, the homemade crosses flower in increasing numbers every year. Now, out of the original three hundred purchased clones from various sources, only a dozen remain with me. The months of October and November, when every morning new seedlings flower for the first time, are truly exciting. It is indeed the godlike delight of creation: the spirit brooding upon the waters.

Nerines, like many plants and some people, give no trouble provided that they are given precisely what they want. They do not ask for much, but what they demand they must have. The growing season is from October until May, during which period a temperature between 9 and 13 degrees Centigrade (48–56 degrees Fahrenheit) will be best. During the first two months of this period they need a great deal of water while they make up to six new leaves. In their native South Africa they are mountain dwellers and therefore in cultivation they must have all the air they can get. The cozy atmosphere of a greenhouse closed against the winter chill, so congenial to the gardener, is death to them. There is a rest from May to September,

My hybrid nerines during the resting season. The mystery of a package of stored life from which a gorgeous flower followed by green leaves would explode.

PLATE 53 Hybrid nerines raised at Vico Morcote: *above* 'Tai Missoni'; *below* 'Rosita Missoni'.

PLATE 54   *above* 'Vanishing Dreams'; *below* 'Dreams'.

PLATE 55 *above* 'Claudine Laabs'; *below* 'Yoshiko'.

PLATE 56 Vico hybrid nerines: *above* 'Sarah'; *below* 'Amelia'.

during which period a little water, preferably from below by capillary action, will be valuable about once in three weeks, gradually diminishing through the summer. This simulates residual moisture deep in the soil of their native habitat. Soil need not be rich and all fertiliser is dangerous, encouraging basal rot and virus. Neither is a problem here. The only pests to watch out for are nematodes which can be controlled.

Small pots are preferred and though nerines probably grow somewhat better in clay, I use plastic for ease of manipulation. Repotting is necessary only when it is physically imperative to avoid crowding. Contrary to the accepted wisdom, these plants do not mind being repotted in the very least, provided that care is taken to preserve the roots. I prefer to repot in late May as soon as the leaves have withered. After repotting the plants are watered and kept as cool as possible. A flush of new roots will result. Otherwise repotting can take place at any time during the summer until late August when the bulbs are beginning to wonder about flowering.

This sounds very positive, but in the cultivation of these plants there remain many enigmas which the scientists have not solved for us. It is fortunate if as many as eighty per cent of flowering size bulbs actually bloom. Why do not all of them do so? It is clear that blooming is precipitated by a drop in temperature. After the first cold night the plants no doubt think "Aha! Cool weather. It will soon rain and then we must get busy while the rains last." For this reason nerines in England bloom earlier than they do here, where the onset of cool weather is delayed. But the flower bud is formed in the bulb in autumn, to flower either one or two years later in the months of September, October and early November. The scientists have not yet been able to tell us what conditions favour the first initiation of these flower buds within the bulb. It will be nice when they do so.

It is difficult to judge one's own products, the result of much concentrated thought and effort over a long period. We therefore have an annual Beauty Contest, in which the best of my new seedlings are put on show. Some forty or so friends, not necessarily involved in gardening, are invited to form a jury. They are asked to forget about any consideration except beauty as they see it: there are no rules for judging other than that. There is a highly secret ballot! It is entertaining to see the excitement with which the voters follow the result of the poll, to find out whether their selections have won a place in the first three. The results go into the computer and are an indication of the popular appeal of the plants chosen.

Of course I have formulated my own criteria for evaluating my seedlings.

They get up to five marks for each of the following points: colour, form and size of floret, number of florets, shape and size of flower head and length and strength of stem. It will be noticed that colour comes before form. Specialists have sometimes reversed this order with unfortunate results. At one time the breeding of *Cymbidium* hybrids concentrated almost entirely upon form at the expense of colour, and the result was beautifully formed flowers in very uninteresting shades. The public had not read the rules and were bored. Like me, they are impressed first of all by a fine colour and they look at the form afterwards, if at all.

My greenhouse is not a large one. Every square foot is needed for young unflowered seedlings which will bloom into the next century if given the chance. This imposes a strict discipline, and any new seedling which is not a marked improvement on what already exists is given away if it has merit and is thrown away if it does not. Every morning in the months of October and November I have to sit in judgment.

Far too many nerines have been named, but the temptation to name one's best plants after friends is difficult to resist. There is also another reason for naming. It is difficult to associate characteristics with a number, but quite easy to do so with a name. The process of match-making can be calculated by the computer, but it still remains elusive, something in the mind which happens in the small hours of the morning as well as in the greenhouse in the presence of the open blooms. Sometimes there are complications. My first hybrid to be named was called for Ken Scott, famous Milan designer of flowered fabrics. Two later hybrids were called for Rosita and Tai Missoni, connoisseurs of colour and design par excellence in their knitwear products sold world-wide. In the course of hybridisation, without thinking about the implications, I bred Ken Scott to Rosita Missoni. A visiting 'investigative' journalist, noticing this, inquired, "Does Tai know?"*

---

* The print out of my nerine breeding programme is deposited annually in the Lindley Library of the Royal Horticultural Society. This shows all crosses made, all seedlings selected with brief descriptions, and all selected seedlings which have been subsequently discarded because they have been rendered obsolete by later breeding.

CHAPTER 15

Taking Palms to Palm Beach

A BOLD SIMPLICITY OF DESIGN
GIVES THE PALMS THEIR IDENTITY,
THEIR GRACE AND THEIR MAJESTY

Palms had fascinated me ever since I saw them growing wild for the first time on the long drive from Washington to Mexico City. They were sabals, fan palms growing in colonies in the desert plains of northern Mexico. So different from the carefully cultivated palms of the French Riviera, they were the symbol of a new world which I now entered for the first time. After I crossed the Tropic of Cancer and approached the foot of the Sierra Madre the landscape changed to luxuriant jungle country. A number of more beautiful palm species came into view, and, of course, the ubiquitous coconut. There were roadside stands loaded with a dozen or more kinds of banana, papaya and pineapple. But the palms were the emblem of the world in which I was to live and luxuriate for the next four years: the tropics.

That first night in the tropics I lodged in the little village of Tamazunchale in a deep valley at the foot of the Sierra. Next morning I would ascend the winding road on my up way to the Mexican Plateau high above, driving up through the clouds which usually encircled the upper slopes and emerging into the sunlight. Now I would spend the night in a delightful little colony of cottages surrounded by coconut palms and some large trees. I washed down a good dinner with two mugs of excellent draught beer brewed in the Mexican city of Monterrey by people who had once been German. Something about the place seemed familiar, *gemütlich*. I suddenly realised that my hosts were Germans. I was at war with Germany: that was why I was there. The atmosphere was friendly enough, but still . . . What would 'Uncle John' think about it? When I went to bed I put my .45 automatic under my pillow.

I was woken in the middle of the night by a very loud noise which in my half-awakened state sounded all too like a pistol shot. This would not be highly unusual in Mexico, but still . . . and 'Uncle John' seemed to be expecting me to react to the situation. Now everything was deathly silence. I cocked my automatic and moved stealthily onto the verandah and looked about me in the bright moonlight. Nothing stirred. It was very beautiful and I lingered, savouring the tropical night. There seemed to be no alternative but to go back to bed, which I did. I had not been long asleep when the same performance was repeated. Again I moved stealthily onto the verandah, but as before, there was bright moonlight and deathly stillness. Not even a dog barked. When I was awakened for the third time I remained in bed. Whoever was causing the trouble evidently did not have me in mind. When day broke I dressed and prepared to breakfast on the verandah before leaving on the long climb to the high plateau 7,000 feet above. It was then that I saw three coconuts and some very large avocados which had fallen from the big trees onto the roof of the bungalow and now lay on the ground. The avocados, though wounded, looked deliciously appetising. This was my new life in the tropics.

I met the palms in many different circumstances. By the coast I would delight in drinking the water of the green coconut, the world's most delicious drink bar none, in my opinion. In Costa Rica I would guzzle the fruit of *Bactris gasipaes*, the delicious Pejibaye, which was enjoyed by everybody from the President downwards. In Cuernavaca I tried to grow a few palms but there was not really room for them, neither were many interesting palms available. I promised myself, nevertheless, that somehow, somewhere, some day I would grow palms in earnest. Thirty years later I found myself in Palm Beach, Florida.

It surprised and shocked me that in gardens in Palm Beach there were so few species of palm. There were plenty of unhappy looking coconuts growing too far north for their own good, excepting only in one or two sheltered sites where they looked happier. Plants under stress, they were being attacked by the lethal yellowing disease. Royals and Queens were plentiful and happy and so were the commoner species of *Caryota*, the fishtail palm. Everywhere were the native sabals. A few miniatures and a few clump-formers, and that was about all. Admittedly Palm Beach was near the northern limit of the area where an extensive range of palms could be grown. A few miles further north at Hobe Sound the vegetation told me that the winter was a little colder. This seemed to be a good reason to try to grow more palms in Palm Beach.

What is the allure of the palms? Not perhaps the suggestion of sunny beaches and Planter's Punch, though in Europe on a grey January day that plays a part. For me, their beauty consists in the simplicity and boldness of the design. Unlike a great oak growing from a thousand points, the palm has staked everything on a single shoot. If the shoot perishes it is a bleak outlook for the palm. However large, with very few exceptions, each palm is but one growth system. It has gambled everything on a single throw of the dice of fate. This bold simplicity gives the palms their identity, their grace and their majesty.

Ann Norton lived in a house with a couple of acres of garden on the Inland Waterway in West Palm Beach. She was a highly distinguished sculptor who had constructed great brick creatures, for lack of a better word, in her garden. There were eight of them and a group of giant sculptured figures. Some were twenty or thirty feet high. A mystic, influenced by the Dalai Lama who was a friend, her sculptures had a significance quite different from anything I had seen before or have seen since. They were nearer in spirit to some of the Maya monuments than to anything of European origin. By any measure they were works of art of great importance. This frail little woman had sat by the work site day by day supervising their construction. The designs, at first sight deceptively simple, were on analysis extremely complex. As I worked around them in the years ahead each would assume a personality of its own. It would hardly have surprised me if one of them had spoken to me, though in what language I cannot imagine. Perhaps an inarticulate squeak or grunt or rumble would have been appropriate.

The large garden was filled with a miscellany of plants including far too much Ficus and that noxious indestructible weed from Australia, Casuarina. Ann was dying of cancer, far too young, her work unfinished. The garden was now beyond her to manage. I was approached for advice.

After a couple of days meditating in the garden I drew up a proposal. There was very little money, so the garden must be densely planted in the manner of Vico Morcote, to reduce labour. The purpose of the garden was to display the sculptures, so the planting must set them off to the best advantage without distracting attention from them. (PLATE 58) There would be no brightly coloured flowers or pretty effects. The design must be such that dense luxuriant foliage would conceal and then at the turn of the path suddenly reveal each sculpture. One would come upon each of them by surprise. The element of mystery which the sculptures themselves diffused must be played up. A first meeting with each one must be an event, almost a shock.

But what to plant? Certainly some native Florida trees, but the selection was limited. The main vegetation would consist of a collection of palm species, thickly planted so that they would provide a dense and luxuriant green background for the sculptures. The texture would be varied and beautiful and the subtle differences in colour would be interesting without distracting attention or dominating the scene. (PLATE 59) This would enhance the importance and increase the impact of the sculptures. At the same time it would create a palm collection of exceptional interest, second only to the greatest collection in the USA in the Fairchild Garden at Miami to the south in a slightly milder climate.

I went to read the paper to Ann Norton who was now near death. She listened attentively and when I had finished she tried to tell me that she would die that much happier in the knowledge that her sculptures, her life work, would be displayed in a way of which she approved. We were both deeply moved. She died ten days later.

I began planting at once. There was $500 for plants and after that it was up to me. The Fairchild Garden in Miami had an annual sale of seedlings from its collection including many rarities, and there were two palm specialists who sold plants, also in Miami. One of these was Carol Graff. She had been an airline stewardess, and was sometimes left over in South America between flights. She had become used to living with palms. Then she married and had two children. The marriage broke down and she and the children were on their own. Money was scarce. Walking the streets in the neighbourhood of their little house in South West Miami they noticed many palm seeds lying in the road. With the children she collected them, put them in pots, and offered the seedlings for sale. There was soon a brisk business. Carol's 'yard' filled up rapidly and she began the search for seeds of scarce palms from other parts of the tropics and sub-tropics. By the time I began planting she was an internationally known source of rare palm species, selling to Botanical Gardens and specialists in many countries. She was my best source of new material for the Norton Sculpture Garden.

In the Sculpture Garden it was hard going in the sandy soil of what must once have been sea bed. Over a period of four planting seasons I managed to buy and set out about two hundred different palms. I was encouraged and supported throughout by the Curator of the Sculpture Garden, Comtesse du Boisrouvray. The heavy work was carried out by a devoted French-Canadian gardener, Jean, who became my fervent supporter, fiercely resisting attempts to interfere with my plans for the garden.

But I was only in Palm Beach for a couple of months each winter, and although the palms were growing well the whole thing was getting beyond me. Then one day as I worked on the palms Monique du Boisrouvray said, "There is a girl who would like to see the garden, have you a moment to show her round?" The girl, who lived in Palm Beach, turned out to be English, Veronica Boswell, blonde, beautiful and charming. I agreed with what I hope was not unseemly alacrity.

All gardeners know that one can tell instantly whether a new acquaintance is really a gardener or only just an enthusiast. After about five minutes I was convinced that my blonde companion was not only an enthusiast but a very knowledgeable and dedicated gardener. Half an hour later when we got back to the house, I told Monique that I would be handing over the garden to Veronica. They both looked very surprised. I had not had time to discover whether there was a husband. If so this might cause problems. Would he agree to his wife spending a substantial part of her time directing Jean and generally caring for the young palm collection? Well, there was indeed a husband and Veronica was now Mrs Jim Butler. Jim was an American business man living in Palm Beach. He would have to be consulted.

Not only did Jim Butler approve the project, he volunteered to start a group of Palm Beach businessmen who would be called 'The Gentlemen of the Garden'. They would aim to raise money for the garden and would have a very convivial time together in doing it. What more could I ask? Clearly nothing. My cup was running over.

Under Veronica's care the garden has prospered exceedingly and the number of different palms growing there is now 334. (PLATE 58) It is probably the best American palm collection outside of the Fairchild Garden. And then the Fairchild Collection was devastated by a hurricane which passed through the middle of it, flattening many palms. The Norton palms assumed an increased significance. The Palm Society, a worldwide body with many members in Florida, agreed to help in the garden, many of the members working there at weekends. Some donated rare and valuable palms. The 'Gentlemen' bought one or two outstanding specimens. The collection is now meticulously labelled and in excellent condition. The spectacle is one of great beauty and interest, and if the palms set off the sculptures to advantage the sculptures add by contrast to the beauty of the palms.

Palm Beach is indeed as far north as it is possible to go with a big palm collection. This makes the Ann Norton Sculpture Garden of exceptional interest. If a palm dies of the 'cold' such as it is, this is not so much a failure as a piece of important information to be recorded for the benefit of other growers. The collection is a northern testing ground for many species. As a matter of fact there have been surprisingly few losses to the cold, though some to other causes, and most of the palms have grown well. Visitors get ideas for planting new and better species of palm in their own gardens.

As for me, I had fulfilled my dream of many years before: that of planting an extensive collection of palms. I had also had a new and delightful adventure. That adventure consisted in seeing the foundations which I had laid built upon and brought to perfection by a friend. In its present state the garden is firmly established as a unique contribution to American horticulture and it is significant for tropical and subtropical gardens throughout the world. It is extremely beautiful. I am certain that Ann Norton would be happy with the result.

Palms growing in the Norton Sculpture Garden, West Palm Beach: 1994

Aceloraphe wrightii
Acrocomia aculeata (Macaw Palm)
Acrocomia mexicana
Aiphanes caryotifolia
Aiphanes erosa
Aiphanes lindeniana
Aiphanes vincentiana
Allagoptera arenaria
Archontophoenix alexandrae
   (Alexander Palm)
Archontophoenix cunninghamiana
   (Piccabeen)
Archontophoenix kuranda
Archontophoenix sp. Mt.Lewis
Areca camarinensis
Areca catechu (Betel Nut Palm)

Areca ipot
Areca vestiaria
Areca vidaleana
Arenga ambong
Arenga australasica
Arenga brevipes
Arenga caudata
Arenga engleri
Arenga hookeriana
Arenga microcarpa
Arenga obtusifolia
Arenga pinnata
Arenga tremula
Arenga undulatifolia
Arenga westerhoutii
Astrocaryum huicingo

Astrocaryum macrocalyx
Astrocaryum mexicanum
Astrocaryum standleyanum
Astrocaryum sp.
Asterogyne martiana
Attalea allenii

Bactris gasipaes (Peach Palm)
Bactris sp.
Balaka seemannii
Bentinckia nicobarica
Bismarckia nobilis
Borrassodendron machadonis
Brahea aculeata
Brahea brandegeei
Brassiophoenix schumanii
Butia capitata (Jelly-Wine Palm)
Butia yatay

Calamus caryotoides (Hairy Mary)
Calamus hollrungii
Calamus moti
Calamus longisetus
Calyptronoma sp.   Costa Rica
Calyptrocalyx spicatus
Carpentaria acuminata
Caryota baconensis
Caryota cumingii
Caryota elata
Caryota obtusa var. *aequatorialis*
Caryota maxima
Caryota mitis (Fishtail Palm)
Caryota new species
Caryota no
Caryota rumphiana
Caryota rumphiana   Papua
Caryota rumphiana   Philippines
Caryota sp.   China

Caryota urens Mountain Form
Caryota sp. Thai Mountain Giant
Chamaedorea alternans
Chamaedorea arenbergiana
Chamaedorea brachypoda
Chamaedorea cataractarum
Chamaedorea concolor
Chamaedorea deckeriana
Chamaedorea elegans (*Neanthe bella*)
Chamaedorea ernesti-augustii
Chamaedorea erumpens or *C. siefrizii*
Chamaedorea neurochlamys
Chamaedorea fragrans
Chamaedorea geonomiformis
Chamaedorea glaucifolia
Chamaedorea metallica
Chamaedorea nationsiana
Chamaedorea oblongata
Chamaedorea pochutlensis
Chamaedorea sartorii
Chamaedorea stolonifera
Chamaedorea tepejilote
Chamaedorea vistae or
    C. woodsoniana
Chamaerops humilis (European Fan
    Palm)
Chambeyronia macrocarpa
Chambeyronia macrocarpa var.
    Hookerii
Chelyocarpus chuco
Chuniophoenix humilis
Chuniophoenix hainanensis
Chuniophoenix nana
Chrysalidocarpus cabadae
Chrysalidocarpus lucubensis
Chrysalidocarpus lucubensis × *cabadae*
Chrysalidocarpus lutescens (Butterfly
    Palm)

Chrysalidocarpus madagascariensis
Coccothrinax alta
Coccothrinax argentata (Silver Palm)
Coccothrinax barbadensis
Coccothrinax crinita (Old Man Palm)
Coccothrinax crinita brevicrinis
Coccothrinax inaguensis
Coccothrinax guantamensis
Coccothrinax litoralis
Coccothrinax miraguama
Coccothrinax proctorii
Coccothrinax readii
Coccothrinax scoparia
Coccothrinax spissa
Cocos nucifera Jamaica Tall
Cocos nucifera Dwarf Golden
Cocos nucifera Dwarf Green Malay
Copernicia alba
Copernicia baileyana
Copernicia bertroana
Copernicia burretiana
Copernicia gigas
Copernicia glabrescens
Copernicia hospita
Copernicia macroglossa (Petticoat
    Palm)
Copernicia prunifera
Copernicia yarey var. *robusta*
Copernicia rigida
Corypha taliera
Corypha umbraculifera
Corypha utan
Crysophila albida
Crysophila argentea
Crysophila guagara
Crysophila warscewiczii
Cyphophoenix nucele
Cyrtostachys elegans

Desmoncus orthacanthus
Desmoncus sp. Acasha
Dictyosperma album aureum
    (Hurricane Palm)
Dictyosperma album rubrum
Drymophloeus subdistichus

Elaeis guineensis (African Oil Palm)
Elaeis oleifera (American Oil Palm)
Euterpe edulis (Jucara Palm)

Gastrococcos crispa (Cuban Belly
    Palm)
Gaussia attenuata
Gaussia princeps
Gaussia maya
Guihaia argyrata
Gulubia macrospadix

Heterospathe sibuyanensis
Heterospathe humilis
Howea forsteriana
Howea forsteriana Pink Petiole
Howea belmoreana (Belmore Sentry
    Palm)
Hydriastele kasesa
Hydriastele wendlandiana
Hyophorbe lagenicaulis (Bottle Palm)
Hyophorbe revaughnii
Hyospathe lehmanii
Hyphaene coriácea (Doum Palm)
Hyphaene dichotoma
Hyphaene thebaica
Hyphaene turbinata

Jubaea chilensis

Kerriodoxa elegans

Latania loddigesii (Blue Latan Palm)

Latania lontaroides rubra (Red Latan
  Palm)

Latania verschaffeltii (Yellow Latan
  Palm)

Licuala grandis

Licuala lauterbachii

Licuala lauterbachii var. *bougainvillense*

Licuala paludosa

Licuala peltata

Licuala peltata var. *Sumawong*

Licuala ramsayii

Licuala sp.   Indonesia

Licuala sp.   Thailand

Licuala sp.

Linospadix minor

Livistona alfredii

Livistona australis

Livistona benthamii

Livistona chinensis (Chinese Fan
  Palm)

Livistona decipiens

Livistona drudei

Livistona sp.   Fern Valley

Livistona mariae

Livistona merrillii

Livistona muelleri (Dwarf Fan Palm)

Livistona morrisii

Livistona rigida

Livistona robinsoniana

Livistona rotundifolia (Footstool
  Palm)

Livistona rotundifolia luzonensis

Livistona saribus (Taraw Palm)

Livistona sp. 186–489

Livistona sp. 87–145

Livistona woodfordii

Lodoicea maldivica

Loxococcus rupicola

Marojejya darianii

Neodypsis decaryi (Triangle Palm)

Neodypsis lastelliana (Teddy Bear
  Palm)

Neoveitchia storckii

Normanbya normanbyi (Black Palm)

Orbignya barbosiana

Orbignya cohune

Paralinospadix stenochista

Phoenicophorium borsigianum (Thief
  Palm)

Phoenix acaulis

Phoenix rupicola (Cliff Date Palm)

Phoenix canariensis (Canary Island
  Date Palm)

Phoenix macrocarpa

Phoenix sylvestris

Phoenix theophrastii

Phoenix zeylanica

Pholidostachys pulchra

Phytelephas macrocarpa

Pinanga cochinchinensis

Pinanga sp.   Celebes

Polyandrococos caudescens (Buri Palm)

Prestoea montana

Pritchardia affinis

Pritchardia aylmeri robinsonii

Pritchardia gaudichaudii

Pritchardia hillebrandii (Loulu Palm)

Pritchardia kaalae

Pritchardia lanaiensis

Pritchardia lowreyana

Pritchardia martii (Loulu Hiwa
  Palm)

Pritchardia nicholai
Pritchardia orericalux
Pritchardia pacifica
Pritchardia praemorsum
Pritchardia remota
Pritchardia thurstonii
Pritchardia woodfordiana
Pritchardia vuylstekeana
Pritchardia sp.
Pseudophoenix sargentii (Buccaneer Palm)
Ptychosperma burretianum
Ptychosperma caryotoides
Ptychosperma elegans (Solitaire Palm)
Ptychosperma furcatum
Ptychosperma kakabona
Ptychosperma latius
Ptychosperma ledermaniana
Ptychosperma lineara
Ptychosperma macarthurii
Ptychosperma microcarpum
Ptychosperma nicolai
Ptychosperma propinquam
Ptychosperma praemorsum
Ptychosperma salomonense
Ptychosperma sanderianum
Ptychosperma schefferi
Ptychosperma takasi
Ptychosperma tenaru
Ptychosperma waitianum
Ptychosperma sp.

Raphia australis
Ravenea rivularis (Majesty Palm)
Reinhardtia gracilis
Reinhardtia gracilis var. *gracilior* (Window Pane Palm)
Reinhardtia rostrata

Rhaphidophyllum hystrix (Needle Palm)
Rhapis excelsa (Lady Palm)
Rhapis leoensis
Rhapis sp.   Thailand
Rhapis subtilis/humilis
Roscheria melanochaetes
Roystonea altissima
Roystonea borinquena
Roystonea elata (Florida Royal Palm)
Roystonea oleracea
Roystonea princeps
Roystonea regia (Cuban Royal Palm)

Sabal bermudana
Sabal blackburniana
Sabal causiarum
Sabal domingensis
Sabal etonia
Sabal jamaicensais
Sabal mauritiiformis (Savannah Palm)
Sabal mexicana
Sabal minor
Sabal palmetto
Sabal parviflora
Sabal princeps
Sabal pumos
Sabal sp.   Riverside
Sabal rosei
Sabal yapa
Salacca rumphii
Salacca wallichiana
Salacca glabrescens
Satakentia liukiuensis
Scheelea brachyclada
Schippia concolor
Serenoa repens
Siphokentia beguinii

Siphokentia dransfieldiana
Syagrus romanzoffiana ×
   camposportoana
Syagrus flexuosa
Syagrus oleracea
Syagrus macrocarpa
Syagrus picrophylla
Syagrus pseudococcos
Syagrus coronata
Syagrus romanzoffiana (Queen
   Palm)
Syagrus sancona
Syagrus schizophylla

Thrinax morrisii
Thrinax parviflora
Thrinax radiata (Florida Thatch
   Palm)
Trachycarpus wagnerianus

Trithrinax acanthocoma
Trithrinax braziliensis

Veitchia arecina
Veitchia joannis
Veitchia macdanielsii
Veitchia merrillii
Veitchia montgomeryana
Veitchia winin
Verschaffeltia splendida

Wallichia disticha
Wallichia caryotoides
Washingtonia robusta
Washingtonia filifera
Wodyetia bifurcata (Foxtail Palm)

Zombia antillarum

CHAPTER 16

Adventures in the Garden with a Camera

THE JOYS OF GROWING
A FLOWER AND THEN OF
ILLUSTRATING ITS BEAUTY

It must have been in the spring of 1932 that I was walking down Oxford High Street from Magdalen College when a most extraordinary object caught my interest in the window of the photography shop. I had never seen anything like it. I went in and asked what it was. "A camera," they said, "the new German Leica." I was convinced by the sales talk, and being a rather extravagant young man I bought it. I took it immediately to the Oxford Botanical Garden, opposite Magdalen, and photographed a plant of *Iris pumila* in full bloom. Then the film had to be sent to Montreux in Switzerland to be developed: there was no facility yet in England. When the prints came back I was astonished at their quality. I took a portrait of my grandmother, a very beautiful old lady, and was astonished again. A Leica went with me everywhere after that: through the war, through Mexico and Central America. After the war it went with me into the garden and I compiled a photographic index of my plants. Then it was replaced by the Leicaflex, a weighty monstrosity though of fine quality. I deserted to the lighter and very competent Olympus.

It was in 1978 that some of my pictures were in a laboratory in West Palm Beach for processing. One of America's leading bird photographers, Claudine Laabs, saw some of the prints. She told the lab that I should get in touch with her. I did.

"What are you doing with your photography?" "Doing? Well, I take it home. Is that all right?" "No, it is not all right. These pictures are 'art' and you should be using them." I think this is an accurate summary of what proved to be a fateful conversation. Frankly I was skeptical, but Claudine

188

was not only distinguished but also attractive. I promised to think the matter over, still unconvinced.

At that time the Royal Horticultural Society had an annual exhibit of painting, drawing and photography. It was in February when plant material to fill the flower show is scarce. I noticed that the rules said that paintings and drawings were eligible for an award, but not photography. The point seemed academic so far as I was concerned: I doubted my work was worth showing at all, but I must keep my promise to Claudine. I took a few pictures of tree peonies to the Society's hall, hung them up and went off to lunch. When I returned – I looked a second time in disbelief – there was a gold medal on my stand. I sought out a member of the committee. "You cannot give me a medal: it's against the rules." "When we saw your photographs we decided it was time to change the rules." My head must have swelled visibly as I stood there.

Now there are seven gold medals, the Grenfell medal, and twenty-three one-man shows, in the United States, France and Italy, including the National Academy of Sciences in Washington, the Petit Trianon at Versailles and Bagatelle in Paris, the Italian 'National Trust' and many museums and botanical gardens. I recite this history partly out of vanity but also to encourage gardeners not to underrate their photographic skills. I had no idea that I was a photographer until Claudine told me so, and even then I did not really believe it. There are remarkably few fine flower photographers working today.

All my photography is of my own plants. There they were waiting in the garden. This is a great advantage, because there is only one day or perhaps two when a flower is at the peak of its beauty. It is the day when the girl at the centre, the pistil, and the surrounding boys, the golden stamens, are ready for one another and only awaiting a bee or a puff of wind to get them together. It is the wedding day. The commercial photographer who must buy his flowers in a shop is at a big disadvantage. Shop flowers are selected and grown for ease of culture and for 'shelf-life'. My flowers are selected and grown with only one thought in mind, their beauty. Some are ephemeral, only lasting a single day, some only a few hours during the night. Such things are certainly never destined to be sold in a shop. With others I can wait for the wedding-day when they are looking their very best, and then take my photograph. Gardeners have a great advantage over other photographers.

To begin with I concentrated my work on tree peonies and magnolias. Their response was wholly different from one another. With the tree peonies, the larger my portraits of individual flowers became the more beauty they revealed. At four feet by five they were still improving, such is the sophistication and complexity of the flower, the subtlety of its petal structure. I reflected that generations of devoted Chinese and Japanese gardeners who for two thousand years had grown, bred and loved these beautiful plants, had never seen what my photography was now revealing. In theory, if one took a magnifying-glass to the flower one would be able to observe the same amount of detail. They had no magnifying-glasses. But even so, to examine each detail one by one would be a very different matter from seeing the entire array displayed simultaneously in a single image five feet across, so that it could be taken in as one, a single impact. The impact of these giant flower portraits astonished even me, as they have many other people.

The magnolias turned out to be quite different subjects. After a magnolia flower is magnified over a certain size, there is nothing more to be gained unless one is looking for an effect similar to that obtained by the great flower painter, Georgia O'Keefe. If a magnolia is to be really effective as a big print it must be a picture of a portion of the tree in bloom. Then it can be most impressive.

The conclusion is that for purposes of portraiture, some genera or species are more photogenic than others. Only experiment will establish which they are though a guess is often right. It is also the case that with flowers, as with people, some individuals are more photogenic than others, and, as with people, each must be approached in its own way. As I walk round the garden an exceptional flower will catch my eye. Off with it to the studio!

It is important to keep an open mind in the choice of subject. Neither *Allium giganteum* (PLATE 26) nor *Garrya elliptica* 'James Roof' (PLATE 28) would at first sight seem particularly photogenic. But approached in different ways both yielded attractive results.

The angle of approach is critical. Shooting for a television film series in Brooklyn Botanical Garden I was provided with a very experienced and competent movie cameraman. He was not about to take lessons from me. Flowers were easy! They did not throw tantrums like actresses. If the flower was not quite at the right position, give it a tweak or tie it in with string. With flowers you just wheeled the camera up to them and shot. What more was there to it? As I expected, the entire shoot was a waste of money. Flowers grow in relation to the light. They must be photographed in that relationship.

I had not 'asked' to be a photographer of note: it had just happened. And now my photography took control. I found myself changing my attitude to the subjects and changing my methods. The Olympus was relegated to the taking of snapshots, which are sometimes required, and for this purpose it has now been replaced by a Nikon. Many images taken with these two excellent instruments are included in this book. But for my exhibition photography I turned to a medium-format camera: a Rolleiflex 6006 with Zeiss optics. This wonderful electronic camera had a small square screen on which one could view the image. This was a great advance on squinting through a viewfinder. Composition of a picture became a more leisurely and considered process. I liked the new system so much that I soon felt convinced that a larger screen would be better. After much thought I ordered a 'Zone VI' large-format Field Camera with a viewing screen 4 × 5 inches. It was hand made by craftsmen in Vermont, constructed from mahogany and brass. (PLATE 57) It contained no electronics. All the adjustments must be made by hand.

Most people take this camera to be an antique, but it is nothing of the kind. So sophisticated are its manual controls that it can do everything that a highly automated electronic camera can achieve, but I, not the electronics, must figure out how to operate it. Electronics can be relied upon to produce a competent picture if correctly operated, but they can never replace the judgment of the photographer.

Mastering the controls turned out to be much simpler than I had supposed. The image on the large ground-glass screen was incomparably easier to compose than had been the case with the Rollei, and it was another and a better world from squinting through a viewfinder. Furthermore, in the large-format camera the image is viewed upside down. This alarms the uninitiated, but in fact it assists in composition. One is divorced from all surrounding distractions. The image seems to float in a void without irrelevancies. Of course such a large camera must be used on a strong tripod. This means that after working on the image, if it is not quite to my satisfaction, I can go away, have a cup of coffee, and come back for a fresh look and to try again.

With a camera of this kind one may select one's own optics. I chose Schneider Kreuznach, and for almost all my work I use an APO Symmar of 210 mm focal length. This superb piece of modern science and craftsmanship is one of the gems of the optical industry. I also have a wide-angle lens, useful for landscape, a 120 mm Super-Angulon, also by Schneider Kreuznach. But for flowers I use nothing but the APO-Symmar. For travel the Field Camera folds up into a small compact square not easily damaged.

I had begun by photographing out of doors in sunlight. I disagree with the accepted wisdom, which is that flowers and gardens should be photographed in subdued or diffused light. With the Field Camera I continued to use direct sunlight. But gradually the desire to have total control of the image drove me indoors to an improvised studio. A powerful Bron flash on a stand gives me the control I need. It can be placed at any angle but in general it will pretend to be the sun and will be at an angle similar to natural illumination. Once again, the accepted wisdom called for diffused light: a diffuser was supplied with the flash. I found this to be quite wrong and discarded it. For all practical purposes the sun is a point source and the flash should be the same.

Using flash, the Apo-Symmar can be stopped down to the extremely small aperture of f. 64. This gives great depth of field which is necessary for close-up photography. To obtain the necessary illumination the flash can be fired several times. With my highly automated 35 mm Nikon the temptation is to go on pressing the button, taking multiple exposures, and choosing the best. In the studio with my ground glass screen and total control of lighting, a film is only wasted if I make a mistake. Normally one exposure would be enough, but as I often require duplicate transparencies and as the best duplicate is another exposure, I normally take three of an important image. These will be taken at slightly different exposures to give the printer a choice of density.

The film is Fuji Velvia Professional with a speed of ASA 50 though I may now turn to the new Fuji Provia with a speed of ASA 100. I do not need the extra speed since my images, unlike Claudine Laabs's birds, stand still. But the colour rendition seems to be even better than in the older slower film. The whole operation is therefore international: the camera American, the optics German, the illumination and light meter Swiss, the film Japanese and the photographer English.

Though this book is illustrated with many pictures taken on 35 mm film with my Olympus or Nikon cameras, and a few with the Rollei, the most important images are all taken with the 4 × 5 inch Field Camera. I cannot imagine any greater pleasure in photography than that of working with this beautiful instrument. But the taking of the image is only the beginning of a process. The translation of the image onto a base for presentation is a complex matter in which much of the beauty of the original image can be lost.

To make very large prints, perhaps as much as six feet in length, requires plenty of space and very large equipment. This was beyond my resources or indeed my wish to supply. I needed a good laboratory. But the process of transferring an image from a transparency to a paper or plastic base is not something which can be left to an automatic process, or to the judgment of the laboratory operators. Every print, in the present state of the photographic industry, is a compromise. If the reds are right the blues will be wrong or if the dark portions are right the whites will be burned out. Choosing the exact compromise is something which I must do myself, working with the laboratory technicians until I obtain what I want. This is not something which every laboratory is willing to undertake: there is not much money in it.

In Atlanta, at Meisel Photochrome, I found a technician in charge, Brian Sims, who was willing to admit me to the laboratory and, with his fellow technicians to use their resources and skill until I obtained the result which I had hoped for. We would start with machine-made contact prints of many images which would be posted to me in Switzerland. From these I would select a few for trial prints of about 8 × 10 inches, made by Meisel in the light of notes from me as to what they should look like. From these perhaps half a dozen would be selected for large printing and for that purpose I would visit Atlanta and work with Brian and his staff until we got a print which satisfied my desires. In the course of this partnership I came to have a good understanding of the technical problems which confront a laboratory in this kind of work, and I was therefore able to modify my photography to make things easier for the laboratory operators. Several fine exhibitions were prepared and presented in this way. Meisel then passed into different hands and Brian moved to Modernera Laboratories, also in Atlanta, where the same process was repeated. I think that the technicians in both laboratories enjoyed our work. They are almost always engaged on commercial images, which have a certain flat quality about them. The making of prints which had no other purpose than visual beauty was in itself a challenge and a fascinating exercise.

But however good the laboratory may be, there is nothing to be done unless the photographer has succeeded in creating a beautiful image. What is it that makes an exceptionally beautiful picture of a flower? Not the camera or the film or the lighting, though the photographer must be master of his tools as in any other art. Not the accurate portrayal of the flower parts and colours: that is botanical illustration. It is something which resides in the photographer. At my very first showing of pictures, at the Royal Horticultural Society, a lady whom I did not know and who did not know that I was the photographer, was standing beside me. Pointing to a picture of a white tree peony, *P. suffruticosa* 'Renkaku' (Flight of Cranes), she said to her companion, "That picture was taken with love." I was startled and much moved by the penetration of her remark. It revealed to me something about myself which I had not taken into account. Perhaps only a woman would have perceived what she saw. She was right, but it was still not the whole story.

I have been looking attentively, yes, lovingly at flowers since I was very young. I know them so well and expect so much of them. I know and must try to reveal their individual poise and character and texture, in short the individuality not just of the variety as I know it but of that particular flower. Only if I can do that can I hope to capture its full beauty on film. Quite often I shall fail. Sometimes I shall succeed. Very occasionally the result will be an outstanding image, much above the general level of my photography. What has brought this about? I cannot tell. If I tried to repeat it with another flower and another shoot I know that I could not do so. It is a mystery. Exciting? (PLATE 57)

Peter Smithers Photographic Exhibitions and Awards

1984   Oklahoma Art Center, Oklahoma City

1985   Norton Gallery of Art, West Palm Beach, Florida
Musée Cernuschi, Paris
Bois des Moutiers, Dieppe
Brooklyn Botanic Garden
Casa Communale, Vico Morcote, Switzerland

1986   Pennsylvania Horticultural Society, Philadelphia
The American Peony Society, Minneapolis
The Pacific Asia Museum, Pasadena, California

1987   The Kirkpatrick Museum, Oklahoma City
The British American Center, New York

The Fernbank Center, Atlanta
Missouri Botanic Garden, St. Louis, Missouri

1989   Atlanta Botanic Garden
The Retrospective Gallery, La Jolla, California
The National Academy of Sciences, Washington DC

1990–91 The Neuhoff Galleries, Dallas

1992   Bagatelle, Paris: by invitation of the Mairie de Paris
Chelsea Flower Show, by invitation of the Royal Horticultural Society
Orangerie de Jussieu, Versailles: for the Amis de Versailles

1993   Villa della Porta Bozzolo, by invitation of the Fondo per l'Ambiente Italiano
Missouri Botanical Garden, St. Louis, Missouri

1995   Associazione Luca Signorelli, Orvieto, Italy

Awards for Photography

1981   Gold Medal, Royal Horticultural Society: Tree Peonies
1983   Gold Medal, Royal Horticultural Society: Tree Peonies
1984   Grenfell Medal, Royal Horticultural Society: Magnolias
1985   Gold Medal, Royal Horticultural Society: Hybrid Hibiscus
1989   Gold Medal, Royal Horticultural Society: Nerines
1991   Gold Medal, Royal Horticultural Society: Hybrid Epiphyllums
1992   Gold Medal, Royal Horticultural Society: 'A Bouquet from Vico Morcote'
1992   Gold Medal, Royal Horticultural Society Chelsea Show: Flower Portraits

CHAPTER 17

Dreams

OF MY GARDEN
AND OF LIFE
ITSELF

I must confess to being an introspective gardener. Not for me the tour, now so popular, by a group of companions to visit distinguished gardens. Many such groups come here, and they are most welcome. It is a personal pleasure to receive them and it is always instructive. But the garden is the dream within which I live, all absorbing in its interest, both in detail and in impact. To leave it at any time is a sacrifice, and the sacrifice is greatest when other gardens – and my garden – are at their best. To leave until the nerines have finished flowering in the second week of November would be unthinkable. Then life in the garden slows to a crawl. By early January the new season is in full swing.

Matters are complicated still further by the midwinter bloomers. As they brave the December and January weather, flowering profusely whenever there is a sunny day and carrying excellent perfumes, they have a special value unlike that of other plants. Perhaps in summer they would pass unnoticed but during the dark days when life slows down and old folk die, they are treasured. Several varieties of *Hamamelis mollis*, of which in my opinion 'Pallida' is the most beautiful, and with a delicious fragrance, flower in the ravine. *Chimonanthus praecox*, the winter sweet, has a first-class sexy scent if ever there was one. Its equal never came out of a bottle. But there is a catch here. I have two plants, both of the pale coloured form which is reputedly more fragrant than the darker yellow one. This is true, but not all of the pale forms have the same quality of scent. The one growing by the entrance to the house so that it is readily sniffable, is far superior in fragrance to the apparently identical plant which grows down in the valley. If ever I had to buy a chimonanthus again I would want to nose it first.

At the same time there is *Abeliophyllum distichum*, a powerful fragrance. Picked before the buds open, perhaps in early December, they will expand in the house to perfume a room with a fragrance which I would place in the upper second class. *Camellia* 'Show Girl' begins to flower in the patio in late November and continues to bloom until March. If the snow comes and goes so does a fresh crop of bloom. The flowers are not the giants of the Chinese parent, nor are they the miniatures of its Japanese parent, but in between the two they cover the tree: for such it is at twenty-five feet, grown clear out of the patio and above the roof. On a sheltered wall *Camellia granthamiana* opens its very large white flowers and nearby the camellia cousin, *Gordonia axillaris* produces a profusion of crisp white flowers with shiny bright green leaves. *Iris unguicularis* in several forms is already in full flower wherever some sunshine remains. *Mahonia lomariifolia* is in full bloom. Here and there throughout the garden a plant of *Daphne bholua* Daman form has already begun to perfume the air.

When it is necessary to step outside the world of my garden the interval between the last nerine and the hamamelis is the only time when it is tolerable to do so. But leaving the much loved winter bloomers is not easy. Who knows how often I may see them again?

Some years ago I was honoured with a visit by the Association de Parcs Botaniques de France. This organisation, which in American parlance would rightly be described as 'prestigious', is not an association of Professors of Botany though some are to be found within it. It comprises most of the famous and distinguished private gardens of France. The year following their visit I was invited by the Association to pay a visit to gardens in Normandy and Brittany. The temptation was too great: I abandoned my garden full of flowers for a truly rewarding ten days.

The English are exquisitely polite to people whom they do not know, but with their friends they are relaxed to the point of being somewhat offhand. The French are sometimes downright rude to those whom they do not know, but once a friend, they are your most considerate and generous friends for life. French hospitality now rose to the occasion.

Every visit was memorable. I saw half of the great garden made by Princess Sturdza at Le Vasterival. It would have taken another day to see the other half of that immense collection of fine plants. The beautiful seaside garden of Jean Laborey, with dense dwarf vegetation of great beauty running down to the edge of the low cliffs, is unforgettable. The intimate secluded garden of Jean-Marie and Brigitte Fourier on the Atlantic Coast was full of interesting plants. The garden of Dr Favier in the Carentan Peninsula, with an immense collection of carefully selected rarities was one of the most delightful and interesting that I have ever seen. The house and garden of Robert Mallet, Bois des Moutiers near Dieppe, might well have been on the Dorset Coast. The beautiful house is by Lutyens with a noble Burne-Jones tapestry hanging on the stair. The landscape garden sweeping down to the distant sea, mercifully preserved with broad open spaces, is by Gertrude Jekyll. Of many views of the ocean which have brought a lump to the throat of a frustrated sailor, this was perhaps the most deeply moving. It is approached in memory only by the moment when I reached the crest of the mountains on my way to Acapulco, then a small village, and for the first time looked upon the Pacific Ocean. The garden of Robert and Annique Lasson, Le Hutrel, was not far from Mont St. Michel. It had been newly planted with many interesting magnolias. But it is something else which springs to mind at Le Hutrel.

The August weather was cool though not cold, nevertheless when my wife and I came down to dinner a log fire was burning on the hearth. Not strictly necessary, I thought, but pleasant. The reason for this was soon apparent. After an aperitif Robert left the room to return with a very large flat wire cage with a handle. It contained a magnificent turbot. This he proceeded to arrange upon the embers of the fire. Another aperitif while we contemplated the turbot, and then to the dining table at the other end of the room. Various hors d'oeuvres were served, and then Robert rose from table and at the fire-place turned over the turbot. Back at the table, the soup was served. That finished, the moment had arrived. The turbot was removed from the fire and from the cage and carefully dissected. A noble fish, superbly flavoured. In the memories of a long life there dwells only one unforgettable fish, a turbot.

But to return to gardens. In ancient Celtic Brittany the village names are almost the same as those in ancient Celtic Cornwall. The two are separated by the English Channel – La Manche to the Bretons. Both share a mild maritime climate in which fine gardens and mythology proliferate side by side. When I entered the garden at Kerdalo Braz I understood immediately that I entered another man's dream. Since the end of the Second World War Prince Wolkonsky had created one of the most distinguished of modern gardens – a model of what a large garden should be in the second half of this century.*

* This account of the garden at Kerdalo Braz is adapted from an article written by me for the International Dendrological Society.

PLATE 57 Japanese tree peony 'Tamafuyo'.
Very occasionally I shall achieve an image
much above the general level of my photography.
What has brought this about? I cannot tell. If I try
to repeat it with another flower and another shoot
I know that I could not do so. It is a mystery. Exciting?

My Zone VI Field Camera, hand-made in Vermont.
Most people think it is an antique but it is nothing
of the kind. So sophisticated are its controls that it
can do everything that an electronic camera can
achieve. The judgment of the photographer replaces
the automaticity of electronics.

PLATE 58 The Anne Norton Sculpture Garden with a background of palms. One comes upon each sculpture by surprise.

Veronica Butler is dwarfed by the giant fronds of *Bismarkia nobilis*.

PLATE 59
The beauty of luxuriant palm foliage in the Anne Norton Sculpture Garden.

PLATE 60 *Nelumbo nucifera*, the Sacred Lotus of the Orient. Mysterious and beautiful. A plant loved and
cultivated from time immemorial, for whom girl babies are named in the hope that
they too will grow up gracious and beautiful.

That which carries the really great garden beyond one which is competently designed and beautiful, is always and only the creative genius of the owner. It is part of himself, expressed in stone and brick, in air space and in water, in green and growing things. No other living being could have created it. By an astonishing tour-de-force the garden at Kerdalo Braz is four different and distinct gardening traditions combined into a single harmonious whole, and much more. It is with a scintilla of this much more, a fleeting dream by a great gardener, that I approach the final conclusions of this book of adventures.

Picture an intimate verdant wooded valley. At its head stands the old stone house, unpretentiously beautiful, sheltered and set off by forests on the hill behind. No other dwelling is in sight. A perpetual spring flows from the valley head through the garden and down to the river estuary in the distance. In front of the house lie two geometric parterres, open-air rooms. The first is severely functional, its form dictated by the house to which it gives access. In the second, at a lower level, are English herbaceous borders rich in colours and fragrances: just the place for an intimate stroll in the perfumed after-dinner dusk. Beyond, on the sides of the valley to right and to left is informal landscape planting in the grand manner. At the lower end of the valley, before the woods which line the river estuary, is the lake. The entire garden is a museum of living plants, each chosen and placed by a master hand. All four elements are perfectly matched and combined to create a dreamlike illusion of remoteness and peace.

And now for the discovery of the much more. It lies still hidden from the view of those who have entered this secret magic valley. It is beyond the upper and the lower terraces, beyond the middle distance of gently sloping park land, beyond the lake where the valley ends and the stream pours into the river. You would not suspect that it is there, so secret is the place. You come upon it when you are convinced that you have seen all, for through the trees you already glimpse the broad waters of the estuary close at hand.

To find it you must now make your way upon a narrow track to your left through dense greenery: immense leaves of *Gunnera* as big as beach umbrellas. There is the sound of water. Not the plash of splashing water, not the gurgle of a flowing stream, but the sound of water gently poured upon itself. Then you see it – and yet you are not there, for you must first pick your way to it along the stepping stones which lead you up the middle of the stream. It is a place enchanted. Certainly a naked water nymph will flee your presence in shocked surprise. There is utter silence broken only by that sound of gently pouring water. You step gingerly, silently, as if in the presence of some unknown invisible creature. The effort of balance slows your progress to a respectful pace. You push open the wrought-iron gate and step inside. In the flash of an eye you possess the secret of the falling water.

On the wall of the tiny temple and directly in front of you is a dazzling circle of sunlight from an opening in the roof. In its midst a ribbon of falling water flashes as it is poured forth as if by an unseen hand. It falls, perfectly formed and unbroken into a great stone shell. Then another step forward – and suddenly you are surrounded on all sides by naked nymphs, shadowy spirits of the flowing waters, begotten by the imagination of the garden's creator playing upon the timeless Breton woods and streams. And then you see that the cold glistening nymph flesh is made of sea shells from the estuary near by.

I spent a couple of hours with the nymphs attempting to picture them with my camera. The whole thing had been a surprise and I was technically ill-prepared for such an adventure. Besides, it is well known that naked nymphs are by their nature timid and unapproachable. I began to realise that it was the nymphs, not I, who ruled here. I should have known. Little by little they came alive before my eyes. Little by little I fell under their spell, or perhaps I should say under the spell of one of them. What if she had the feet of a bird and grotesque ears and was made of sea shells? For she was wild and yet gentle, part animal part spirit, fugitive yet beckoning and somehow beyond my reach or comprehension. She was the ideal woman for whom men search, never to find her because she does not exist – except as sea shells.

The evening sun no longer played upon the falling water and the images of the nymphs began to fade. I packed my modest equipment, closed the iron grill and turned to cross the stepping stones. There was no sound but that of water pouring into the great shell. For an instant it was transformed to laughter, the shrill mocking laughter of young girls. And then, once again, it was just the sound of pouring water.

The sun was now about to set. I was deeply moved. I strolled slowly up the valley, past the lake, through the woods scented with the leafy fragrance of the dusk, past the herbaceous borders fragrant with the scent of flowers after the heat of a summers day, and across the lawn of the open air rooms; but I saw none of this. Only the mocking laughter of the nymphs still echoed in my ears.

The sun had now set and I looked back down the valley. Nothing was

Suddenly you are surrounded by naked nymphs, shadowy spirits
of the flowing waters, begotten by the imagination of the garden's
creator, playing upon the timeless Breton woods and streams.

to be seen but the darkening lake and the woods and a hint of the estuary
beyond. Perhaps it had all been the imagination of an old man. Yet the dial
of my camera told me that I had photographed something. Time would tell.

Back in the comfort of the house, glass in hand, I taxed my host with
the nymphs he had created to adorn the temple which he had designed. He
was surely in love with them, I said. He looked extremely surprised, and
then amused, and laughed merrily at my impertinence. But when the artist
dreams, who is to say whence his dreams come? And perhaps the artist is the
last to know?

I also dreamed a dream. My garden was never a static thing: it was created as an organism, a living creature, destined to pass like life itself through different phases from birth to death. All were due to disappear as the ecosystem grew. Now they are only a lingering dream, but a delightful one. I rejoice in the pleasure which they once gave to me and to others. But the system was under way. There was much less work now. I was a little older and glad to spend more time enjoying my plants and visiting them with others and to spend less time working with them.

Now that I am eighty years old I and my garden are both in the final phase. I have had to recognise some miscalculations and some failures, but they have been fewer than might have been expected. The ecosystem has reached a stable maturity: it only needs occasional adjustment. Here and there, as in any aging system, there has been a death or a local disaster, but they have not been numerous. I can rely upon the community of plants to provide beauty – and excitement – without taxing my reduced stamina. As the ecosystem has stabilised and occupied much less of life the sedentary but delightful task of breeding hybrid nerines in the greenhouse leading off my study has occupied a larger proportion of time.

Not long after beginning the garden I started a new love affair. This time it was with an adolescent computer living in my study by the greenhouse door. I told myself that the fascinating machine would catalogue the garden, transferring the entries from my manuscript register onto diskettes. It would also help in my nerine breeding, keeping check of the crosses and their results. And of course it would write all my letters and keep records. This was in very early computer days. There was no tuition available locally. The computer manuals were written by experts who could not imagine that a user of their machine would need to learn the basics. The mental effort of doing this was immense – and salutary. The sense of triumph was rewarding. The adolescent machine did everything that I had expected and more besides. Only one of my friends had a computer. The infant computer press told me that my computerless friends were 'techno-peasants'. I did not realise how young and innocent my machine was, neither did I realise that I was in love, until it was too late.

In three years the adolescent was also obsolescent. It would not run the new operating system, DOS. DOS had not been around when it was born. I write this book on my fourth computer, a grown-up Pentium machine, an adult marvel of speed, sophisticated design and elegance of operation. The computer, which grew out of the garden, has become a world in itself within which I could live, infinitely expandable and enabling me to perform tasks undreamed of when I fell for the adolescent. Long forgotten is the excuse that a computer would help in the garden. It does indeed do so, but it has also become an implement in the art of living, a replacement for my failing memory, an extension of my personality, a buttress of the intellect, an invitation to creativity and a playmate. It has added a new dimension to life by making the whole world accessible to me from my desk by way of Compuserve and the Internet. At Compuserve 100436,163 you, the gardener reader, may contact me with your computer from anywhere in the world for the price of a cup of coffee. This miracle is part of the last phase of life, refreshing and exciting.

As for my garden it remains a dream and dreams vanish into the thin air, but not until memory itself fails. I do not know whence the dream came, for it was I who dreamed. But it became a part of a philosophy of existence. I have been exceptionally fortunate in living my life in very different phases and in different places and societies, touching the physical world and the realms of the intellect at many points. Yet throughout it all there remained the tranquil continuo: the love of green and growing things. I was pruning my standard roses when the telephone call came from Downing Street to ask if I would join the Government. Now the garden at Vico Morcote is the setting for the last phase in life or perhaps for the last but one. I cannot tell: I still do not know. But in either case the dream will remain with me.

Looking back down the years, through so many experiences, infinitely varied, often fascinating, sometimes exciting, sometimes very beautiful and from earliest youth always supported by the love of others, the past phases remain vividly real, and yet they have a dreamlike quality. In spite of the images in memory it is hard to convince myself that it all really took place, that I was really there. What then does the future hold?

It must have been in the middle fifties of this century that I was in India as a member of a Parliamentary Delegation. An earnest politician in search of the truth, I noticed the absence of the Anglo-Saxon apparatus for rescuing the elderly from boredom while they await death: the Country Club, the Old Folks Colony, the special programmes for Senior Citizens and all the rest. Our guide was a young Indian woman of perhaps twenty-seven. I asked her how Indians confront the problems of old age. She replied immediately in three words: "They turn inwards." Then she added, "Away from material things." It was evident that she accepted this as the pattern of her own future life. Of course, it was ancient Bhuddist wisdom, predating her Hindu philosophy but a part of it. The beauty and simplicity of her reply has illuminated life ever since. She, like me, was a passenger from birth to death. She already knew how she would handle the last phase of the journey. Like so many Anglo-Saxons, I had given no thought to the subject. I have thought about it ever since. A turn inwards? Away from material things? The idea has great attraction.

So thought the 'Shining Prince', Genji, a thousand years ago in Heian Japan. I suppose that every man who reads the massive *Genji Monogatari*, one of the world's greatest works of fiction, will recognise in the Shining Prince most of his own strengths and weaknesses, aspirations and disappointments. Murasaki Shikibu did not think fit to tell us the manner of Genji's death. We cannot know whether he succeeded in the turn inwards for which he longed or whether he died still engaged with material things. She left us to make the choice for him, and for ourselves.

I sometimes reflect upon the unreasonableness of the Psalmist who addressed the Almighty with the words, 'Lord, let me know mine end and the measure of my days.' Of course I too would be grateful for the same information. It would simplify investment policy, and it would be helpful in family matters and in the planning of garden activities. As I cannot obtain this useful information, I must rely upon the optimistic speech made to me each autumn by Dr Schwarzenbach as I climb off the Ultrasound machine. He tells me that I am very fortunate and I believe him.

Joseph Addison, reflecting upon these matters, expressed the wish to die in the summer, surrounded by the beauties of nature, adding, deferentially, "If it so please God." Apparently it did so, for he died in June 1719, surrounded by the midsummer beauty of the gardens of his home at Holland House, at the age of forty-nine. It would be nice to end life surrounded by the beauty which is my garden. But should this not be possible it would not matter greatly. As long as memory lasts my garden will remain with me, like my own past life, a delightful dream which once I dreamed here on this mountainside.

PLANT INDEX

GENERAL INDEX